[THE FAILURES OF INTEGRATION]

[THE FAILURES OF]

INTEGRATION

How Race and Class Are
Undermining the American Dream

SHERYLL CASHIN

PublicAffairs
New York

Book design by Mark McGarry
Set in Sabon

Library of Congress Cataloging-in-Publication data has been requested
ISBN 1-58648-124-X

FIRST EDITION
10 9 8 7 6 5 4 3 2 1

For my father, Dr. John L. Cashin, Jr.,
who taught me first to care, and then to agitate.
And in memory of my mother, Joan Carpenter Cashin,
who loved by letting me be.

CONTENTS

PART 3:
OUR FUTURE

INTRODUCTION

On May 17, 1954, the Supreme Court declared in its landmark unanimous decision, *Brown v. Board of Education,* that
separate schooling of black and white children was inherently
unequal, marking the dawn of the modern civil rights movement. Over the next twenty years, the civil rights revolution
put in place laws that attempted to guarantee, essentially for
the first time since our nation's founding, that no one should
be restricted in their access to education, jobs, voting, travel,
public accommodations, or housing because of race. For most
people, this was what integration meant. Blacks, whites, Latinos, Asians, and Native Americans might not share social
space, but our public institutions, our workplaces, and our
schools were no longer to be divided into separate domains,
with access to the best opportunities determined by skin color.
The promise of civil rights laws was that only the most private
institutions—and the hearts and minds of would-be discrimi-
nators—would remain unregulated.

Fifty years after *Brown v. Board,* we now profess to believe that the United States should be an integrated society and that people of all races are inherently equal and entitled to the full privileges of citizenship. Here is the reality: While we accept these values in the abstract, we are mostly pretending that they are true. At the dawn of the twenty-first century, the ideals of integration and equality of opportunity still elude us, and we are not being honest or forthcoming about it.

There is a national cognitive dissonance when it comes to integration. It shows through in a *New York Times* poll on racial attitudes: 85 percent of whites said in response to a poll question that they did not care whether they lived in an area where most of their neighbors were white or where most were black; but in response to another question, 85 percent of whites also said they actually live in areas where they have no or few black neighbors.[1] The majority of Americans say they support integration.[2] But this is not the reality that the majority of us actually live. Most of us do not share life space with other races or classes. And we do not own up to the often gaping inequality that results from this separation because, being physically removed from those who most suffer the costs of separatism, we cannot acknowledge what we don't see.

Even as our nation diversifies at a dizzying pace, we are haunted by old paradigms and old ways of thinking. In 1954, about 87 percent of the population was white, 10 percent was black, and the small remainder was composed of Latinos, Asians, and Native Americans. Our national struggle with race relations was rendered starkly in hues of black and white. Fear and animus toward integration of black people into white neighborhoods and white institutions colored how America came to be ordered. The predictable patterns of urban concentration of blacks and the minority poor and suburban concentrations of whites and the affluent emerged through conscious public policies and a great deal of discrimination against black people. In short, America had a "Negro problem."

Five decades later, our nation is infinitely more diverse; Latinos now outnumber African Americans and we are headed toward a new social order. By the end of the new century, we will be a majority-minority nation with whites composing only 40 percent of the national population. American separatism, however, endures, and its class dimensions seem to be growing. We have not yet figured out how to break out of separatist patterns burnished in less enlightened times, and we rarely, if ever, have any explicit discourse about it.

Ironically, while the nation has not yet moved beyond a fundamental hurdle regarding integration—the discomfort of many with large numbers of black people—some of the most admired and respected national figures in the United States are black. White America embraces Colin Powell, Oprah Winfrey, Tiger Woods. They admire Michael Jordan, Bill Cosby, Condoleezza Rice. There are enough examples of successful middle-class African Americans to make many whites believe that blacks have reached parity with them. The fact that some blacks now lead powerful mainstream institutions offers evidence to whites that racial barriers have been eliminated; the issue now is individual effort. In December 2001, when Richard Parsons, an African American, was named the CEO of AOL Time Warner, then the largest media company in the world, it was not an earth-shattering event. Not much was made of the fact that President George W. Bush chose a black woman, Condoleezza Rice, to head his National Security Council or that Colin Powell was the first black Secretary of State. As a nation we seem to have moved past the era when the "first black" is noted, celebrated, or even explicitly discussed. For many, if not most, whites, words like "segregation" and "inequality" are old, finished business. And words like "integration" and "affirmative action" are beyond the point.

That whites are now tired of black complaints may stem from the fact that they are rather misinformed about how well African Americans are doing. Depending on the question, in response to opinion polls, between 40 and 60 percent of whites say that blacks are faring as well as, if not better than, they are in terms of jobs, incomes, education, and access to health care. No doubt, African Americans have progressed, but the closing of social and economic gaps is mostly in the minds of white Americans. According to a recent survey, half of whites believe that the average black person is as well off as the average white person in terms of employment, even though blacks are about twice as likely as whites to hold lower-paying service jobs and more than twice as likely to be unemployed. Four in ten whites incorrectly believed that the typical black earned as much as or more than the typical white, even though black median household income is about 64 percent that of whites—$29,500 compared to $46,300 for whites. (The disparity in terms of wealth, as opposed to income, is much worse: Black median wealth is about 16 percent that of whites.[3]) There were similar gaps of perception and reality concerning education and health care.[4] The odd black family on the block or the Oprah effect—examples of stratospheric black success—feed these misperceptions, even as relatively few whites live among and interact daily with blacks of their own social standing. We are still quite far from the integrated, equal opportunity nation whites seem to think we have become.

Black people, on the other hand, have become integration weary. Most African Americans do not crave integration, although they support it. What seems to matter most to black

people is not living in a well-integrated neighborhood but having the same access to the good things in life as everyone else.
There is much evidence of an emerging "post–civil rights" attitude among black folks. We are ambivalent integrationists. In
opinion polls, the majority of African Americans say that they
would prefer to live in an integrated neighborhood; but for
some of us integration now means a majority-black neighborhood—one where you are not overwhelmed by white people
and where there are plenty of your own kind around to make
you feel comfortable, supported, and welcome.[5] Across America, wherever there is a sizeable black middle-class population,
suburban black enclaves have cropped up that attest to the
draw of this happy "we" feeling.

This is not separatism in the classic sense. Black people
want the benefits of an integrated workplace; we want the
public and private institutions that shape opportunity to be
integrated. More fundamentally, we want the freedom to chart
our course and pursue our dreams. We bang on the doors and
sometimes shatter the ceilings of corporate America not
because it is largely white but because this is how to "get
paid." We want an integrated commercial sector because we
want banks and venture capitalists to lend to us and invest in
our business ideas. We want the option of sending our children
to any college we desire but for many of us Howard, Morehouse, or any number of historically black colleges are at the
top of our list. We want space on the airwaves for our music,
preferably aired by black-owned radio stations. We want space
in Hollywood and on the big screen for our films. We want to
see and celebrate ourselves on television, but we do not particularly care that there was not a black friend on *Friends;* most
of us didn't watch it and didn't understand its appeal.

Even at the height of the civil rights era, socializing with whites was never a goal in itself for black people, and undoubtedly for many, it is not one today. There are counter examples, but we all know they are fairly rare. For those blacks, like myself, who attended primarily white schools, the dominant pattern of socialization was that blacks hung with blacks. And at most social gatherings that I attended then and those that I attend now, one race overwhelmingly predomi-nates. Even when I attend functions that might be described as well integrated, I often observe the phenomenon of blacks pairing with blacks and whites paring with whites. Obviously there are exceptions. I am necessarily writing about generali-ties. But these generalities reflect certain truths—typically unspoken ones—about the limits of integration in our nation.

In 2004, then, we face a number of ironies. Despite *Brown v. Board* and the civil rights laws that followed it in later decades, our schools and neighborhoods are still decidedly seg-regated. The various races and ethnic groups may come into contact in the world of work and in some diverse public spaces—the streets of large, dense cities come to mind, as do sporting events—but we largely live and recreate apart. Most American children learn apart. Race is still a fault line in America, and class separation is widely accepted as the "natu-ral" order. Americans seem to have come to a tacit, unspoken understanding: State-ordered segregation has rightly been eliminated, but voluntary separation is acceptable, natural, sometimes even preferable.

In this book I argue that our tacit agreement to separate along lines of race and class means that the experience and privileges of American citizenship typically vary greatly, depending on what side of the race or class line you are born on. Sometimes the political, social, and economic dividing lines that separate us are quite stark. It is the difference, say, between Hempstead and Garden City, New York, two cities on Long Island—reportedly America's most segregated suburb—that share a political boundary but not much else. As recently reported in the *New York Times:*

> Garden City is home to many executives. It has a median family income of $120,305, houses that look like pages out of decorator magazines, downtown businesses like Saks and Fidelity Investments and a population that is 92 percent white. The mayor and village and school board members are all white. Hempstead is a working-class community. It has a $46,675 median family income, midrise apartment buildings, generic middle-class homes, a downtown with storefront churches, thrift shops, and Spanish restaurants, and a population that is 51 percent black and 32 percent Hispanic. The mayor is black, as are all but one of the village and school board members.[6]

The differing realities of two families from these neighboring towns illustrate our national conundrum perfectly. The Tomlins, a black family, and the Midwoods, a white family, live on the same street but are separated by a hedge and the political boundary line that identifies Hempstead, where the Tomlins live, and Garden City, where the Midwoods live. The Tomlins' side of the street is cracked and potholed. Mrs. Tomlin complains to a *Times* reporter that plows rarely show up after a snowstorm. But on the Garden City side, the pavement is smooth; when a large tree limb falls, village workers arrive within hours to haul it away. The Tomlins want their two daughters to go to college and feel compelled to pay $10,000 a year for private school. Mrs. Tomlin's frustration is palpable. She knows that if the Garden City marker were moved a short distance to include her house, her property value would jump by as much as $200,000; she would then be able to send her daughters to the high-quality Garden City public schools, save the money spent on private school, and feel confident that her children would be well prepared for college.[7] Of course, the Tomlins could not gain access to these benefits just by moving a city marker. A move to Garden City would require them to pay a steep premium in the form of much higher housing costs, assuming they could afford it, and they would have to be willing to live in an overwhelmingly white city. They would have to be willing to be integration pioneers—a "been there, done that" experience for many black people.

Usually the race and class lines that divide us are not so clearly drawn. But most Americans experience forms and degrees of separation. Racial segregation is still pervasive, and class segregation seems to be an accepted norm. Across America's metropolitan regions, there are neighborhoods for the rich and neighborhoods for the poor. Such separation is so endemic to American life that we rarely question it—at least not when we benefit from it. In fact, one might argue that our balkanized social structure is a salutary, critical feature of our system of benefits and incentives. Choosing a neighborhood that separates oneself and one's family from "worse" elements farther down the economic scale has become the critical gateway to upward mobility. Like it or not, this is the established path to better schools, less crime, better services, and stable property values. We seem to understand, if not accept, that the opportunities and amenities available in a neighborhood, as well as the responsiveness of local government to its needs, are often closely calibrated to its racial and economic makeup. We may not agree with this system. We may even decry its unfairness. But when it comes to our personal choices about where to live, our primary motive is to maximize benefits and comfort for ourselves and our families. The white liberal, for example, who chooses a majority-white, affluent enclave, or the middle-income person who chooses the neighborhood with the best public schools she can afford, is taking advantage of a system that creates "desirable" neighborhoods and schools in part by excluding certain populations, usually poor minorities.

As I explain in this book, we are all making choices about where to live in a market system that values racial and economic homogeneity, at least of the white kind, over racial and economic integration. This balkanization comes with very steep, long-term costs, particularly for black and Latino children. Black and brown public school children are now more segregated than at any time in the past thirty years. Typically they are relegated to high-poverty, racially identifiable schools that offer a separate and unequal education. Many poor African Americans live in isolated ghetto neighborhoods that offer violence, weak schools, few jobs, and limited avenues for escape. Of all of our tacit understandings about separation, the supreme, cardinal principle seems to be that poor black people are to be avoided and that society is better off shunting them into their own neighborhoods, far away in particular from sizeable white populations. Indeed, one could argue that the subconscious raison d'être of our separatist system is the bulwarking of white families with children into "safe" havens.

Although we are loathe to admit it, the United States, much more than any other developed Western nation, is premised on the idea of there being winners and losers. Our separatism plays into this. Our acceptance of pervasive racial and increasingly stark class separation creates communities of abundance and communities of need. The 7 percent of the population of large metropolitan areas that live in affluent, job-rich, predominately white suburban enclaves are the biggest winners. They are typically the families of corporate executives and entrepreneurs who are at the top of the income and wealth scale. Everyone else gets a very different deal; the black poor get the worst deal, often being relegated to hypersegregated neighborhoods that are incubators of extreme social distress. Our tortured racial heritage—one that initially was premised on blacks being unworthy of the privileges of full citizenship—masks our winner-take-all system. Middle-income whites cannot appreciate that their daily anxiety about just trying to stay ahead in America has a lot to do with how we have chosen to order ourselves. It is easier for suburban whites in less favored communities to associate themselves with the "winners" than to see that a system premised on separating people based upon their racial and economic status limits opportunities for everyone, including themselves. With the expensive price tag attached to exclusive "winner" neighborhoods, it is increasingly difficult for middle-income whites to afford the trappings of middle-class status, which includes a home in a "safe" neighborhood with "good" schools along with the ability to pay for things like college tuition and health care.[8]

There are multicultural, socioeconomically integrated islands that buck the dominant trend of race and class separation. Neighborhoods such as Adams-Morgan in Washington, D.C., Jackson Heights in Queens, and Fruitvale in Oakland are home to a rich mélange of races, languages, and cultures. But such inclusive neighborhoods are the exception, not the rule, in American real estate markets. Those home buyers who set out to live in an integrated neighborhood are often surprised by the lack of offerings. And frequently in integrated communities, like West Mount Airy in Philadelphia, the schools are becoming more segregated and impoverished. Even among the universe of families that choose to live in integrated neighborhoods, parents with options, especially white and black professionals, often bypass the public schools.

My aim with this book has been to offer a thorough factual account on where we are in upholding the integrationist, egalitarian ideals we claim to believe in. I come to this as a scholar but also as a black woman who values black institutions and communities even as I advocate for race and class integration. These are highly emotional issues. They go to the very core of our social structure. I hope the book makes unassailable points based upon research even as much of what I say may be inconvenient and discomfiting. Ultimately, I argue that unless and until we complete the unfinished business of the civil rights movement, meaningfully integrating our public and private realms in a way that gives all Americans, especially those who have been most marginalized, real choices and opportunities, we will not solve the conundrum of race and class inequality in America. For far too many Americans, race and economic status defines what type of neighborhood they will live in, what type of education they are able to acquire, and ultimately, their life chances. Beyond the inequality that results from our separation, this stratification is contributing to a corrosive politics of selfishness. Communities of abundance compete with communities of need for limited state, federal, and private resources. The communities of abundance are winning, but over the long term, as gulfs of opportunity begin to entrench classes of "haves" and "have nots," we risk a stark failure of our democracy project.

At the dawn of the twentieth century, W.E.B. DuBois predicted that only a complete transformation of American society would bring about equality for black people. I am arguing that in the twenty-first century we still need a transformation—a jettisoning of the common assumption that separation is acceptable—in order to solve the riddle of inequality and unfairness in America. Our public policy choices must be premised on an integrationist vision if we are to achieve our highest aspiration and the promise that America says it embraces: full and equal opportunity for all. Integration should be viewed as inherent to American citizenship. This is a necessary shift in thinking if we are to harness the beautiful diversity of America and be an example to the world on how to transcend differences of race, class, ethnicity, nationality, and religion.

This book proceeds in three parts. Part I presents the facts about the limits of integration; it explains the extent of our separatism and the reasons for it. Chapter 1 illustrates how and why racial integration of our neighborhoods and our life space still eludes us. Chapter 2 offers a happier portrait, one of integrated, multicultural islands that are hopeful exceptions to the dominant trend of separation; it explores the challenges of creating togetherness among strangers. Chapter 3 explains the extent of race and class separatism in our neighborhoods and demonstrates that it is not inherently natural but the result of conscious public and private policy choices.

Part II examines the costs of our separatism for the whole of society. I contend that we are creating a separate and unequal opportunity system and illustrate this primarily by comparing the life space and residential returns experienced by suburban blacks and whites who live in separate enclaves of their own kind. Chapter 4 tells the story of predominately black middle-class communities in Prince George's County, Maryland, illustrating the dilemma of the black middle class, who must decide whether the psychic benefits of "we-ness" are worth the costs of racial isolation. Chapter 5 documents the heavy costs of separatism to white America—the often elusive quest for a sane middle-class quality of life. Chapter 6 tells the story of separatism in American public schools, which are rapidly becoming more separate and unequal, underscoring the profound costs to American school children and society. Finally, Chapter 7 examines the cost of the black ghetto, for those who live its cruel reality and for the rest of us, who distance ourselves from that reality but suffer its indirect effects.

Part III examines the current and future implications of our separatism. What does it mean and what should we be doing about it? In Chapter 8, I illustrate how our separated condition is fraying the social contract and altering politics, which now heavily favors the desires of white suburban voters and implies that they need not be a part of or contribute to larger society. In the final chapter of the book I address solutions. Chapter 9 presents my optimistic vision for an America that has made its core ideals true for everyone: a new, integrated reality that might be achieved in the twenty-first century. In positing how we might achieve such a seemingly utopian vision, Chapter 9 examines the grassroots, cross-cultural coalitions that have been forged around issues of equity and sustainable development and suggests revolutionary policy directions for such coalitions to pursue. Ultimately, I conclude that we cannot solve the problem of grave inequality of opportunity or stem our drift toward a "winner-take-all" society without meaningful race and class integration, particularly of the institutions that foster upward mobility, such as schools.

A hopeful shift in public attitudes occurred in the twentieth century. As a nation, we embraced the ideal of equality and came to believe that integration was the best route to this ideal, as well as the best way to ensure domestic tranquility and prosperity. At least that is what the majority of us profess to believe.

Our growing diversity presents an opportunity to make this abstract vision much more of a shared cultural value. But this is not where we are headed. The current trend is one of enclave formation and pronounced class separation, leading to separate and unequal realities. A more hopeful destiny will only come about as the result of a conscious effort to change our public policies and culture. We managed a revolutionary shift in national consciousness as a result of the civil rights movement. Lifting the physical and psychic shackles of Jim Crow produced a sea change. My hope for America in the twenty-first century is that she fully completes the transformation.

PART 1

FACTS ABOUT THE
FAILURES OF INTEGRATION

CHAPTER 1

WON'T YOU NOT BE MY NEIGHBOR?
Race and Housing

HOUSING—where we live—is fundamental in explaining American separatism. Housing was the last plank in the civil rights revolution, and it is the realm in which we have experienced the fewest integration gains. When it comes to integration, housing is also the realm in which Americans most seem to agree that separation is acceptable. We may accept, even desire, integrated workplaces and integrated public spheres. But when it comes to our private life space, more visceral personal needs of comfort and security take precedence—especially for families with children. In this context, for many, integration is simply irrelevant or perceived as a threat to more fundamental concerns. Yet segregated residential housing contributes to pervasive inequality in this country and to social gulfs of misunderstanding. Where you live largely defines what type of people you will be exposed to on a daily basis and hence how well you relate to different types. It often defines what schools you will go to, what employers you will have access to, and whether you will be exposed to a host of models for success. We seem to ignore the obvious when it comes to race relations in this country. From civil rights leaders to the average Joe, the issues of where we live and why go unexamined, even as they have seminal consequences for society. I begin with these questions precisely because they are so ignored yet so fundamental.

How do you decide where to live? Eleven years ago, I bought a lovely bungalow in Shepherd Park, an integrated, albeit majority-black, upper-middle-class neighborhood in the northwest quadrant of Washington, D.C. This was my first foray into home ownership. My goal at the time was to acquire a house in the best and safest neighborhood I could afford. The race or class of my would-be neighbors was not at the forefront of my thinking. But many communities were beyond consideration. As a committed urbanite and a hater of traffic, living outside the Beltway was out of the question. As a black woman with a strong racial identity, I found the overwhelmingly white neighborhoods west of Rock Creek Park, such as Georgetown, American University Park, and Bethesda, inherently unattractive. I was not prepared, even if investment wisdom counseled otherwise, to make the profound personal sacrifice of living totally among "others" with whom I could not identify and who likely could not identify with me. Implicit in my choice about where to live was the understanding that I wanted to be among more than a just a smattering of black people. If I had been forced to describe my ideal neighborhood, I suppose I would have said it was an integrated one. Shepherd Park seemed ideal when I moved in and still does today. Its tree-lined, quiet streets are on the edge of a swath of neighborhoods known as the "Gold Coast," the territory where upwardly mobile black people in the District staked their claim decades ago. It is not perfect. We have had our issues with drug dealers, burglars, and car thieves. I was burglarized twice in the early years before I wised up and began using my alarm consistently. And the public schools are stronger in the "white" areas of town. Still, if I were a parent I would rather work to improve on the strengths at Shepherd Elementary or, should I lack such faith and courage, pay for private school tuition than live totally among whites.

If you had asked me at the time I bought my home what the racial makeup of my neighborhood was, I would have told you that it was about 60 percent black and 40 percent white. I remember telling friends that I had bought into one of the few well-integrated neighborhoods in the District. I thought it might even come close to a 50–50 breakdown. I was quite surprised to learn, when I later accessed the census data, that the area I live in is 72 percent black and 21 percent white. In fact, I could find only one census tract in the District of Columbia that came close to being a true melding of the races. As of 2000, Census Tract 50, which includes the rapidly gentrifying Logan Circle neighborhood, was 26 percent white, 36 percent black and 29.5 percent Latino. But it is doubtful that this racial equilibrium has endured. With gentrification, inevitably, the area has become whiter and wealthier. Stable racial integration is much more elusive in Washington and elsewhere in the nation than I had imagined.

When I bought my house I had no illusions about *economic* integration. To be honest, I was not seeking it. There were great deals to be had in other parts of the District in 1993—if I had been willing to be an urban pioneer. But as a single woman living alone who might be coming home late from work, I was not willing to live in rougher areas, although I had done so as a renter. For two years I had rented a garden apartment in the Hillcrest area, a middle-class, predominately black enclave in what was otherwise the District's poorest ward, Ward 8. I had also rented a basement apartment for a brief stint in the early 1990s in rapidly gentrifying LeDroit Park, near Howard University. In those days, the sound of gunfire was not unusual, although the couple who lived above me had cultivated a highly calibrated ear and could tell me with assurance that the gunshots I had just heard were five blocks away. This was a little too much of the hood for my taste. For a black southerner like myself who had grown up in middle-class neighborhoods of detached houses and big lawns, the bourgeois, leafy streets of the Gold Coast felt safer and more familiar.

My thought processes in purchasing a home were not that different from those of most Americans who have choices. In theory I wanted to live in an integrated neighborhood, but one where people of my own race were well represented. I was not willing to buy in a neighborhood with a large number of low-income people because I feared crime and because I wanted to protect my precious property investment. I recognized that gentrifying areas might pay off handsomely, but I feared living in a transitional neighborhood. And so I chose the smallest house in the best block I could afford, in a neighborhood where I also felt comfortable socially. This was my way of maintaining the resale value of my investment.

No doubt, my sense of where I am willing to live, and the type of people I am willing to have as neighbors, is shaped by my relatively privileged economic status. My blackness—or rather my strong identification with being black—also greatly shapes my locational preferences. The only difference between me and Americans of other races who have real choices about where to live may be their distaste for black neighborhoods.

Personal preferences *and* discrimination help explain why so many of us end up living in neighborhoods where our own race and social class predominates. An article in the *Detroit News* tells the story of two middle-class families in search of a better life. Both families wanted to live in the suburbs; both had roughly equal middle-class status, but they ended up in very different neighborhoods, one overwhelmingly black and the other overwhelmingly white. Michael and Caroline Mallory, who are black, moved from Detroit to suburban Southfield. Their new neighborhood is 62 percent black, and they say being in majority-black surroundings offers them a certain comfort. Janine and Andrew Gurka, who are white, chose to build a home in suburban Livonia, which is 95 percent white. Their new 1,600-square-foot rancher is a step up from their former cramped home in Dearborn Heights. In other cities throughout the region, they said, "everything was worse than what we had or too expensive." The Mallorys asked about the color of their neighbors when they looked for a home. The Gurkas said they didn't.[1] But it is hard to imagine that, in the bundle of tastes and preferences that went into their choice about where to live, the racial composition of the community they chose (and of those they would not consider) was not a factor, consciously or otherwise. Being overwhelmingly white, Livonia was likely well within the Gurkas' comfort zone in a way that a majority-black or even a well-integrated neighborhood in Southfield likely would not be.

The premium that whites tend to place on such comfort shows up in the costs of predominately white neighborhoods. A working-class African American can find a home in Redford for $112,000 that would probably cost him $160,000 in Livonia. Wayne County executive Ed McNamara sums up his feeling about why racial segregation exists and in his mind should not be viewed as an issue, telling the *Detroit News:* "Why should an individual pay $50,000 or $60,000 more to live in a community that is ethnically different than they are, and maybe not feel as comfortable?"[2]

Beyond personal preferences, discrimination is also contributing to Livonia's overwhelming whiteness. When Deano Ware and his family, who are black, initially searched for a home in Livonia, they were surprised by the stares they received as they drove through its tree-lined neighborhoods. They were confronted with a remarkable number of homes that already had offers when they inquired. In the end, they gave up on Livonia and gave in to exhaustion. "Sometimes it's like everyone is on a conveyor belt carrying you where you are supposed to go," Ware confessed to the *Detroit News.* "After a while, it's just easier to go where it's most comfortable." Even though he was willing to try to go where others of his race were not going, Ware acknowledged that he was stymied by barriers that were thrown in his path: "I have to rely on the white homeowners, realtors and mortgage companies. If it breaks down anywhere along the line, you're stuck. I can't change the system alone."[3]

It is not surprising, then, that neighboring towns can evolve into very different racial and economic milieus. These differences often develop out of different cultural histories and are encouraged by planning choices made by city leaders. Southfield, which was initially a heavily Jewish suburb, has something of a tradition of nonhostility toward blacks. But in Livonia, real estate brokers were known to convey the message that blacks were not welcome. Ware's real estate agent, who was not white, kept telling Ware and his family that Livonia was racist and that they should try Southfield or Redford. Ultimately, the Wares decided they could get more for their money in Redford Township and settled on a house that was almost across the street from Livonia. The mayor of Livonia, Jack Kirksey, says his city has never had ordinances or covenants that dictated where blacks could live. But he admits that the biggest problem with integrating Livonia is its lack of apartments or low-income housing—a policy decision made fifty years ago. "You pretty much have to be a homeowner to live here," Kirksey acknowledges to the *News*. And with undeveloped lots selling for $150,000, many middle-income folks will be priced out of Livonia.[4]

The story of the Mallorys and Gurkas repeats itself over and over in the millions of individual choices that make up real estate markets in the United States. The pull of personal preferences and the push of discrimination can lead to racially polarized private realms, even on the same street. In the Detroit metropolitan area, for example, Alter Road serves as the boundary line between Gross Pointe Park and Detroit, Michigan. The Detroit side of Alter Road is 79 percent black; the Grosse Pointe Park side is 93 percent white.[5] The two cities are worlds apart in terms of racial and socioeconomic composition, as well as the opportunities available to their inhabitants.

There are at least five influences that contribute to such separation:

1. *Blacks face integration exhaustion.* African Americans are increasingly reluctant to move into neighborhoods without a significant black presence. They prefer places that are recognized as being welcoming to blacks and seem less willing than in the past to be integration pioneers and move into neighborhoods that might be hostile to their presence.

2. *Whites place a premium on homogeneity.* Whites are less likely than blacks to want to live in diverse neighborhoods. Studies show that whites are willing to pay a 13 percent premium to live in all-white neighborhoods. Three Harvard economists have concluded that this willingness to pay more to live in predominately white areas best explains the persistence of segregated neighborhoods.[6] Overwhelmingly white areas are less affordable to racial minorities, who tend to have less income and wealth to underwrite their housing costs.

3. *Racial steering thrives.* Racial discrimination is still very prevalent in the real estate industry, with blacks and Latinos frequently being steered to areas perceived as acceptable for them.

4. *Private institutional practices support homogeneity.* Real estate developers, financial institutions, insurance companies, retailers, and even land-use planners have come to rely on a system of racial and economic profiling of neighborhoods to decide where to invest, develop, and do business. Profiling databases establish a hierarchy of neighborhood types that skew investment decisions heavily in favor of predominately white suburban communities. Neighborhoods that cannot be easily categorized, that is, well-integrated neighborhoods, are at a disadvantage, as are predominately minority neighborhoods, which receive lower-quality commercial and public amenities as a result of such profiling.[7]

5. *Public policy choices support homogeneity.* A host of public policy choices made in the twentieth century have created a systemic bias in favor of socioeconomic separation rather than integration. While official government policy no longer supports racial restrictions or

"redlining" of neighborhoods, as it did in the past, our policies promote local autonomy in land-use planning and zoning in a way that has detrimental effects.

I explain the private and public institutional choices that contribute to race and class separation in more detail in Chapter 3. Suffice it to say that individuals in search of homes must operate in a market environment that decidedly undervalues racial and economic integration and, frankly, overvalues whiteness. The end result is separatism. We say we support integration, but most of us—even those of us who might genuinely prefer to live in an integrated environment—are not truly living integrated lives at the neighborhood level. Still, individual attitudes—what we feel in our hearts and minds—color the choices we make and determine whether we will be open or resistant to living among people of a different race or class.

The Pull of Personal Preferences: Black Ambivalence and White Fear

How do most blacks, whites, Latinos, and Asians really feel about integration? Two consistent, warring themes come through in surveys that attempt to gauge the extent of Americans' racial tolerance.[8] On the one hand, Americans overwhelmingly say they are committed to integration. Fully 75 percent of us claim to believe in something approaching Martin Luther King's vision of an integrated, beloved community in America.[9] We embrace the ideal of integration much more now than in past decades. In 1958, when nonblacks were asked if they would move away if great numbers of black people moved into their neighborhood, a resounding 80 percent of poll respondents said yes. By 1997, only 18 percent of nonblacks would claim this view.[10] Most of us are also against "segregation" per se. Seven out of ten of us view the prevalence of segregation as a "bad thing."[11] But on the other hand, we do not seem to think that integration should be the focus of social policy. Blacks and whites tend to disagree on many things, such as whether affirmative action should be continued, but when it comes to integration they are similarly dissonant. Nearly identical percentages of whites (73 percent) and blacks (76 percent) support integration in the abstract.[12] But when asked to choose an objective for achieving racial equality—integration, equal opportunity, or equal results—whites and blacks also had near identical responses: 60 percent of whites and 62 percent of blacks chose equal opportunity over the 5 and 6 percent respectively who chose integration.[13] In a post–civil rights era, where official racial barriers no longer exist, we feel we can give in, without self-consciousness or guilt, to the fundamentally human tendency to seek community among people who are familiar to us. Although in opinion polls the majority of all races say they would prefer an integrated neighborhood, similar majorities also state a preference for living in a neighborhood in which their own race is a majority or plurality. Neither whites, blacks, Latinos, nor Asians wish to be vastly outnumbered by "others." That prospect of being outnumbered is inherently threatening, particularly for whites.[14] So residential integration necessarily has been limited. And much of this limitation seems to be tied to the comfort level of nonblacks with blacks.

White Fear: Society's Discomfort with Blacks in Numbers

I have my own informal means of observing the consistent discomfort with African Americans on the part of nonblacks. It is a phenomenon that, ironically, I greatly benefit from. I call it "Southwest Airlines First Class." My husband and I enjoy this inside joke when flying Southwest, a dependable, cheap airline that allows passengers to seat themselves on a first come, first served basis. We always hope that there will be a black person far ahead of us at the front of the line; a dark-skinned young black male is best. At least four out of five times, we can depend on the seats next to that black person being empty, even if his row is far up front, begging for the taking. I am always happy to take this convenient seat, feeling grateful for the discomfort of others and marveling at the advantage they are willing to pass up due to their own social limitations. I smile warmly at my black brother as I plop down next to him.

In my view, racial separation is animated by a similar fear of or discomfort with black people. I am reminded of the story a Harvard-trained black lawyer once told me. She and all the black summer associates at her law firm went to lunch together. When they returned, they happened to be the only people in the elevator. The elevator door opened, and a white female attorney was taken aback to be confronted with a bevy of well-dressed, not unfamiliar black people. She blurted out defensively, "What is this? A BLSA meeting?" She later apologized to the group and confessed that she felt "threatened"— threatened by the mere presence of a number of black people whom she was acquainted with and who worked in her own firm. I've seen this uncomfortable, fish-out-of-water expression on the faces of many white people who are unexpectedly thrust into a situation where they are in the minority in a room full of black people, a very rare occasion for most white people.

When I have a party at my home, I feel compelled to go through a racial calculation to accommodate white or non-black friends who may not be comfortable being one of the few nonblack people there. I don't worry about white friends who have worked for black organizations or causes or who have somehow imbibed black culture in a way that makes them totally comfortable, even delighted, to be the honorary brother or sister in an otherwise all-black crowd. Former President Bill Clinton is a member of that rare club. But for white friends who don't fit that category, which seems to be most white people, I find myself trying to be sure there are enough whites invited so that those who do come will feel comfortable. I don't feel the need to go through this racial calculus for Asian or Latino friends, who seem to have acquired more cultural dexterity. But, if it seems I won't have enough whites attending to make it a truly racially mixed event—I do an advance poll to check availability—I simply let it be an overwhelmingly black affair, which means colleagues from work won't be invited. All of this would be easier if the vast majority of the people I spend social time with were not black. But my social set mirrors who I am, just as my white friends' predominately white social sets mirror who they are.

I don't think my white friends ever go through this racial calculation on my behalf when they invite me into their homes. It is not at all unusual for me to be the only black person in a predominately white social setting. I, like so many black people who constantly move back and forth across the color line, am quite used to serving as the integrationist who bears the burden of adjusting to another culture. Whites are so used to racial minorities bearing this burden that it probably does not occur to most of them that they should work at integration too. I don't step into an all-white situation and experience fear, because I am used to being one of the few darker spots in a crowd. However, I believe a lot more integration between the races would occur if whites experienced being outnumbered more frequently and were therefore forced to adjust to and learn about people who may or may not be very different from them.

Our real estate markets mirror this fear of blacks in numbers. This fundamental, never-discussed problem at least partially explains why we do not have more racial integration of our neighborhoods. And it does not matter whether the blacks are affluent or poor. Affluent black people in the Los Angeles area, for example, are more segregated than poor Latinos.[15] When Matteson, Illinois—a white-collar suburb south of Chicago—experienced an influx of middle-class black people in the mid-1990s, whites started panic selling, even though the blacks moving in shared the same, if not higher, socioeconomic status of the whites who lived there.[16] If blacks exist in large numbers, say, more than 20 percent of the metropolitan population, they are likely to live in predominately black neighborhoods. Half of all black people live in a metropolitan region with extremely high segregation levels.[17] No other racial minority in our nation is singled out for this degree of separation.

Whites are not free to express ambivalence about integration. The risk of being labeled a racist is too great. In my numerous dialogues with predominately white audiences, however, I have encountered a range of attitudes: from the rare, ardent integrationist who believes I should be exhorting whites to integrate, to the guilt-ridden commentary about how integrated neighborhoods don't offer quality schools, to a seemingly resigned acceptance of the fact of our separation ... to silence. In conversations with white colleagues or in one-on-one conversations with whites, I have been offered a few candid assessments about what they think other white people think. One colleague who lives in an overwhelmingly white community told me she thinks that most whites don't really care about integration; she thinks whites would just like a few more black faces in their neighborhoods so they would feel less guilty. Another white woman I talked to after a lecture confessed that she thinks the fear factor among whites about living among blacks or about being outnumbered by racial minorities is very real. Her claim is certainly consistent with opinion polls in which a majority of whites expressed unease about the changing demographic composition of our country and expressed the least willingness among the races to move into integrated areas.[18] A *Detroit News* survey is also quite telling. When whites were asked about their own attitudes about who they would be willing to live among, the answers were predictable: The overwhelming majority would not mind living in an integrated or even a predominately black area. But when asked how they think other whites would feel about such racial integration, they were much more cautious and attested to a likely ambivalence or discomfort on the part of many whites with very much racial integration of their life space.[19]

As a black person who is rarely privy to candid conversations among whites on these issues, I can only speculate about the factors that drive any caution whites may feel about integration. I suspect many whites would claim that their choice about where to live has nothing to do with race; they are only seeking the best schools, the best amenities, a newly built house, a suburban lifestyle, safer, crime-free environments, more house for the money, and so on. The list of racially neutral explanations for why most whites live in predominately white surroundings is endless. All of these ostensibly race-neutral factors do tend to steer white movers to predominately white areas. But if white movers were completely honest with themselves, I believe many would have to admit that areas

with significant populations of racial minorities or black people are beyond their comfort zone, for reasons both natural
and insidious.

Black Separatism, Black Ambivalence?

In research surveys, all nonblack groups—whites, Latinos, and
Asians—display a consistent strain of antipathy toward integrating with substantial numbers of African Americans.[20] Black
people likely sense this and are weary of dealing with it. When
confronted with the option of integrating with whites, in at
least one national survey in the 1990s, blacks preferred a heavily black neighborhood—one that was three-quarters black.
Latinos and Asians, by contrast, preferred 50–50 integration
with whites to a neighborhood in which their group overwhelming dominates. But blacks have also maintained the more
idealistic position in response to other surveys, stating a preference for a neighborhood that is 50–50 or that has a slight pre-
dominance of blacks.[21] What is clear is that black people are
reluctant to place themselves in situations of hostility. For a
black person in America, the idealistic 50–50 neighborhood is a
rare, elusive option. Realistically, most blacks generally have
one of two choices: an almost all-black neighborhood or one
where blacks are few.[22] Knowing the history of discrimination
and hostility against them, it is not surprising that many blacks
would consider an overwhelmingly black neighborhood more
attractive than an overwhelmingly white one.

Faced with such trade-offs, many black people appear to
have adopted a "post-integrationist" mind-set, and now most
value living among themselves, even as they exhibit a high tolerance for living among other groups. This phenomenon is
particularly evident among the black middle class. Across

America, in most of the metropolitan regions populated with a sizeable black middle class, there are suburban communities where black professionals have formed enclaves built on a "we" feeling. A proud resident of Brook Glen, a middle-class black suburb of Atlanta, attests to the psychic balm her neighborhood provides from the daily struggle of being black in a predominately white workplace. She tells writer Sam Fulwood:

> There are not any white people around here staring us in the face and trying to prove we don't matter. So much goes on at the job that we have to endure, the slights and the negative comments, and feelings that we're unwanted. When I have to work around them all day, by the time I come home I don't want to have to deal with white people anymore.[23]

Alvin Thornton, former chair of the school board for Prince George's County, Maryland, the highest-income majority-black county in the United States, draws a clear distinction between the legally mandated segregation of old and the voluntary separation of today. He calls his county's racial separation "apartness," something that cannot be contested legally, and he vigorously defends it. "There are some people who want to live in majority black communities," he declared to the *Baltimore Sun*. "Why wouldn't you?"[24]

This new or renewed concern with the benefits of "we-ness" is not grounded solely in a defiant separatism. African Americans perceive more discrimination against themselves than do other racial minorities, and some discrimination studies bear out this perception.[25] Perhaps in preferring a black neighborhood many African Americans are just anticipating what they already know to be the truth: that negative racial attitudes and barriers still exist; that being an integration pioneer can be wearing on the soul; that being in a warm and welcoming community that understands you implicitly is inherently attractive and achievable in a way that the fantasy of residential integration is not. This post–civil rights attitude may also arise from the modest successes of the civil rights movement itself. In a world where official racial barriers have been eliminated, some of us black folks actually do have a choice about where to live, where to work, and definitely with whom to socialize. Separatism is a luxury because we now have choices. But any voluntary separation on the part of a black person is more likely to be animated by pro-black feelings than anti-white ones. As John Edgar Wideman once eloquently stated: "I don't need to hate white people in order to love myself. But I also don't need white people to tell me what I am or what I can strive to be or tell me if I've made it or not. I don't need to know a white person or know white people to make a good life for myself or be happy with myself or to love other people whatever color they may be or not be."[26]

Such expressions of confident separatism on the part of black people can be highly discomfiting to nonblacks. A twenty-four-year-old African American journalist named Natalie Hopkinson created something of a local furor when she wrote openly about these feelings on the editorial pages of the *Washington Post* one Sunday in June of 2001:

> In the small act of choosing to buy our home where we did, I believe that we became part of a growing group of African Americans who are picking up where the civil rights movement left off. From our perspective, integration is overrated. It's time to reverse an earlier generation's hopeful migration into white communities and attend to some unfinished business in the hood.[27]

Hopkinson struck a nerve because she was brutally honest, some would say anti-white, in her view about the effects of white gentrification on the black central city neighborhood that she had moved into with her husband and six-month-old son. Using rather incendiary rhetoric—"We damn sure are not about to let white folks buy up all the property in D.C."—she articulated the views of many post–civil rights babies. Her trajectory was quite typical of her generation. She and her husband are "twenty somethings who were raised in neighborhoods where there were few black families." As a child she lived "the pernicious side to pioneer integrationism"—the harassing phone calls and the steely glares that constantly demanded, "What are you doing here?"—and she refused to subject her son to that experience. Like many of her black elders, she lamented what the black community lost when black professionals like her parents moved out of cities, taking the gains of the civil rights movement with them.

Ms. Hopkinson made an "in your face" statement that there was a lot more to be gained by living among your own and by making a commitment to help stabilize black communities than by living among white people. In her parting shot that "whiter is not necessarily better," she expressed an uppity, defiant black separatism that was profoundly alienating to many white readers. I suspect it was her arrogance and indifference to what whites felt that most rankled. The *Post* received such a torrent of mail that its ombudsman felt compelled to write twice to defend the paper's decision to run the piece.[28] But while whites of all political persuasions were outraged that their infiltration of black central city neighborhoods was being met with such hostility, many black people were passing Ms. Hopkinson's separatist manifesto around on the Internet and quietly agreeing with its core sentiment.

Whites tend to feel a group solidarity too, but our collective racial history simply does not allow whites to express it.[29] White conservatives sometimes enter this fragile territory, usually to a torrent of knee-jerk reaction. One of Ms. Hopkinson's few white supporters came from the cyber pages of the *National Review*. A cherub-faced Jonah Goldberg, speaking with the honesty of a younger generation, shouted solidarity with Ms. Hopkinson. In his view, maintaining cultural norms and traditions by imposing a certain social order within a community was a wonderful American tradition. "Let's not kid ourselves" that sometimes maintaining social cohesion requires "letting strangers know they're, well ... strangers," he argued.[30] Perhaps one of the few safe spaces to express ideas like this to people outside one's own tribe is from the insulation of one's personal space, at the keys of a computer and out into cyberspace.

Black people, I suppose, are given more license to write or talk openly about separatism because of their unique history of subordination. African Americans were not the authors of slavery or Jim Crow and do not have a history of limiting the opportunities of another race, based on race. So black statements about the benefits of living among one's own do not carry the imprimatur of a racist past. But they can, admittedly, be animated by a present, racist feeling. My reading of honest, separatist statements by most of the black people who express them, however, is that they are animated by a love and longing for a vibrant, stable, healthy, and nurturing black community. In the voices I read and listen to, I sense a nostalgic cry for an intact, pre-integration black community that may never have been as good as it seems from the distance of time. I also sense a human draw toward the familiar—a love of and comfort with "my black self." Put differently, in choosing to move to a majority-black neighborhood, many black movers are simply asserting the inherent legitimacy, even superiority, of "things black."

I experienced this way of thinking firsthand growing up in the house of an admitted "black supremacist." My father, Dr. John L. Cashin Jr., founder of the National Democratic Party of Alabama and a 1970 gubernatorial candidate against George Wallace, had a colorful theory of natural selection for black people in Alabama. He figured that the gene pool that survived the Middle Passage, three hundred years of slavery, and the unreconstructed violence of the segregated South had to be superior to any other race of people. He certainly believed that blacks were capable of forming and leading a coalition of blacks and progressive whites to counter the hegemony of the Wallace-dominated politics in Alabama. But this "black supremacist" lived a more integrated existence than most people, black or white, in Alabama in the sixties and seventies. Our family was the primary source of integration at the local Unitarian church. Our house was always flowing with guests of all races and classes, and my parents broke the color line of white neighborhoods and white schools in an early move to get their kids into the better public schools of my hometown of Hunstville. Dad's assertion of black identity and supremacy was not inconsistent with the incredibly integrationist, cross-cultural life he led.

My point is not to validate or invalidate feelings of separatism but to underscore that they are there. Much of our daily lives reflects separatist choices, whether they are made consciously or unconsciously. Separatist values are felt passionately by some people of many hues, and they are a phenomenon that must be reckoned with if a more perfect, integrationist union is ever to be achieved in this country. The chief irony in this post–civil rights era is that African Americans, the group that fought most mightily for entry into mainstream American society, now seem most ambivalent about what integration has wrought. When the Reverend Joseph Lowery, a lieutenant of Martin Luther King in the movement, says that "[i]ntegration no longer means the moving of everything black to white,"[31] or when the Reverend Andrew Young, one of King's intimates, says that [i]ntegration is not about sitting next to white people or going to the same school [but] having equal access to the resources,"[32] it seems that there is some buyer's remorse in the civil rights community about integration.

In truth, what comes through in the voices of black people is a frustration with the unmet promises of integration. As John Hope Franklin, the eminent historian and leader of President Clinton's "One America" race initiative dryly suggested, perhaps racial integration has failed because it has barely been tried.[33] Denise Brown, who spearheaded discussions about race throughout the city of Louisville, Kentucky, echoes the same sentiment, contending in the *Boston Globe* that some "blacks are rethinking integration for the simple reason that it never happened."[34] Her argument, which has shown up in a host of books by black authors such as Ellis Cose, Sam Fulwood, and Lawrence Otis Graham, is that many blacks feel that whatever integration has been achieved has been the result of blacks assimilating into white domains. Integration that happens only through subjugation of black identity, and on terms that meet white comfort levels, is too much to ask. Perhaps even more profoundly, many blacks simply feel that we have a lot less integration and openness than white America thinks we do. The boardrooms, professional partnerships, and middle and upper echelons of corporate America are just not that diverse.

A palpable frustration on the part of black professionals spills out in conversations and interviews. They see a private workplace that is still not color-blind when it comes to promotions and that can still be quite tribal in terms of who is mentored and who gets the best opportunities for advancement.[35]

A friend of mine—a tall, confident black male and a Rhodes Scholar with four degrees from elite universities—wearily attests to his constant struggle working in the corporate world. He often sees whites whom he views as mediocre advance because of their connections. And he believes there are few companies that are truly comfortable letting a black man be exactly who he is without requiring that he somehow subjugate himself. My friend may be confusing personality conflicts with racism in some circumstances, but I don't for a minute doubt that there is a kernel of truth to his experience, one echoed by black professionals in opinion surveys and discrimination complaints. In a recent survey of all black alumni of Harvard Law School, for example, over half of the respondents stated that they have experienced expressed racism, and 88 percent of respondents thought that black lawyers still face significant discrimination in the workplace.[36]

Thus for some blacks, the choice to live in a black neighborhood may constitute acceptance of defeat in trying to fully enter the American mainstream—a recognition that integration as assimilation is neither possible nor desirable and that a degree of independence and a welcoming personal life space are necessary, salutary, spirit-saving strategies. Sadly, such defeatism can have a self-fulfilling quality to it. Acknowledging the probable limits of how far white America is willing to go with integration may ensure that such limits will always be there. If the group that has most made integration possible—the willing black integration pioneers who boldly pushed their way into white neighborhoods, white schools, and white workplaces—is now less enthused about integration, this has ominous implications for a society on the precipice of majority-minority nationhood.

While a frustration with the failed promises of integration or a simple weariness with carrying the assimilator's burden may be motivating some black people who choose to live in black enclaves, many black movers also express an affirmative delight in simply being among people like themselves. The black professional class that has benefited most from the civil rights revolution seeks out black enclaves because black socialization is now harder to cultivate in a more integrated society. Longtime summer residents of Sag Harbor on Long Island, New York, or of Martha's Vineyard, Massachusetts, testify to this phenomenon. Elite black families who live in overwhelmingly white neighborhoods or who send their children to overwhelmingly white schools in order to ensure they have the best possible education maintain their tribal roots and provide a positive black cultural grounding for their children by vacationing with their own. "We want to be around other black families, other people who look like our kids," a young black mother who lives with her husband on the Upper East Side of Manhattan and "summers" in Sag Harbor attests. In this way, her two children, one of whom is the only black child in her preschool class and who comes home saying she wants blond hair, will "know different is good."[37] Indeed, when I have visited Martha's Vineyard in August, I have been overwhelmed by feelings of positive reinforcement. It is a place where two-parent black families abound, where community ties are strong, the web of relationships among blacks are extensive, and evidence of black success overflows. One feels love, support, and pride. The spirit is happy. The black children and adults who

return to the Vineyard year after year and decade after decade
are cultivating a support network and positive black identity
that cannot be recreated in a predominately white or maybe
even in an integrated setting. The positive impact of being
together with one's own attests to the critical role of black
enclaves and black institutions in an otherwise integrated
world. Those parents who live permanently in black neighborhoods don't have to worry about questions like, "Who are
your children going to date? Who are their friends going to be?
Will your children be accepted?"—concerns one black resident
of Hempstead, New York, cited for her reluctance to move to
whiter environs that might afford her children better schools.
She concludes that full integration is not her goal, implicitly
suggesting that the psychic benefits of a black enclave trump
any educational or other benefits her family might reap from a
white neighborhood. From her perspective, "it does not matter
if it's separate as long as it's equal."[38]

So residents of black enclaves want to reap the perceived
benefits of "we-ness," but they also want equal opportunities.
Whatever ambivalence black people feel about integration,
they are unequivocal about this desire for equal opportunity.
The hope, voiced by some, is that black communities can
somehow recapture the economic integration that made black
institutions most viable in the era of Jim Crow. Charismatic
local leaders, usually elders who experienced both Jim Crow
and integration, and who are involved in efforts to stabilize or
restore black neighborhoods to their former glory, express this
sentiment. Reverend Raymond Hammond, a black minister
and local organizer in Boston, obviously doesn't want to
return to Jim Crow but tells the *Boston Globe* that "the ideal
of integration" needs to be reexamined, that the "ideal of
opportunity" is still necessary, and that a community works
best economically, educationally, and socially if it stays

together.[39] W. W. Law, an unsung, now-deceased civil rights soldier who was attempting to revive the historic black business district in Savannah, told the *Globe* he favored "opportunity" over "integration," and Jim Goodwin, a black Tulsa attorney attempting to redevelop "the black Wall Street" along Greenwood Avenue, is content to rely solely on black entrepreneurs, a black bank, black investors, and eventually black patrons to make his development successful.[40] Similarly, former pupils of Charlotte, North Carolina's beloved and segregated Second Ward High School cherish the "nourishing and nurturing" they received in Second Ward classrooms in the fifties, believe that "black on black" would be "better than what it is now," and "don't mind resegregation if the schools are equal—and children have the same opportunities."[41]

Sentiments like these are not limited to black elders. As with Ms. Hopkinson, post–civil rights babies can be just as passionate in their affirmation of the benefits of separatism. A friend of mine, a thirty-seven-year-old African American graduate of Morehouse College, fits the mold. He is openly dubious about the integrationist choices of his father's generation. After attending elite private schools and a freshman year at an overwhelmingly white private university, he sensed he was missing something and chose to transfer to Morehouse, the venerable historically black male college in Atlanta, Georgia, that produced Martin Luther King, Spike Lee, Maynard Jackson, Edwin Moses, and Dr. David Satcher, to name just a few. He says he experienced "enlightenment" at Morehouse, developing a confidence in the intrinsic abilities of black men and black institutions. He chooses to live in a black neighborhood, parks his money in a black-owned bank, invests with a mutual fund, Ariel Capital, that was founded and is managed by an African American, counts successful black entrepreneurs among his closest friends and allies, and struggles with the relevance of integration, even as he has worked for both black businesses and predominately white employers.

It is not hard to find black people who express sentiments like this, although I do not intend to suggest that African Americans are monolithic in their attitudes about integration. I know and encounter black people who value living in integrated communities, and I do not believe their preferences are an aberration. Again, the vast majority of blacks, like the vast majority of Americans, support integration in the abstract. However, it is hard to find ardent black voices for integration and amazingly easy to find ambivalent ones. In my own nonrepresentative, nonscientific survey—in the course of writing this book I have had scores of conversations with black people about their personal attitudes toward integration—the sentiment about wanting equal opportunities is virtually universal, as is the rather obvious point that no one wants to return to the days of official segregation. But in conversation after conversation with black friends, acquaintances, and strangers, integration is simply not a priority in the way that getting ahead is. What black people now seem most ardent about is equality of opportunity. As one black acquaintance once put it, rather than wanting to integrate with whites, black people now seem more interested in having what whites have. In 2004, "separate but equal" may not sound so bad to many a black ear because, after the civil rights revolution, it can no longer mean state-imposed segregation, and the hope is that maybe this time around "equal" really could mean "equal."

Negotiating the Separatist Impulse:
The Challenges of Transcending Difference

Between black ambivalence and white fear about integration is a still extensive chasm that must be bridged if Martin Luther

King's vision of a beloved community in America is ever going to truly come to pass. At present, most of us are separatists with a small "s" and integrationists with a small "i." We believe in both ideologies to a degree, and we "multitask" when it comes to race relations, to the extent that we really attempt to relate to the "other" at all. We move back and forth between our frequently homogenous personal life space into sometimes integrated work and public spaces. In my experience on the East Coast, a truly integrated social gathering outside of work or a professional event is rare enough that one notices it when it happens. My sense is that this pattern of separate social space is more pronounced in areas with large black populations, where it is quite possible to form an extensive racial enclave both in neighborhoods and social circles, and where the presence of sizeable black populations raises the likelihood of fear of being overwhelmed on the part of other races. Our separatism is less pronounced in areas of the West and Southwest with small black populations.

Still, we all have a tendency to regard other groups and their tribal space with caution. We do not put ourselves in situations that will be too discomforting. In particular, all non-black groups are still most perplexed and fearful when it comes to black people, even as they can be fascinated appropriators and consumers of black popular culture. We have not yet solved the riddle of how to accomplish a being *together* of strangers in this country. Instead we have created mostly balkanized neighborhoods of race and class that can provide much positive reinforcement within particular communities but also have the effect of creating social distance that can be hard to bridge.

We do not emerge from the womb with separatist attitudes. The least race-conscious people in our society are children, whose main agenda is typically, "Do you want to play?" As we grow up we lose this playfulness and sense of adventure about difference. By middle school we begin to take on adult ways and adult-created stereotypes. We also begin to discover and explore personal identities, trying to decide who we are, where we fit in, and in what social milieu we will be accepted. Some argue that self-segregation among teenagers is a normal, necessary part of their psychological development.[42] Unfortunately, racial lines tend to be definitive in this process, and those kids who attempt to straddle these lines seem to have the hardest time. Our society tries to force them to choose. "Are you black? White? Puerto Rican? What *are* you?" "Why do you, a black girl, act white? Why do you talk proper?" Those who do not follow the conventional path or don't fit into a neat category, such as biracial children, can find this racial gauntlet exhausting and alienating.

There are a lot of factors both insidious and natural that lead to social and spatial separation of the races. It is human nature to identify with people with whom you share a common culture. It is not surprising that at an ostensibly "integrated" party of teenagers, all the black kids end up dancing in the basement and the white kids stand around upstairs and talk.[43] "Black" parties and "white" ones do tend to be quite different as a matter of culture and style. It is disturbing, however, that a degree of orthodoxy and social categorization can be imposed or inculcated as a result of groupthink. The racial drifting apart that tends to happen in the early teen years is animated just as much, if not more so, by black kids pulling away from others as the others pulling away from them. Whether animated by the draw of a hip-hop culture and style, in which white culture is largely irrelevant or uninteresting, or the need for a safe haven from the insults of a predominately white world, or a simple happiness with the familiarness of one's "boys," a powerful separatist current holds sway over many black kids in their teens.[44] But something else tends to happen in middle school that brings the insidiousness of the world of adults into the innocent world of children. In schools, children are typically assigned to separate academic ability tracks. That group tracking quickly separates mostly white kids into honors classes and mostly black kids into lower-level classes. It sends a corrosive message of difference that may explain why some black students start to believe that behaving like an honors student is "acting white." A friend of mine, a brilliant computer scientist who attended an integrated public high school in Washington, D.C., and went on to graduate from MIT, deftly negotiated this social tension. As a survival strategy, she learned to shed her upper-middle-class dialect when needed and learned how to "hang" with other black students, even as she attended honors classes. She says a relative of hers who did not learn to speak "Ebonics" and who maintained a very integrated social set was taunted unmercifully by black students in her high school. I, too, was a culturally dexterous kid in middle and high school. Like both my parents, I was an honors student who worked hard but also played hard and mastered the fundamentals of both black and mainstream culture in a way that enabled me to relate to many different social groups.

Moving beyond our separatist impulses is a formidable challenge. I see both promise and peril in demographic trends. As we evolve into a majority-minority nation, there is a risk that many whites will continue to follow the way of the bulwark, responding to fear rather than working to forge a new, twenty-first-century dynamic of diversified oneness. There is also the risk that black communities, particularly poor ones, will become even more marginalized in a nation that has moved on to other things and begun to respond to the political demands of other minority groups. The promise of a majority-minority nation, however, is that once no one racial group constitutes a majority, perhaps the fear factor or the defensive or indifferent response to difference can be reduced and replaced with a more positive acceptance, even celebration of difference.

Obviously whites and blacks are not the only players in our increasingly multihued, polyglot mixture of languages, cultures, skin colors, hair textures, dress, and varied sexual, social, political, and economic preferences. The black-white paradigm that has colored most civil rights and race discourse no longer fits our changing demographic reality. Still, blacks and whites tend to be at polar opposites along a racial spectrum that defines the dominant white culture on the one hand and the historically oppressed black masses on the other. In between are other groups emerging and laying claim to their own unique ethnic-American identity and dealing with their own struggles to be assimilated or not, embraced or not. Their striving for respect and equal opportunities mirrors the struggle of black people in this country in some ways but diverges radically in others.

The Push of Discrimination: Racial Steering

In November 1999, Lisa Lincoln, a Japanese American woman, inquired about a two-bedroom apartment in the Lakeview neighborhood of New Orleans, Louisiana. Lakeview is a moderately wealthy neighborhood of frame cottages and brick ranch houses. According to the latest census, it is 94 percent white, in a city that is 67 percent black. Upon inquiring,

Lincoln was told the apartment was available. When she showed up with her boyfriend, Don Weaver, who is black, they were told that someone was already holding a deposit on the place. Don had been interested in Lakeview because he was wanted to be near a park where his young son could play. Being suspicious, Lincoln and Weaver arranged for a white friend to inquire about the apartment, who, as they predicted, was told that it was available. Lincoln and Weaver then contacted the local fair housing agency, which sent testers to look into the apartment. All of the black testers were told that the apartment had been rented while all of the white testers were told that it was available. Weaver, an Army and Coast Guard veteran, described the entire experience as "culture shock" after "growing up here and going other places around the world and seeing people getting along." Lincoln and Weaver's lawsuit resulted in a jury verdict in their favor, with punitive damages of $100,000.[45]

Lovie Fisher-Townsell and Bernard Townsell, a black couple, learned by telephone in 2001 of an apartment available in Chicago's wealthy Near North Side area, which is 93 percent white according to the 2000 census. When they arrived to inspect the apartment, they were told falsely that it had been rented. The Townsells complained to the Leadership for Metropolitan Open Communities, which sent five testers to the eight-unit building. Only the whites were told that the apartment was available. The owners of the building settled the Townsell's lawsuit for $100,000.[46]

In 1999, the Justice Department resolved a lawsuit brought under the Fair Housing Act against Choice Property consultants. Choice was a company that landlords used to list rental properties. They would code the properties to indicate to whom landlords wished to rent. The code words "Archie" or

"Archianna" were used to indicate landlords who did not want to rent to blacks or Latinos.[47]

In 1996, Mary Holley, who is black, and her husband David, who is white, decided to look at houses in Twentynine Palms, a small town in southern California. They contracted Triad Realtors, the leading real estate firm in town, and indicated they could afford to spend $150,000. Triad agent Grove Crank showed them only a few smallish homes in their budget and others that were well out of their price range. While driving around in town, the Holleys spotted a home under construction. They knew the builder, Brooks Bauer, who told them he was asking $145,000 for the home, which was listed with Triad. The Holleys arranged to take a tour with a young agent and liked what they saw. They told the agent they wanted to make a down payment of $5,000 and would pay the remaining $140,000 when the house was completed. That evening, however, the agent who had shown them the house called to say that more senior agents, including Crank, found their down payment insufficient. A few months later, when the builder ran into Mary Holley at a store, he expressed surprise that she had not put an offer on the house. Holley told him that Triad had refused their offer. Bauer was quite upset, especially when he stopped by to discuss the matter with Crank, who referred to the Holleys as a "salt-and-pepper team," among other things. By then, Bauer had already sold the house for $20,000 less than the Holleys were willing to pay. Bauer reported the incident to a fair housing group, and Bauer and the Holleys eventually sued.[48]

In another incident, P. R. Hall, a real estate agent, successfully sued her employer, Lowder Realty, for violating the Fair Housing Act. She proved that the company matched the race of customers with the race of real estate agents and gave black agents business only in predominately black neighborhoods of Montgomery, Alabama. The end result was racial steering of all customers. In April, 2002, a jury awarded Hall $100,000 in damages.[49]

Stories like these are not unusual; in most of these cases, fortunately, the victims of discrimination were suspicious enough to seek the assistance of fair housing organizations that could send out testers to confirm that discrimination on the basis of race was occurring, or they discovered their mistreatment by happenstance. Many other victims of discrimination who ask about the availability of a house or apartment that is suddenly "no longer available" have no idea that they are being denied an opportunity or a choice typically freely available to a white person.

The most recent national audit of racial discrimination in housing, conducted in 2000, shows that although there has been considerable improvement since the last audit in 1989, whites are still consistently favored over racial minorities. Researchers for the study, commissioned by the Department of Housing and Urban Development, sent minority and white testers out to attempt to rent or purchase homes in twenty-three metropolitan areas with significant black or Latino populations. The test partners had virtually the same income, assets and debt liabilities, and education levels. Overall, *Latinos experienced more discrimination than blacks.* The group most discriminated against were Latino renters; landlords favored whites over this group one-quarter of the time. They favored whites over black renters one-fifth of the time. In particular, whites were more likely to receive information about available housing units and had more opportunities to inspect available units. The numbers were only slightly better for blacks and Latinos seeking to buy, rather than rent, a home.[50] The research evidence also suggested that blacks and Latinos experienced adverse treatment compared to equally qualified whites about half the time they visited real estate or rental offices in any major metropolitan area.[51] Asians and Native Americans do not escape housing discrimination; there is just less empirical data available regarding these groups. Pilot studies in a few select cities, however, also found systemic discrimination against Asian and Native American home buyers and renters.[52]

Although most measures of systemic racial discrimination declined in the 1990s, the study found a significant increase in what is known as "geographic steering," whereby minorities and whites are provided information about houses for sale in different types of areas. The study found that white and black home buyers were consistently steered to neighborhoods that promote or perpetuate segregation. The most prominent form of steering was gratuitous editorializing on the part of real estate agents, particularly those operating in areas with a high percentage white population. Overall, agent editorial comments were significantly more likely to encourage segregation rather than integration of the races. Agent commentary also tended to promote class separation; real estate agents "systematically offered editorial comments that encouraged white testers to choose homes in neighborhoods and school districts with lower poverty."[53] Such steering was most pronounced between black and white home buyers and neighborhoods and less often observed among white and Latino testers. But there was still some evidence of racial steering of Latinos.[54]

Discrimination also occurs in other dimensions of the housing market, such as mortgage lending. Even after controlling for differences in creditworthiness, studies have found large differences in mortgage loan denial rates between minority and white applicants. And often minorities who are successful in obtaining a mortgage receive less generous loan amounts and terms.[55] According to an analysis of mortgage lending in thirty-five cities between 1995 and 1997, African Americans were 210 percent more likely to be rejected than whites, and Latinos were rejected 176 percent more often than whites.[56] Blacks living in predominately black neighborhoods are frequently redlined by mainstream mortgage lenders and are forced to rely on the predatory loans made available by the subprime market. Half of all refinancings by minority borrowers are serviced by subprime lenders, with attendant usurious rates.[57]

Several researchers believe that discrimination and racial steering in real estate markets are the definitive forces that create segregated neighborhoods. Discrimination shapes the options available to racial minorities and hence likely shapes perceptions about what areas are welcoming to minorities. Whatever individual preferences or fantasies we each harbor concerning an "ideal" neighborhood, those racial minorities that attempt to buck the trend of racial separation in seeking a home are likely to encounter discrimination in some form, although they may not realize it is occurring. Some researchers argue that discrimination has a greater influence than individual preference.[58] Discrimination is a stubborn presence that we have not succeeded in eradicating. And housing is a realm where its perpetrators are perhaps most motivated and can easily escape detection. As my law professor colleague, John Calmore, once said: "Housing is the civil rights area that has most been plagued by slow, small advances, where the possibility for real change is viewed as most remote."[59]

Race and class segregation, then, is borne of both personal preferences and rank discrimination. Both reflect fundamental human impulses, one seemingly benign and the other nefarious. Is segregation an inherently natural consequence of human nature? I think not. There was a time, at the dawn of the twentieth century, when the natural tendency of American real estate markets was integration and heterogeneity. As I describe in Chapter 3, it took decades of affirmative public policy choices to develop a separatist bias. It might take several more decades to return America to an integrationist impulse.

CHAPTER 2

BUCKING THE TREND
Racially Integrated Communities and Racial Integration

THE ALBINA neighborhood in Northeast Portland defies our separatist tendencies. It is a multicultural island—a bohemian mélange of art galleries, organic co-op grocery stories, and black beauty salons. It wasn't always so. Oregon had its own unique take on the "Negro problem." It was the only state to be admitted to the Union with a clause in its constitution that mandated the exclusion of black people from the entire state. Once Oregon's exclusion law was repealed in 1926, other tactics to contain blacks were put in place. Racially restrictive real-estate covenants and racial steering gave blacks who migrated to Portland few options on where to live. Pullman porters and others who came to Portland to take advantage of job opportunities in the city, especially during a booming wartime industrial job market in the early 1940s, were steered primarily to Albina—a community that was, until the late nineteenth century, a stand-alone city. Midcentury, a series of large public works projects in the name of "urban renewal"—

the city coliseum in the 1950s, the I–5 interstate highway in the 1960s, and a major expansion of Emanuel Hospital in the 1970s—mowed through the black neighborhoods of Albina, over the protest of its black citizens. A relatively tepid, two-day riot in Albina in August 1967, like larger conflagrations elsewhere in the country during those long hot summers, was a display of black frustration. With the social upheaval from such displacement, withdrawal of investment, and other woes, Albina followed a familiar pattern of urban blight that took hold in the 1960s. A steady loss of population, housing, jobs, and businesses continued and even accelerated in some neighborhoods that, by the late 1980s, were associated with drug-related gang activity.

But things changed dramatically in the 1990s. Black-white segregation fell 23 percent in Portland, primarily because of an influx of mostly childless whites into neighborhoods once dominated by the city's small African American community. Albina has now become a magnet for nonblacks with open minds and a willingness to live in or near a black bastion that claims MLK Boulevard as its major thoroughfare.

This is a story that has played itself out in countless other American cities. It remains to be seen whether Albina will become a rare example of a population influx that results in stable diversity rather than mere displacement of one race by another. It may well. Portland is only 3 percent black. Like other western cities with small black populations, it has fewer challenges to negotiate in creating stable, integrated spaces. It will take many more individuals choosing to live in integrated settings and much more of an institutional shift in support of integration to make neighborhoods like Albina the stable, successful norm rather the exception.

I begin this chapter by attempting to quantify how many

American neighborhoods actually achieve stable integration. Next I describe the two kinds of integrated communities that have emerged since the 1960s: biracial middle-class enclaves and, more recently, multicultural islands. I then explore the type of people who tend to be integrators in American society—the relatively few ardent integrationists who believe in integration, seek it out, and live it as a personal value, as well as the accidental integrationists, who find themselves in integrated settings and make an affirmative choice to stay and make it work. Finally, I address the challenges inherent in creating or maintaining integrated communities and argue the case for integration. As with a marriage, successful stable integration requires work.

The Extent of Racial Integration

How much stable integration is there in America? It is a difficult question to answer, in part because defining "stable integration" is itself a challenge. In a society that, as of June 2003, was roughly 68 percent white, 13.5 percent Latino, 12 percent black, 4 percent Asian, and 2 percent "other," what constitutes meaningful integration?

The answer to that question is subjective. Any definition of integration will necessarily be arbitrary and value laden. Some academics define racially integrated neighborhoods as ones that are between 10 percent and 50 percent black.[1] Yet that definition excludes, for example, any neighborhood that might be 51 percent black and still very mixed racially. It seems to buy into the dangerous logic that a predominately black neighborhood cannot be an integrated one. On the other hand, by focusing on the degree to which blacks are present, this definition implicitly recognizes that incorporating African Americans into other people's life space is the great challenge of integration. In 1990, according to one observer, 19 percent of all neighborhoods met this definition of "integration." In that year, about 15 percent of whites and a third of blacks lived in neighborhoods that were 10 to 50 percent black.[2] But to be understood as racially stable, a neighborhood should have had roughly the same racial composition in 2000 as it did in 1990.

A more pointed, and I think accurate, way of determining the extent of racial integration has been offered by another research team. Recognizing that diversity in a neighborhood is likely to be the ephemeral result of racial transition, these researchers reasoned that if the majority of neighborhoods within a socially recognized community have a racial/ethnic percentage that roughly mirrors the city's overall racial/ethnic averages *and* if the community is recognized as diverse by people who live and work there, it probably is diverse. Researchers using this definition of integration "conservatively estimate that more than 10 million Americans are living in relatively stable diverse communities."[3] At the time they made this estimate, in 1998, our national population was approximately 272 million. In other words, according to this conservative estimate, less than 4 percent of Americans lived in stable integrated surroundings. I most prefer this definition because it accounts for the differing racial makeup of individual metropolitan areas—what counts as "integrated" in one region may not elsewhere. Still another research team that quantified the extent of integration defined "integration" in terms of city blocks with at least 20 percent blacks and 20 percent whites. Looking at the fifty largest cities in the United States, they found that only 9.4 percent of citizens lived on such "integrated" blocks.[4]

No matter how you define it, it appears that the universe of stable racial integration in the United States is a small, exceptional parallel to the dominant, separatist universe that the majority of Americans experience. Truly integrated neighborhoods are rare. Maybe that is why people who live in such communities tend to embrace and brag about their diversity. They frequently work to promote and nurture this identity. Likewise, people who live elsewhere typically can identify the rare multicultural island or integrated neighborhood surrounded by a sea of separation.

The Characteristics of Integration: Biracial and Multiracial Communities

To the limited extent that they do exist, there are two main types of stable integrated neighborhoods, one older and another that is emerging but has been in existence for over a decade. The first type, which researchers classify as diverse "by direction," tend to be older suburbs that border a central city. They tend to be biracial, that is, black and white, rather than multiracial. They also tend to be decidedly middle class both in perspective and in demographics, with higher median incomes than the regional average. Most of these are older, inner-ring suburbs that managed to stem the tide of neighborhood transition that rolled through so many places in America when black people began to exercise new liberties and choices that came with fair housing laws and emerging middle-class status. Black and white leaders in these communities consciously articulated diversity as a goal in the early stages of community transition and developed a civic infrastructure, a web of community organizations and social arrangements as well as a social and political atmosphere intentionally aimed at creating and sustaining diversity. These are places like Shaker Heights and Cleveland Heights outside of Cleveland; Southfield outside of Detroit; Oak Park and Park Forest outside of Chicago; Maplewood–South Orange outside of Newark, New Jersey; Fleetwood (Mt. Vernon) outside New York City; Ferguson outside of St. Louis; Sherman Park in Milwaukee; Vollantine-Evergreen in Memphis; Park Hill outside Denver, and West Mount Airy in Philadelphia. In all these communities, individuals and institutions understood that diversity tends to breed instability and that extraordinary effort and sustained attention were necessary to cultivate a positive ethos that would sustain intergroup relations and hence integration.[5]

The second type of stable diverse neighborhood, described as diverse "by circumstance," tends to be multiracial (or multiethnic) and multiclass. These are poorer communities compared to the Shaker Heights and West Mount Airys of the nation, but they represent what may be a more common possibility in our majority-minority future. They are most common in cities or areas with an abundance of affordable rental housing that have become a magnet for recent immigrants. Diversity in these communities is a by-product of social and economic forces that were initially beyond the control of residents: an influx of immigrants, an aging white population that moves or dies out, making way for new and different residents, or a reinvestment in a formerly rundown neighborhood that invites a modicum of white middle-income residents but not a wholesale gentrification. The lack of a numerical and hence political dominance of any one racial, ethnic, or class group in such neighborhoods can mean a peaceful coexistence for all. Examples include Adams-Morgan in Washington, D.C.; Jackson Heights and Fort Greene in New York; Rogers Park, Edgewater, Uptown, and Chicago Lawn in Chicago; San Antonio and Fruitvale in Oakland; and Houston Heights in Houston.

So we have two primary models of integrated neighborhoods, both of which either directly or indirectly assuage the fear element that can contribute to separatism. The first involves a melding of people of different races along a common bond of middle-class experience. In established, predominately white suburban communities, an influx of professional black middle-class movers is less threatening to white suburbanites. There is a natural selection of sorts among integration pioneers. Educated middle- and upper-middle-class black movers tend to be the ones willing and able to "invade" majority-white middle-class territory. Communities like West Mount Airy in Philadelphia and others show that a stable, if fragile, coexistence between whites and blacks can be forged with a high degree of social engineering and intent—when the black folks involved also share a middle-class perspective. This is not easy work. Indeed, it is probably more difficult than the second possibility: the multicultural island. In a multicultural neighborhood, where no one group dominates, no one seems to feel threatened, even when low-income minorities are part of the mix. I find this second possibility more promising, but both types offer object lessons about the project of integration and its challenges. I will now examine these two models more closely, presenting first the biracial example of West Mount Airy and then the multicultural example of Southeast Seattle.

Biracial, Middle-Class Enclaves

West Mount Airy in Philadelphia is an often-lauded example of middle-class mixing of blacks and whites, a community where stable integration came about because of sustained efforts of community leaders and institutions. Located in the northwest reaches of the city of Philadelphia, West Mount Airy is roughly half black, 44 percent white, 2 percent Latino, 1 percent Asian, and 1 percent "other." It is buffered to the west by overwhelmingly white and upper-class Chestnut Hill and the overwhelmingly white middle- and working-class communities of Roxborough and Manayunk. It is buffered to the east by the overwhelmingly black communities of East Mount Airy and Germantown. Germantown, East Mount Airy, and West Mount Airy all started out as all-white communities. The racial transition that began in the 1950s in these communities was mediated in West Mount Airy because of a combination of lucky circumstances and aggressive intervention. The communities that border it are a window onto the racial homogeneity that it narrowly escaped; they suggest quite clearly that separation is our ultimate tendency, particularly in a bipolar dynamic between two races and particularly where one of those races is black. In such a milieu, in the absence of aggressive countermeasures, separation seems inevitable.

West Mount Airy has many of the characteristics that are common to other older, intentionally diverse communities. Its housing stock is diverse, architecturally varied, and pleasing. West Mount Airy has single homes, duplexes, and apartments in addition to grand historical houses. The wide variety of home prices and styles enable a degree of economic diversity. The community has a country-village feel because of its grand stone mansions and charming row houses, amidst trees and yards in close proximity to parks. It is also one of the most historic areas in Philadelphia. The Pelham Road area, known as the Pelham district, is a community of carefully designed Victorian hybrids from the early twentieth century that was created to attract homeowners of diverse tastes and backgrounds.

The neighborhood is lush and suburban in feel and is complemented by close proximity to Fairmount Park, the largest landscaped urban park in the world with 8,900 acres of winding creeks, green meadows, and rustic trails. It is not a high-density community. There is a sense of space. It has been argued that East Mount Airy did not fare as well in countering white flight because of its much more densely developed row housing, suggesting that it is harder to live with "the other" when they literally are right next door.[6]

Although there is a relatively diverse income range in the community, the predominant middle-class background and perspective of blacks and whites living or moving into the community has minimized any potential social gulf. As with all other older diverse communities, West Mount Airy boasts a number of institutions that offer "social seams" for social and cultural interaction. There are more places for differing groups to come together on a regular basis here than in most other communities, including grocery stores, shops, relatively integrated schools and parent teacher associations, parks, interfaith religious services, community days and neighborhood festivals. These are the stuff of community, a web of interconnectedness that is developed and palpable in older stable diverse communities. Finally, and perhaps most importantly, West Mount Airy has a history of activism and intervention to support and nurture its integrated identity.[7]

Regarding its demographics, West Mount Airy seemed to benefit from having—to be blunt—just the right type of white and black folks to make stable integration possible. In the 1950s, as is the case today, its white community was heavily Jewish, very educated, and liberal.[8] The West Mount Airy community has earned the moniker of "Ph.D. ghetto" because it attracts a disproportionate number of highly educated people who are affirmatively committed to living in a diverse community. Many white residents are apt to cite the community's diversity as its main attraction. Researchers have argued that the many higher-income white residents of West Mount Airy also enjoyed a level of economic security such that any possibility of a decline in housing values due to a black influx could be buffered with other economic resources. (In fact, after some initial softness in the housing market when blacks started moving in, housing values remained stable and have increased over time in West Mount Airy.) The community's many high-income whites could also afford private school, so that any concerns about the public schools were not a barrier to living in West Mount Airy. Also, the economic security and educationally elite status of many white West Mount Airy residents was such that they would not be concerned with a "loss of status," which whites of lesser means might associate with living in an integrated neighborhood.

The black people who live in West Mount Airy, on the other hand, do not cite diversity as their main rationale for living there. For them, the affordable housing stock, the relatively high-quality public schools, the community's upwardly mobile profile, and its reputation for racial tolerance are more important factors. In fact, empirical research suggests that most minority families that seek out integrated neighborhoods do so not because of any ideological commitment to diversity but because they believe these places will offer enhanced opportunities and resources.[9] Minority movers understand intrinsically the way of markets and political influence: A neighborhood that is home to some upper-middle-class white people or prominent white families is likely to do better in the competition for resources. I wish this were not so in America, but it is.

These dominant perspectives among black and white residents of the West Mount Airy neighborhood underscore the degree to which class can be an essential link to mutual under-standing between the races. Let's face it: Racial integration with black people is not a natural inclination for the vast majority of white people in this nation. People who wonder aloud about why all the black students are sitting together in the cafeteria never seem to acknowledge or perceive that there is a sea of white students also sitting together. Whites with higher educational backgrounds and greater economic means may be more disposed to an integrationist mind-set. Or rather, it may be easier to cultivate an integrationist ethos among whites who feel a certain security of status. But everyone has a comfort zone, the limits of which are defined by each individ-ual's history and experience. It takes an unusual person to go boldly where others have not gone before, to step out of a seemingly natural pattern of being with one's own, to, say, walk over to the "black table" and have a seat. The baby steps a white person may be inclined to take in the direction of inte-gration are certainly made easier if they are moving toward people of another race who share similar values and perspec-tives, which is to say, if they share the same class.

This certainly seems to have been the experience of West Mount Airy and virtually all of the older, intentionally inte-grated communities formed by blacks and whites in the '60s and '70s. I do not think it is mere coincidence that many of the well-known integrated communities that are held up as exem-plars of successful integration—such as Hyde Park in Chicago and Oak Park in its suburbs or Cleveland Heights and Shaker Heights outside of Cleveland—share the same demographic profile: middle and upper middle class, highly educated, pro-fessional. For high-income, educated whites seeking a diverse alternative to separatism and a striving black middle class on a quest for quality of opportunity, these relatively few integrated communities have offered a logical common ground.

The same could happen for any two racial or ethnic groups with similarly congruent aspirations. Integrated neighborhoods can offer something that people of both races want, although primary motivations may differ slightly. Either way, an integrationist mind-set is required to live in these communities. Above all, an integrator possesses a willingness to be with and among people who are different to some degree and a willingness to work at negotiating those differences.

Among the many organizations that nurture diversity in the community, perhaps the best known is West Mount Airy Neighbors (WMAN). Founded in 1959 specifically to deal with fostering integration, WMAN focused in its early days on unethical real estate practices like racial steering and blockbusting, urging realtors not to engage in such practices and lobbying the city council to ban or limit "For Sale" signs and to use the zoning code in ways that fostered rather than inhibited integration. WMAN was also an early advocate for desegregation of West Mount Airy schools. More recently it has been deeply involved in promoting revitalization and beautification of Germantown Avenue, a major commercial thoroughfare. It has also sponsored numerous Mount Airy events to enhance social interaction, most prominently, "Mount Airy Day," a joint effort with East Mount Airy Neighbors that celebrates diversity and unity.

West Mount Airy's religious community has also worked to cultivate integration in the community. When African Americans first began moving into the neighborhood, synagogue and church leaders were among the first to assuage rising alarm in the white community. The Germantown Jewish Centre, built just a few years before black movers started arriving, had a vested interest in keeping and attracting Jewish members in the neighborhood. Its leader, Rabbi Elias Charry, along with religious leaders from varied synagogues and churches threatened with the loss of membership from any suburban exodus, went door to door to try to persuade white residents not to leave the neighborhood. To this day, the religious community remains active on issues of diversity, be it through a workshop on diversity training sponsored by the Unitarian Church, or the Lutheran Seminary's work with schools on such issues, or the simple effort of many congregations to incorporate diversity values into regular worship.

Hence, in West Mount Airy, as well as other established integrated communities, community and religious organizations' direct interventions on behalf of diversity are broad and deep. Some communities have organizations devoted solely to promoting diversity and offering programs designed to ensure inclusion. Others have organizations devoted to easing intergroup or black-white tensions. In Oak Park, Illinois, for example, a suburb of Chicago, residents have used a variety of methods to prevent racial flipping. They banned "For Sale" signs to keep whites from panic selling. They offered equity insurance packages to homeowners who were convinced their property values would plummet as racial minorities moved in. They currently counsel both blacks and whites to consider moving into integrated neighborhoods, and they redraw school boundaries when racial balance in any one of the elementary schools begins "looking less like the community as a whole."[10] Such efforts are part of a complex web of sustained efforts in these older suburban or semi-suburban enclaves of integration.

Some may wonder whether such intentionality is worth it. When people have to be given financial incentives to move onto blocks where another race predominates—as is offered in

Shaker Heights, Ohio—and a degree of separatism still pervades many neighborhoods and most social settings, it certainly raises questions as to whether this energy is well spent.[11] Many intentionally integrated communities, such as Oak Park, the Nineteenth Ward of Rochester in New York, and Sherman Park in Milwaukee, Wisconsin, have experienced racial change in the typical "invasion-succession pattern"—one race "invades" a neighborhood and ultimately becomes the dominant or sole occupier—despite conscious strategies designed to maintain integration.[12] Communities that work extremely hard at maintaining integration still experience a slow "blackening." Integrated communities that attract large numbers of African Americans are swimming against a tide of institutional and individual predisposition toward separation. Those victorious communities that manage to achieve reasonably stable diversity have built an extended institutional framework for intergroup communication, for articulation of and dealing with critical community issues, including, when necessary, offering a strong lobbying voice vis-à-vis elected officials and city government.

The Multicultural Island

A different, perhaps more common scenario for integration in the future is the multicultural island. Southeast Seattle embodies this possibility. Of 70 percent of the neighborhood's blocks, at least two of the three major ethnic groups in Seattle—blacks, whites, and Asians or Pacific Islanders—make up at least 20 percent of the block. It has attractive physical characteristics that home buyers of all races, particularly whites, often want, such as high bluffs that offer views of Lake Washington, the mountains, or the city skyline.

Southeast Seattle became integrated over time mainly because of overspill from the Asian neighborhoods of Beacon Hill and the African American neighborhoods of the Central Area. This influx of minorities did not result in white flight. Instead, the housing diversity in Southeast Seattle, coupled with its attractive surroundings and community activism, seems to have given people of all races many reasons to stay. Like most multicultural islands, there is a great degree of income diversity in Southeast Seattle because of the wide diversity in housing. There are many older homes, including fixer-uppers with spectacular views, as well as more inner-city neighborhoods.

Southeast Seattle clearly has developed an identity as an exceptionally diverse part of town, one that seems to attract both activists and those who savor difference. Interracial couples are far more evident here than in other parts of town. One can hear many languages spoken, and foreign language signs abound. Many people seem to come here not just for the diversity but also for the sense of community. One resident commented to researchers studying the community's diversity, "The Southeast may be as important for who chooses to be there as [it is] for what is done through formal mechanisms. It's amazing how many activists live in the neighborhood." Said another: "More than anything else, the value of life in this neighborhood is the sense of the neighborhood itself ... a sense which has been lost in white suburbia [with experiences like] playing cards on the porch up the street or finding a bag of Mrs. Frazier's green beans on their doorstep."[13] A newcomer to the neighborhood described its impact on his outlook toward diversity this way:

> I told [my fiancée] "We can't live in that neighborhood. It's too dangerous. It's just too hard to live there." I had a lot of

baggage, I think, about this neighborhood. . . . When we first got here I used to take the bus to work, and a lot of times I'd be the only white passenger on the bus. Now I actually like the fact that I might be a minority in this neighborhood. And that's something that's, I think, hard to find in Seattle: where a white male is a minority.[14]

Beyond its multicultural character, its established diverse identity, and its diverse housing, Southeast Seattle also has an abundance of community organizations that build community. A representative of the Mutual Partnerships Coalition, a local group committed to making diverse communities work explained to researchers:

When I look at a neighborhood, I don't look at it from the perspective of integration . . . because the goal becomes trying to become integrated rather than trying to develop relationships. I think throughout the whole civil rights movement the issue was not necessarily integration, it was about having equal access, about choice, about education, about economic development. So for me, a neighborhood—I see it from the perspective of people who have things in common regardless of where they're coming from [or] what their ethnic background might be. But they're working toward building a healthy community through healthy relationships. And healthy means when people come together because they care about each other, and they care what's happening in their neighborhood, on their streets, and to each other.[15]

Multicultural islands such as Southeast Seattle may have less need for organizations that deal directly with maintaining integration or negotiating intergroup tensions because, as one

Chicago resident of a multicultural community observed, "What we have in common are our differences."[16] Still, making a diverse community viable requires work on those quality of life issues that make a community attractive: schools, crime, physical surroundings, commercial vitality, and so on. Diverse communities may need to work a little harder at these issues because of the perception by a large number of people that diverse or integrated communities are risky or unstable. As residents of multicultural, multiclass communities experience working together to get something done—be it a neighborhood ethnic festival, a community policing initiative, or an effort to bolster local public schools, like the Powerful Schools coalition in Seattle—they are building bonds across race and class and support the notion that integration can work. As victorious multiracial and multiclass coalitions form and endure, these accidentally diverse communities may evolve into communities more directed at maintaining diversity.[17]

In contrast to the biracial middle-class enclaves, the multicultural islands go against a tidal wave of classism that is evident and growing in the rest of the country. To achieve exceptional race mixing, class mixing must occur. Close observers of stable integrated communities of either type have found that rental housing typically accounts for 25 to 50 percent of the residences in such neighborhoods. To be diverse, a neighborhood needs single-family homes, duplexes, market-rate rental apartments, *and* subsidized housing. The most diverse of all places, the multicultural islands, do not vilify low-income people. They include them. In Jackson Heights in New York and in Uptown Chicago, clusters of higher-income residents live four or five blocks away from low-rent block areas.[18] In Clinton Township, a hamlet described as a "Little United Nations" in Macomb County northeast of Detroit,

low-income apartments can be found just blocks from
$150,000 to $200,000 homes.[19] Each multicultural island has
its own dynamic and means of building bonds across the
chasm of class. Usually there is a positive draw for a variety of
socioeconomic types, be it affordable apartments, scenic views,
or ethnic restaurants. Unlike with the often tense, two-race
dynamic of black-white relations, the lower-income people in
multicultural islands are more apt to find a kinship among
themselves than any schism. One African American man who
lives in the San Antonio district of Oakland described it this
way to the *San Francisco Chronicle*:

> Everyone's riding the same bus, just struggling. Everyone has
> a sad story. It ain't just black people—it's the people who
> don't have, the have-nots. Our neighbors are all Mien, Laot-
> ian, Filipino. The teenagers are all smoking and doing donuts
> [360-degree spins in their cars]. They're doing the quote-
> unquote black ghetto thing. That's the first thing I tripped off
> on—Asian people doing the things I used to do when I was a
> kid. Asians are doing the same thing quote-unquote brothers
> are doing. It's a street thing. It's an Oakland thing ... it's an
> economic thing.[20]

The multicultural islands, then, embody a rare integrationist spirit. Their diversity reflects globalization trends. In
Edgewater and Uptown in Chicago, the students at the local
public high school come from families that speak sixty-five different native languages. In the Jackson Heights section of
Queens, New York, one can take an "International Express"
subway tour, given by locals, that features a dizzying array of
ethnic stores and restaurants.[21] In the San Antonio district of
East Oakland there is a veritable ethnic scramble, or rather, a

Tower of Babel. At Garfield Elementary School, the Spanish-
and English-speaking kids compete with speakers of Mien,
Cantonese, Khmer, Vietnamese, Lao, Tagalog, Arabic, Tongan,
and even one student who speaks Farsi and another who
speaks Bosnian. The San Antonio population itself is 34 percent Asian, 27 percent Latino, 23 percent black, 12 percent
white, and 3 percent biracial. The sum total is "roiling, hot-
blooded, exceptional diversity."[22] It is hard to develop pernicious divisions in such a pluralistic environment.[23] Cultural
differences are so common they are expected. One can't live in
a multicultural island and not develop some cultural and class
dexterity.

The multicultural islands are pioneering their way into new
social and political territory. They are beginning to address
enormously complex challenges of building relationships
across race and class—challenges that the nation itself will one
day be forced to grapple with frontally. Far beyond the bipolar,
black-white dimension of race relations in older integrated
communities, in the multicultural islands, community groups
can find themselves negotiating "White/Vietnamese/new
Latino immigrant/established Latino/African American residential mixes."[24] They are a window onto the cultural shift I
believe the vast majority of Americans need to embrace if we
are to achieve a multiracial, multiclass democracy that truly
does offer equality and equal dignity to all persons.

The Integrators: Ardent and Accidental Integrationists

I take heart in those individuals who choose to go against our
collective, separatist grain. We have a lot to learn from them.
The integrators among us, in my view, are on the cutting edge

of advancing our democracy. Those in the trenches of building relationships across differences of race and class understand better than most the challenges and the delicious possibilities that lie ahead in our diverse future. Integration, as they attest, has its benefits and challenges.

Ardent Integrationists

A woman I know who lives in Brookland, an integrated neighborhood in northeast Washington, D.C., near Catholic University, is an ardent integrator. I will call her Katherine. She describes herself as a "CIA brat." A mother with children ranging in age from five to seventeen, she and her husband are white, as are her children. She is a local activist who has ensconced her family in a heavily black area that has an average income of about $41,000. All of her children have attended D.C. public schools, although lately three of her kids are in public charter schools. She works part-time because, she says, her other "part-time job is to be an active parent," particularly in her children's schools. (It is not lost on me that Katherine can afford to work part-time and devote so much effort to her children's schools precisely because her family has chosen to live in an integrated neighborhood with housing prices at a fraction of the cost of the majority-white bastions in this metropolitan region.) At one of her children's schools Katherine is the PTA president. She is also an insistent advocate—the kind that gets labeled a troublemaker, she says—in some majority-black settings. Katherine admits that she is like many white parents, who, she says are "more likely to expect change [from a school or the school system] and know how to make it change." She is making a cultural, not a derogatory, statement about the different tendencies of black and white school parents. She says she observes many black parents who feel less empowered simply yank their kids from schools where they don't like what is going on.

Katherine has become a student of such subtle cultural and class differences because, through her paid work in public schools and her activism, she finds herself working in all parts of the city. She brings a learned sensitivity to bear in the several multiracial, multiclass contexts in which she finds herself or her children. She says that she has "found the quality" and the "things that work" in D.C. public schools and is very happy with the results for her children, although she admits that "you have to be vigilant and informed about what works." She has had her kids in a public Montessori school for ages three through twelve, a public charter school, and a magnet arts school. Of her oldest, she says she is proud that she has raised an "urban city kid who is a citizen of the world." Katherine worries aloud that her son, who is so ensconced in minority culture, particularly blackness, "won't have the armor" to negotiate the separated adult world he will soon enter.

"I chose to put my kids in D.C. public schools because I want to make a difference for other people's kids," she says. "I chose to live in the city, with its free museums" and abundant culture. "I don't want to protect my kids from the world. I think the world is cool and rich. I want them exposed to that but I want space in the world for them," Katherine laments. Because her children have grown up as the odd white kids in overwhelmingly minority schools and neighborhoods, because they have become completely acculturated to "otherness," because they are so different from most white kids in this respect, she worries about where they will fit in America's racially separated architecture. Still, she would not have it any other way.

"Nothing is more exciting than working for public education," she says with the fervor of an old-line integrationist. She marvels that the birthday parties for kids at her children's charter school can be "in housing projects or half-million dollar homes west of the park." It is wonderful, in her mind, that children of all backgrounds who attend this school can have these common experiences. "If more schools did a better job of making all types of people feel welcome, then diversity could work," she argues, because "the resources of the middle class will be translated to everybody." She admits that her children's school does not always "get it right," but they have a diversity task force, and they work at it.

Katherine has a quick response for other white parents who take a dim view of her choice to place her kids in an overwhelmingly minority school setting. She says she gets comments like "I admire you, but I could not do that to my children" or "I would worry about the violence." Katherine's response is fierce and original: "I am not treating my kids like lab rats. What are you afraid of?" As for the threat of violence in a large, predominately black city, she says, "There are worse things than getting shot. I don't want my kids to grow up being afraid of black people. In a world as rich and diverse as the one we live in, *that* [choosing separation] would be a soulless, impoverished existence." She feels that whites who take the safe, suburban, separated route "have a stingy soul; they are being stingy with the opportunities they have." She makes an affirmative choice to be in the fight for the health of a city and its public school system, even though she could move elsewhere or perhaps opt for private schools. Her characterization of the private school prestige chase that pervades upper-class families in the D.C. area is equally withering. "The pressure on kids at elite private schools, like Sidwell, is so high." An over-elevated "success standard" can be "very limiting for kids," she argues. Instead of focusing on giving kids an "artificial perfection," she wishes more parents would focus on "giving kids the tools to negotiate the world." "What will serve you better for living life? What kind of world are you ultimately going to live in?"

Katherine is asking the hard questions and living integration in a way that precious few Americans of any race do. She is highly unusual, at least in my experience. But after several years of conversations and preparation for this book, I have come across scores of people who are integrators and countless more who would like to be, if society would only make it a little easier.

My colleague Peter Byrne is such an integrator. A member of the Georgetown University law faculty, he and his wife, Karen, who are white, have lived in Capitol Hill neighborhoods southeast of the U.S. Capitol since the early 1980s. They sent all three of their kids to the Capitol Hill Cluster School, the best public school among the city's poorer eastern quadrants and a blending of three formerly freestanding preschool, elementary, and middle schools that was created to keep middle-class white families in the neighborhood. Peter's two daughters attended the school through the sixth grade. In her final year there, the younger of the two was one of only four white children in her class. Says Peter of their experience, "There were real advantages. I would definitely do it again. My daughters developed a perspective on their lives and on other people that was tremendously helpful. They now attend the National Cathedral School, and they are not caught up in the wealth that permeates that school. They have a generous and realistic image in their minds about people of color from having grown up with them." The experience, he says, worked almost perfectly for his oldest daughter, who grew up with and continues to have friends who are about half black and half white. She developed an "easy camaraderie" with the children of firemen, public school teachers, and others in the ranks of the working class. She continues to live an integrated life at the elite, private NCS school.

Another person I recently encountered is a staunch advocate for integration based upon his own personal experiences. A Yale University law student I met when giving a lecture at the school, Jay Readey, who describes himself as a "tall white guy," argues that I should be exhorting white people to integrate: "White folks should find ways to move into integrated communities, and ... when they live in segregated white communities they have an obligation to be receptive and even inviting to people of color in order to create more integrated neighborhoods." He believes that integration ought to be a "white obligation" because "so much of the historical burden of integration has fallen on communities of color." He described his own experience with integration in an e-mail to me:

I grew up sheltered in a 99% white Columbus, Ohio, suburb, then had several transformative experiences concerning race when I came to Yale as an undergraduate.... I majored in African-American and American studies as a result of my experiences.... I have remained in New Haven, spending six years in the nonprofit sector working with young people and [in] neighborhood development before returning to Yale for a JD/MBA. For the first four years, I lived in an Empowerment Zone neighborhood with a group of African-American male roommates, buying and renovating a blighted home. When I got married four years ago, my spouse and I moved 3/4 mile to a more middle-class neighborhood (still in New Haven), one that is fantastically integrated with middle-class

African-Americans, orthodox and conservative Jews, and a
significant portion of others (including me). My experiences
living integration have been powerful and life-affirming, and
I believe there is instrumental and symbolic value in sharing
such realities.

I recall Lynn, a white woman who lives in Arlington, Virginia. Lynn is a professional working woman and a soccer
mom. She and her family live on a major thoroughfare in what
she describes as "an old holdout house," located right next
door to a complex of subsidized apartments and across the
road from an upper-middle-class residential development. The
neighborhood offers "huge variety, kids of all races, languages,
and ethnicities." Lynn grew up in West Mount Airy and
wanted a similarly diverse experience for her children. "I
actively fled neighborhoods that were too white—they made
me nervous—and I have avoided predominately white schools,
including one that is conveniently right down the street in our
neighborhood," she says. Instead, Lynn chose the Key School
for her son because it offered a Spanish-language immersion
program and "a community that validates diversity." She says
the Key School ingeniously turned a large Latino population
that had been an impetus for white flight into an asset by creating the immersion program. As a result, her son, a sixth-
grader, speaks Spanish fluently. He thinks the Key School
environment is the way the world is. Still, Lynn admits that
diversity has its challenges. Her son's soccer team is "very
divided socially, especially along class lines." The Latino kids
"have different expectations about what is important. They
think my son is bookish, and he is bookish." But Lynn's son is
also a mediator, indeed, an integrator on the soccer team and
in life.

Accidental Integrationists

I met Lynn along with of group of nine other white moms, most of whom live in South Arlington. Arlington County, Virginia, is a short drive from the District of Columbia and quite different in terms of its racial and economic makeup and the quality of its public school system. In contrast to the District, Arlington County is majority white and only 8 percent of its population lives below the official poverty line. South Arlington is far more diverse than the county as a whole, being a little more than half white, 30 percent Latino, 18 percent black, and 9 percent Asian. Although there are some pockets of integration in this community, much of the diversity is achieved through small clusters of sameness. Historically, there were areas of the county where freed blacks lived after the Civil War, creating some heavily black neighborhoods, which are now matched by some heavily Latino neighborhoods. The schools in South Arlington are diverse because they are surrounded by middle-class single-family residential developments that are bordered on their periphery by major thoroughfares dotted with affordable apartments, which in turn attract lower-income people, often recent immigrants. As a result, there is no chance of escaping diversity in the South Arlington public schools.

I had to overcome my own initial discomfort in order to have a meaningful conversation with this group. I, the constant integrator, who is so very accustomed to being the sole person of color in a room of white people, felt uncomfortable utterly surrounded by ten women who were all white, all suburban, all moms and, as far as I could gather, all married—four things that I, as a then-single, childless black female who lived in the city, did not have in common with these women.

But I sipped a glass of wine, adopted a "what the hell" attitude, and just started talking with them.

They did not have horns and they did not fit any stereotype. A few were living where they do because they chose diversity. A few found themselves in diverse surroundings by happenstance; the house they bought was affordable, people of color happened to live nearby. Jan moved with her husband from the east side of Cleveland. "We had always lived as adults in diverse neighborhoods. We chose the Claremont neighborhood because it had trees, we could afford it and the house was not falling down, and it was diverse, in that order." Linda, who also lives in Claremont, had to overcome a realtor who tried to steer her to neighborhoods in Maryland. "The realtor told me I would be making a 'mistake' by looking to buy in northern Virginia, since 'all you will be able to afford is South Arlington.'" She says she and her husband "bought the house blind," not realizing how integrated the neighborhood was. But they stayed and are content there.

I got the impression that most of the others in the group did not live on especially integrated blocks. Instead they lived in mostly white neighborhoods in an otherwise fairly diverse area. But all of them had chosen integration in one very important sense. When the time came for their children to enter elementary school, they chose public schools. Many white parents in their circumstances chose to send their children to private schools or to move to north Arlington, where the public schools are majority white and the test scores much higher. These women chose to stay and send their children to schools where they are outnumbered by Latinos and African Americans. They did not see themselves as heroes for doing this. But their decision not to move or to abandon local public schools does reflect a certain conscious idealism about how society ought to be. The other critical choice for these women was whether to stay in the South Arlington public schools once their children had moved on to middle and high school. Several had reached that juncture and stayed the course. In a majority-white, majority middle-class school system, the children of these women attended schools that are mostly Latino, then black, then white, with a few Asians. In most of these schools, as many as half of the students receive free or reduced-price lunch.

The participation of these middle-class white families in Arlington public schools underscores just how critical maintaining quality is to enhancing opportunities for integration. Says one mother, Kari, "I support public education but if it did not meet the needs of my child, I would be out of there." Several of these women were attracted to unique programs, like Spanish immersion at Key and Abingdon elementary schools or a child development strategy at Campbell (formerly Claremont) Elementary that mixes students of different ages and focuses heavily on conflict resolution. Others in the group seemed more willing to stay and fight for diversity in the face of quality challenges. Melinda purposely avoided the special programs within schools "because I saw them as white flight programs." "I chose [Claremont/Campbell] because I thought it would offer a more genuinely diverse environment, but even there the kids that are identified as bright [and placed in advanced classes] tend to be white middle-class kids," she lamented.

All of them admitted a degree of white privilege; the school system has been more responsive to their demands than it has been to meeting the needs of people of color, especially black kids, who are heavily tracked into the basic, less challenging courses. They also felt, however, that they had no choice but to be insistent and demanding in order to get a response from the school system. They were quite clear on the necessity of "working the system," although they wished they didn't have to. Melinda described herself as a "pushy white parent." She told the story of advocating for her child to take intensified algebra. The teacher of the class was resistant because her daughter had only received a "high B" in her previous math course. But Melinda successfully forced the issue, ignoring the teacher's officious tone and veiled threat that her daughter would suffer the indignity of having to be put back in regular algebra if she could not cut it. Melinda learned of a black child who also wanted to take intensified algebra and got the same treatment, but the student said, "no way would my mother call and negotiate with a school official." Another black parent, Melinda said, did in fact make a similar call on behalf of her child, got the same treatment, and backed off. Said Donna of herself and other white parents, "We were people who knew how to work a system and get what we wanted for our children. We were active in the PTA and knew people who could make things happen when we needed it. The schools seem more responsive to our kids as a result."

The "pushy white parent" phenomenon reflects a cultural difference that these women admit is a source of tension at their children's schools. They acknowledge that diversity is challenging. Social separation of students outside the classroom and the tracking of middle-class white students to advanced classes and of minority students to special education and lower-level classes are common. Tension between white-dominated parent groups and minority parents who may feel excluded or unwelcome is another common problem. Said Jan: "Diversity is not a value of the school system. There is no instruction coming from central administration to school administrators to make diversity concerns a priority. This is a resource issue. There are dynamic individuals or schools that are making extra efforts but there is no overall policy or philosophy." Others agreed with her and attested to some of the daily challenges. One mom lamented, "My children lead integrated lives, but none of the activities I am engaged in at the school are diverse." Said Donna, "The PTA is not diverse; Girls Scouts is not diverse; the teachers are mostly white." They all agree that there is a predominately white or predominately middle-class bent to the PTAs they are involved in. The children also have their challenges. "The hardest part is the social part outside of school," said Jan. Trying to arrange play dates with parents who live far away from the middle-class neighborhoods, or who may not have a phone, or who live in neighborhoods where they would not feel comfortable sending their child, or who may not speak English is difficult. So it is not surprising that there can be real strains and social separation among children, even in extremely diverse schools. The mothers observe a shift and change among kids that typically begins in elementary school, as early as second or third grade. Cliques of color and class start to form. Children integrate best in extracurricular activities like sports and music, but social time is often separated. White and black kids at Drew Elementary, a magnet school located in a historically black neighborhood, have had special challenges with the color line. Melinda said she and another parent were so concerned about it that they approached the school principal about how the school might better support building bridges among the children. "The black girls are too proud," Melinda's daughter explained to her. When Melinda raised this with the school principal, an African American, she reportedly responded, "I think that's great that they have pride," meaning esteem.

A common theme among all of these white mothers was that class is the strongest common denominator among children of different races. Where integrated friendships are formed, typically it occurs among children who share similar social norms and perspectives. Jan noted that her child's two best friends are both black, but one is African and the other is Haitian. As a middle-class kid, her child has more in common with these immigrant children than with the lower-income African American children she attends school with.

Despite the challenges, these women attested to certain clear benefits of integration. Jan marveled at her youngest daughter's completely altered worldview. Said Jan of her daughter, "She knows how privileged she is and talks about it all the time. She asks, 'Am I spoiled?' She tells me to take some of her things back and give them to someone else. She has had friends over who don't know what an upstairs is or have never seen a basement or are shocked that everyone has a phone or a TV."

All of these women observed that their children's lives are much more diverse than their own. Linda, whose son has maintained a diverse set of friends from elementary school through high school, was completely perplexed as to how she would begin to form more friendships with people of another race. Her life, despite her child's integrated experience, just doesn't seem to offer meaningful opportunities for crossing racial boundaries. "I can't figure out what keeps us apart. The only friends that I have that are not white are from interracial couples," she said. She mused aloud that she thinks growing up African American in this country is a much different experience and talks about a coworker who experienced racial profiling and discrimination. She said she thinks that such vastly different experiences make it difficult for blacks and whites to relate. She seemed eager to talk to me about these issues, probably because she rarely if ever has such an opportunity or a safe haven to talk openly about her difficulties with race.

These women are laying the groundwork to make successful integration possible in their children's schools and neighborhoods. Unfortunately for them, they are having to make it up as they go along, in a school system that does not yet support integration systemically. Unlike West Mount Airy or Southeast Seattle, South Arlington has not built a civic infrastructure that consciously attempts to build bridges and relationships, whether directly or indirectly, in support of integration. Yet their example underscores that everyone who cares has the power to do something to alter our separatist tendencies. In the individual act of choosing to stay and participate in a majority-minority school, perhaps the accidental integrationist will become the ardent one. And perhaps as a result of their efforts, the children of these women will lead socially integrated lives as adults, sharing life space with people of different races and participating in public institutions in a way that helps them work for everyone.

Trouble in Paradise:
The Challenges Within Integrated Communities

Even with the best of intentions and conscious efforts, integration has its challenges. It takes hard work to negotiate race and class differences successfully. It also takes patience and sensitivity. Those communities that have achieved stable diversity typically have succeeded in creating an environment where people from all race and class backgrounds feel that they can be and are being heard, even if their perspective might not win the day on a particular issue.

A colleague of mine attests to the sensitive work required. She is a white woman who is married to an African American man. She has black in-laws and has more experience than many whites in dealing with people of color. Yet she tells me that even she sometimes feels discomfort when reaching out to black people she does not know. As a PTA president for one of her children's schools, she has felt inhibited when having to "cold call" a black parent she is trying to get involved. She does not feel the same discomfort when calling a new white parent. But she also recognizes that it is important that a PTA at a majority-minority school have the active participation of minority parents. She makes herself stretch beyond her comfort zone to make the calls and reach out to Latino and black parents, who often need extra encouragement to feel welcome and valued at PTA meetings that tend to be dominated by white middle-class parents. Integration simply does not happen naturally, my colleague says, particularly not in institutions. Institutions, such as PTAs, schools, colleges, workplaces, have a way of reflecting the values and needs of the dominant, white culture in our society. It takes care and daily effort to make an institution truly inclusive and truly integrated. Recognizing that such work and sensitivity is required may be half the battle in striving toward successful diversity.

My colleague Peter Byrne broke into a hearty laugh when I asked him what it was like being a white PTA president at the mostly black Capitol Hill Cluster School. Peter was active in both the PTA and the Local School Restructuring Team, a committee created by the school system to give parents a voice in school reform. He said of the experience:

White parents tended to live closer to the school, were more affluent and active. Some black parents were resentful. We actively tried to identify and cultivate some black parents to be leaders. It was very difficult. There were few black middle-class parents because the black middle class does not tend to live on Capitol Hill. White parents had a perception of black parents as uninvolved and unreliable, although clearly many had much more difficult lives and home situations. Black parents had a perception of white parents as control freaks that had an agenda for their own kids but who were not thoughtful about the needs of all children. They also thought white parents were disrespectful of school administrators, who tended to be African American. There was some truth to both perspectives. There was a real desire to create a mixed race group that would be supportive of high standards and of raising money. We were not really successful. It was difficult because we did not have enough time together to dialogue and build trust and a common vision. I understand that it is much better now. A dynamic principal has engaged a lot of parents.

Clearly there are challenges and tensions even in the most successful of stable diverse communities, where clusters of homogeneity, that is, of separation, are not uncommon. It is entirely possible for a neighborhood of thousands of people to appear diverse from a distance but be segregated block by block, with minimal interaction between the races or classes. Even in a community like Clinton Township, which is recognized as a diverse exception to the racial segregation that pervades metropolitan Detroit, the majority of blacks live west of Interstate 94, attending schools in one school district, Clintondale, while the majority of whites live to the east, attending schools in another district, L'Anse Creuse.[25]

All communities in American society struggle with a diminishing civic space and a loss of community engagement. Integrated communities must fight an uphill battle against this trend as well as against our overwhelming tendency toward separatism. Perhaps this explains why stable diverse communities tend to have an abundance of community activists. But even the most successful of these communities have their problems. Constituencies differ not just in their race and class but also in their opinions about what is important and what needs to happen in a community.

Anecdotes confirm what academic researchers have found: "organizational membership tends to be skewed toward the middle strata (that is, professionals and the middle class) with African-Americans underrepresented and wealthy Whites exhibiting little to no participation. African-American participation does increase in the case of town watch groups formed around issues of crime."[26] In Southeast Seattle, several residents described such tensions to researchers. One resident observed:

> My experience, not only in Mt. Baker but in the central area, too, is that when it comes to community activism and who's at meetings about land-use planning and other issues like that, the participants don't reflect the statistics of the neighborhood. I mean it's predominantly White, out of proportion to the neighborhood. . . . Some of the older African-Americans have felt resentful. They think people came in but it really wasn't real integration anyway.[27]

A public official who lives in Southeast Seattle on a very diverse block observed that "his family has White neighbors who send their children to private school, shop on Mercer Island (a less diverse area outside Southeast Seattle), and seem altogether uninvolved in community life." A prominent school principal expressed frustration at people who live in Southeast Seattle but do not contribute to its integration:

> The man that bought that house right there sends his kids to another school. He lives right across the street. Now this is a nationally recognized school, why wouldn't you send your kid [there]? He gets up in the morning; they get in their car and drive their daughter to school. [So if their concern is integration, they should] send their kids over to a school that is ethnically mixed. They're in a neighborhood that is, but they send their kids somewhere else.[28]

In this community, like most of America, the church congregations are mostly made up of a single race. At the local high school, students cluster largely by race. The children's sports leagues are integrated, though, and one can find evidence of diverse race mixing—at the nightly community computer laboratory at the Hawthorne Elementary School, at the annual multiethnic dinner at Maple Elementary on Beacon Hill, at community centers that regularly draw a mix of young people. The youngest children seem to lead the most integrated lives, but this does not necessarily lend itself to adults playing together. Said one resident, "Unfortunately, there isn't as much interaction between adults as you see with the children, and I'm not sure how that can happen."[29]

West Mount Airy experiences similar challenges. The northern section of West Mount Airy is wealthier and whiter than other parts of the community. Germantown Avenue is a major commercial strip that divides West and East Mount Airy. Most of the businesses and shops on the southern end of the avenue are patronized by black people. The more prosper-

ous part of the avenue runs north into Chestnut Hill, attracting a large percentage of West Mount Airy's affluent white residents to its quaint shops and restaurants. The major grocery
store on Germantown Avenue, Acme Supermarket, is patronized almost exclusively by black shoppers. Many white residents buy their groceries in predominantly white Chestnut Hill
or the nearby suburbs. The clientele for the Weaver's Way Co-
op, a bastion of community, is disproportionately white, educated, and professional, though the black educated elite are
also finding their way into the Co-op. Meanwhile, many of
West Mount Airy's black middle-class shoppers are driving to
the Acme in Andorra, a shopping center in a predominantly
white neighborhood, or to Chestnut Hill. If social mixing matters, it does not appear to be happening to the degree one
might expect in such an integrated community.

Part of the problem is class divisions. Class becomes a
sticking point when setting community priorities. Residents of
West Mount Airy experienced this very pointedly when trying
to decide how to bring about a revitalization of its commercial
sector. To stem the outflow of money being spent by West
Mount Airy's more affluent residents in Chestnut Hill, the
Mount Airy Revitalization Team, which is focused on revitalization of Germantown Avenue, developed a plan that essentially called for the development of businesses and arts and
cultural activities at the north end of the avenue that would be
more compatible with the tastes of West Mount Airy's higher-
income residents. The plan devoted considerably less attention
to the southern end of the avenue. Not surprisingly, the plan
was met with much controversy when it was introduced at a
community meeting. Its geographic emphasis was felt to have
racial and class overtones. Some saw the plan as an effort to
force those businesses with a predominantly black clientele off

the avenue through benign neglect. Defenders of the plan argued that it was neither racially nor economically skewed; it merely attempted to build on the community's economic strength, to capture more of its affluent buying power. There were kernels of truth in both perspectives, as is usually the case with any social dispute. The divisiveness of the meeting forced planners back to the drawing board. The incident itself was a critical reminder of the extreme sensitivity organizations must exercise in negotiating both race and class.

The class issue is raising its head in West Mount Airy schools. Why should it surprise anyone that lower-income families of any race would attempt to avail themselves of the public schools with higher performance rankings that tend to be found in middle-class neighborhoods? The two elementary schools in the neighborhood, Charles W. Henry and Henry Houston, have become blacker and poorer over time. The flip side to this development is that there is a strong tradition of private school enrollment among whites in Philadelphia. Although white enrollment at Charles W. Henry School is higher than the city-wide average, many white residents can afford to bypass public schools, which means that school quality will not deter whites from locating in the neighborhood.[30] But as white people opt for private schools, the resegregation and increasing impoverishment of Mount Airy schools means that the community is missing a critical opportunity not just for social interaction but for bolstering the quality of these schools for children of a variety of backgrounds.

Mount Airy schools are not unique in this regard. As I discuss in a subsequent chapter, most American public schools became more segregated in the 1990s. All urban school systems face the same issue. Maintaining a racial balance, much less a class balance, is a Herculean task in any district that has high numbers of poor kids. Both the white and black middle class appear to be abandoning Mount Airy schools, and poor kids from surrounding neighborhoods appear to be finding their way in. As a result, the schools suffer. It is a common phenomenon and challenge in integrated and nonintegrated communities alike.

Montclair, New Jersey, a suburban enclave twelve miles west of New York City that is well known in the region as racially and socioeconomically integrated, has been struggling with similar issues. White and black residents alike admit that the races do not really mix socially or not very often. The supermarkets here also seem to be color-coded. Whites go to King's; blacks go to Pathmark; and Whole Foods might be coded green, for the affluent. The Board of Education noticed that at the middle-school level, students from middle- and upper-class families began leaving the school system for parochial or private schools. This exodus, which the community unfortunately labeled "bright flight," was mostly white, but included a good number of students from the community's well-heeled black families. White or middle-class attrition became the explicit focus of the school board and school superintendent, resulting in a new middle school, Renaissance, that offers smaller class sizes and the kind of educational programming normally associated with private schools—rigorous instruction, longer school days, innovative field trips, and extensive community-service requirements.

Is it successful integration when a middle school singularly achieves majority-white middle-class status in an integrated neighborhood while all the other schools are majority-minority? Building a new school with excellent resources and low student-teacher ratios in order to attract and retain the (white) middle class clearly means a diversion of resources from other schools or priorities. Such trade-offs invariably generate opposition, depending on what group feels they are being negatively affected. At the same time the community was experiencing "bright flight," a wave of lower-income black folks was moving into Montclair, trying to get the benefit of its better public schools. When one teacher declared war on tracked classes at Montclair High, devising a world literature class that was open to everyone, she created panic among some white parents, having pierced the insulated bubble of advanced placement and ability groupings that enabled many of them to comfortably keep their children in public school. The innovation of a challenging world lit class without any prerequisites resulted in an acrimonious debate requiring school board approval, which was forthcoming. But several, mostly white, parents responded by taking their children out of the school altogether.[31]

In schools, as in neighborhoods, we must struggle constantly to overcome an institutional tendency to value certain kids over others and certain perspectives over others. Advocacy on behalf of "other people's kids" is rare. The natural tendency of parents of any race is to want the best for their children. Unfortunately, that singular pursuit will often mean, especially in the case of white parents, an exodus from a public school or a fight against any element that could be perceived as watering down the quality for their kids. As for black middle-class parents, they are worried that teachers have low expectations of their children.[32] The potential flight of the middle classes, coupled with the yearning of lower-income minority families for quality, underscores just how challenging the project of race and class integration is. Add to this mix the scarcity of public resources, or budget cuts, and the problems can be gordian.

The Case for Integration

I think the possibilities for integration could be much enhanced if more white people and more middle- and upper-class people could become comfortable with not always being overwhelmingly dominant in numbers. This does not mean that their interests would necessarily be subordinated. It does mean that they would have to share power, resources, or influence. This is what it means to be a part of a larger community.

This project is easier in multiracial environments than in biracial ones, in my view. White fear of black people is still strong. Integration is most fraught with peril, and a tortured racial history, when the relational dynamic is between blacks and whites. Still, countering the "black" lunch table requires acknowledging that there are many more "white" lunch tables. The weight and onus of integration should not be placed solely on racial minorities; the weight and responsibility should be placed on everyone. Openness to others, coupled with institutional arrangements and commitments that cultivate a coming together of strangers, is needed if the fantasy of integration is ever going to be achieved or sustained in any systemic way.

The stable racially integrated communities that do exist in our nation are far from perfect, but they have built bridges across difference that do not exist in any systemic way in the remaining 90 percent of America's neighborhoods. They should be commended for trying and sometimes falling down, for recognizing that a meaningful, sustainable being together of races and classes requires sustained effort and attention. A testament to West Mount Airy's success in the face of struggles and missteps is that even critics of some organizations' plans have noted that this is the type of community where objections are heard.[33] A mother of a senior at Montclair High School put it

saliently to writer Lisa Funderburg when she emphasized that
there is victory in the day-to-day struggle: "I don't think it happens in your lifetime.... The long and short of it is the contribution you make along the way and the fervor you bring to it.
The fact that a lot of things around here are wrong doesn't
mean for a minute you change doing your best to do right." Or,
as Montclair's Mayor William Farlie put it, "You either believe
in diversity and are prepared sometimes to be disappointed and
other times be elated, or you move to suburban Connecticut."[34]

Unfortunately, there is more demand for racially stable, integrated neighborhoods than there are neighborhoods to fill that
demand. The biases—some would say prejudices—of markets
and market actors work against stable racial integration. A lot
more Americans may have integrationist tendencies than our
life space and neighborhoods reflect. In the final chapter of this
book I suggest some policy alternatives that might reinforce
rather than inhibit integration. To begin to alter our public and
institutional choices, however, will require a cultural and political shift. The starting point is with the hearts and minds of individuals. How might more people be swayed to support or
personally try living in integrated neighborhoods or creating
thoroughly integrated community and public institutions?

We need a more forceful rationale for integration than
Rodney King's plaintive plea, "Can't we all just get along?"
The twentieth-century notion of integration, which reached its
heyday in the 1970s, was one of melding blacks with whites; it
was mainly premised upon opening doors to black participation. Black people were expected to be the integrators, indeed
the assimilators. But this model, which, as this book attests,
has enjoyed only modest success, will not sustain us in the new
century. A call to assimilation will not captivate or empower
the multitudes that will make up the majority-minority nation
we are becoming. More importantly, it places no onus on

whites to adjust and contribute to a new multicultural ethos.

Cultivating an openness to difference is in the collective self-interest. In a society where all races and classes are respected, where children of all colors are believed to be capable of learning and excelling, where the corporate, boardroom, and management doors are truly wide open to the best and brightest of all hues, we will come closest to maximizing our collective potential. The point of integration is not to pursue it for its own sake, although it has its own inherent social benefits. The point of integration is the same as the core motivation of the civil rights movement itself. Integration, then and now, is the best route to equal opportunity for everyone. As I argue in Part II of this book, I have become convinced of this—even as I recognize the nurturing benefits of a racial enclave—because of the virulent inequality that our separation is begetting. I have come to believe that racial and economic integration, particularly of the social institutions that offer pathways to upward mobility, is the best route to closing the egregious gaps of inequality that weaken our nation.[35]

A moral and spiritual case can also be made for integration. Integration is the best route to cultivating an ethos where the individual, regardless of race, is respected, embraced, and loved. The hat trick will be enabling whites to see how they will gain, rather than lose, in such an integrationist society. An opening up of institutions and neighborhoods may be experienced as a loss of status—that is, a loss of the rights, privileges, and entitlements that have been enjoyed by whites. There are seeds of this ethos though. It is there in the homage we pay to the civil rights movement. It is there in the majestic language of Justice Sandra Day O'Connor's opinion upholding the University of Michigan School of Law's use of affirmative action: "We are a 'free people whose institutions are founded upon the doctrine of equality.'... We have repeatedly acknowledged the overriding importance of preparing students for work and citizenship, describing education as pivotal to 'sustaining our political and cultural heritage' with a fundamental role in maintaining the fabric of society."[36] O'Connor goes on to quote the Court's edict in *Brown v. Board of Education* that "education is the foundation of good citizenship."[37] Yet her prediction that, in twenty-five years, affirmative action will no longer be needed to ensure inclusion in higher education will not be realized, in my view, without a significant closure of existing gaps of opportunity in primary and secondary education, which, as I argue in Chapter 6, will require a socioeconomic integration that currently eludes most public schools. We will no longer need to deploy race-conscious measures when the institutions that fundamentally define opportunity are themselves no longer racially identifiable.

American society may never completely eradicate its growing tendency toward "have" and "have not" communities. The open, inclusive, integrated society we purport to have is an elusive fantasy except in the relatively rare multicultural or integrated islands among us. Even these are imperfect universes. But in these places people are dealing with one another. They are fighting the good fight, living the values of democratic participation more forcefully than most places, giving voice to often voiceless people in a context of competition, compromise, and coexistence. I would bet on these places before the separatist ones. I would choose such communities and institutions, even at my own personal expense on some issues, because I know I will gain far more by living in an inclusive community. Society will also gain from a burgeoning of more islands of inclusion and from a swell of individuals affirmatively choosing and supporting integration. I hope many more others will make this choice.

CHAPTER 3

INSTITUTIONALIZED SEPARATISM

IN CHAPTER 1, I explored how personal preferences and racial discrimination contribute to racial separation. In this chapter I begin by examining what the most recent census tells us about the extent of race *and* class separation. There is heightened risk that Americans will view class separation as "natural." To demonstrate that this is not the case, I survey the conscious public and private policy choices that create homogeneous neighborhoods in the second part of the chapter. Our separatism was not always the ingrained tendency in America, and it does not have to be in the future.

Stratification: The American Way?

Since 1970, both the poor and the affluent have become more isolated from everyone else, creating bastions of privilege and pockets of distress in America. At the same time, all neighborhoods have become more stratified along lines of income. Economic separation has become so ingrained in U.S. real estate markets that we seem to accept it as the natural order. The American middle class struggles to stay ahead by buying homes in the best neighborhood they can afford, ones with the best possible public schools.[1] The ability to differentiate "good" schools and neighborhoods from "bad" ones depends on stratification. No one really questions a separatist real estate market because bulwarking strategies—the locking out of low- or moderate-income populations—are tacitly and sometimes explicitly understood as the means to the good life. Havens of good schools, low taxes, low crime rates, and other amenities require economic homogeneity, or rather, not having too many poor people around. This is the American way and the vision that has animated the five-decade outflow of millions of people from cities to the suburbs and often from suburbs to exurbs.

Class separation is a shared cultural value in America. Although we are loathe to admit it, classism is deeply ingrained in our national psyche. We profess to abhor "class warfare" in this country, but in many ways that is exactly what we have. Property owners go to war when threatened with an influx of lower-income people or any group perceived as incompatible with their way of life—such as a group home for the mentally disabled. We erect gates around our communities, twenty-first-century moats, and we willingly pay more, in cost or in commuting times, to distance ourselves from people and—let's admit it—social classes we don't feel comfortable with.

As a result, the geographic separation of the classes in America has become pronounced. In any given metropolitan area there is a hierarchy of neighborhoods that roughly approximates the American income scale and the varying social classes. Racial differentiation is also very much a part of this sorting of the populace. The black single mother who left welfare last year will spend half or more of her monthly income as a hotel housekeeper, child care worker, or baker's assistant for a one-bedroom apartment in a very marginal, inner-city neighborhood, if she is lucky enough to find something "affordable." If she were white, she would be more likely to live in a neighborhood where the people around her exceed her own economic standing. The white poor have more access to the relatively few "affordable housing" units for "moderate"-income people that are built in middle-class settings. The gay childless couple moves into a gentrifying black neighborhood in the city center, following other urban gay pioneers who have raised housing prices and threaten to displace lower-income residents. The elite, professional-class couple with children—the two-parent doctor-and-lawyer family with a combined income in excess of $200,000—lives in a neighborhood with impressive homes. If they live in a central city, they will be well buffered from the minority poor, and they can afford to bypass the typically struggling urban school system in favor of private schools. If they live in suburban environs, they likely have the option of sending their kids to high-achieving public schools. The real middle-class people, the single- or two-paycheck households struggling to maintain a middle-class existence on, say, $45,000, live in shabbier environs. If they are white or Asian, they likely live in an older suburban neighborhood; if they are Latino, they have a 50–50 chance of living in suburbia; if they are black, they are more likely to live in a central city "buffer" neighborhood. Sandwiched between the ghetto and suburbia, these black middle-class families struggle to insulate their kids from "thug life."

The older suburban neighborhoods offer modest homes—split-level ranchers, Levittown boxes—built cheaply three, four, and five decades ago and not standing up well to the wear and tear. Neighborhoods like this are becoming home to people from Vietnam, El Salvador, Mexico, Mali, India, or any number of countries from which immigrant hopes spring. The influx of people with modest incomes and many children threatens to overwhelm a limited tax base. The schools here are bursting at the seams, with average class sizes exceeding those of the better-funded suburban school districts. Those people higher up the "middle-class" income spectrum who can afford it, especially those who are white, are escaping to the newer communities on the suburban frontier. The "exurbs," or "boomburbs," offer bright, shiny new homes with vaulted foyers and palatial facades that can sell, seemingly miraculously, for under $200,000. The schools here are also shiny new bastions of high achievement and little poverty. On this suburban frontier one can also find havens for the more affluent. Gated communities with names like The Gates at North Hills, Acorn Pond, The Hamlet at Jericho, and Turnberry Isle offer $500,000 homes for those who cannot afford the 10,000-square-foot trophy home but who want to feel like they live in one. Then there are the communities for the seriously affluent. The corporate executive paid millions annually will actually live in the 10,000-square-foot trophy home, if not one that is even larger.

How did this stratification become the seemingly natural order of things? Partly, it is because of personal choice. But, as I show later in this chapter, public policies greatly shape the choices that individuals have available to them. I begin by demonstrating the fact of race and class separation in America.

Lessons from the Census

The latest national gauge of our progress in integrating the races and classes is the 2000 census. The framers of our Constitution presciently understood that an authentic representative democracy, however limited the voting franchise was at the time, would require a periodic accounting of America's people. Hence they required a decennial census that would determine the distribution of seats in Congress, based upon a counting that notoriously excluded Indians and two-fifths of nonfree persons. In other words, the framers declared that slaves were only three-fifths of a person for purposes of determining representation in Congress—a provision eliminated when the Constitution was amended to abolish slavery and to grant blacks equal legal protection and full citizenship.

Obviously, much has changed since then. Among other things, black people have transmuted from Africans to Negroes to African Americans. We gained voting rights and are considered full people, worthy of representation. By 2000, the census finally began to reflect centuries-old miscegenation. The 2000 census was the first in U.S. history that allowed its respondents to designate themselves as more than one race. Our national rainbow quickly widened its spectrum. Because of the ability to define oneself in multiracial terms, 126 possible combinations of race and ethnicity were available on the 2000 census form, up from just 6 in the past. Yet, only 2.4 percent of those who responded to the 2000 census chose to identify themselves as multiracial.[2]

I believe the census conveys, in admittedly blunt terms, some essential truths about how our society is ordered. With respect to race, the singular message emanating from the census is our seeming inability to achieve meaningful integration where people of color exist in large numbers.

Race Trends

Demographers have developed certain indices of our separation. One of them, an index known as dissimilarity, measures the degree to which a racial group would have to move in order to be evenly distributed throughout a region in proportions commensurate with the group's percentage of the total population in that region. Detroit, one of the most segregated cities in the United States, has a dissimilarity index of 85, meaning that 85 percent of blacks in the Detroit metropolitan area would have to move in order to be evenly distributed in that region. Chicago's index is 81. Newark's is 80. You get the picture, and you likely have some sense of what these highly segregated places are like. The Midwest is our country's most segregated region, followed by the Northeast. The West is the least segregated region—because blacks are more evenly dispersed where they are fewer in number—followed by the South. In the 1990s, the largest decline in segregation between blacks and other groups occurred in the Sun Belt, below the Mason-Dixon line. For the first time in the history of the census, the Northeast, Midwest, and West each experienced a net decline in black people in the 1990s, while the South's black population rose by over 3.5 million.[3]

The national dissimilarity index for separation of black people from whites is 65. Sixty-five percent of all black people in the United States would have to move in order to be evenly distributed among whites. This figure has been coming down about 4–8 percent per decade since 1970—a reversal of the steady *increase* in segregation that occurred in the first seven decades of the twentieth century. No doubt this represents progress.[4] But at the current rate of improvement, in forty years, when, God willing, I will be an octogenarian, blacks will be just as segregated as moderately segregated Latinos are today.[5]

Something intangible seems to happen when a city or town reaches a black population in excess of 20 percent. In the areas above this threshold of color, where about half of all black people live, declines in segregation have been glacial. Thus, African Americans are equally divided between places that have experienced modest progress in integration and places where progress has been very slender.[6] Almost half of blacks now live in neighborhoods that are not majority black.[7] But the other half lives in places with dissimilarity of 75 or higher.[8] These are places that white people have been fleeing en masse for five decades. In sum, in the metropolitan regions with large numbers of black people, the dominant trend is one of stasis.

There is also a stasis of sorts occurring among Latinos and Asians. Latinos are moderately segregated. About 52 percent of all Latinos in the United States would have to move in order to be evenly distributed among whites.[9] As with blacks, Latinos are most segregated in the urban areas where they are most populous; for Latinos in the 1990s, segregation declined only in areas where they made up less than 2 percent of the population—areas where only about 1 percent of Latinos live.[10]

The story is similar, though better, for Asians. They are the least segregated racial minority; 42 percent of Asians would have to move in order to be evenly distributed with whites. But in areas where Asians are most populous, where 75 percent of Asians live, levels of segregation did not change significantly in the nineties. Only in areas with a population that was less than

2 percent Asian did Asian/white segregation decline significantly in the 1990s.[11]

So as America slowly moves toward majority-minority
nationhood, she seems to be compartmentalizing rather than
melding. In areas where there are many shades of black,
brown, and yellow, America has separated her people. The
people of color, like Hagar's children, still live at some distance
from the most populous race. This separation is occurring even
as, or perhaps *because,* the numbers of racial minorities
explode. The Latino population grew by 58 percent in the
1990s, emerging as our nation's largest minority group. The
Asian population grew by 48 percent, blacks by 16 percent,
and whites by 6 percent. Yet there has essentially been no
progress in integrating Latinos or Asians with whites in the
past two decades. Instead, for the most part, existing Latino
and Asian neighborhoods are simply extending. Granted, these
groups are not nearly as segregated as blacks. But it is surprising that Latinos, the largest minority and fastest-growing
demographic group, are largely being contained by or channeled to their own enclaves rather than being integrated.[12]

Overall, I believe three key lessons concerning racial integration can be distilled from recent census trends:

1. *Communities with few blacks integrate better than
    those with many blacks.* Of the nation's five most inte-
    grated urban areas, none is more than 3 percent black.
    Metropolitan areas such as Salt Lake City, Utah, and
    Portland, Oregon, that saw some of the most impres-
    sive declines in segregation in the 1990s are only 1.1
    percent and 2.7 percent black, respectively.[13]
2. *Communities with a Latino presence seem to integrate
    blacks and whites better than communities without this*

third group. Phoenix, Arizona, Providence, Rhode Island, and Raleigh, North Carolina, all experienced rapid growth in their Latino populations in the 1990s. They also had some of the most impressive declines in black/nonblack segregation. In comparison, only 2.9 percent of Detroit's population and 4.4 percent of New Orleans's is Hispanic, and these cities have dissimilarity indices of 84 and 66.5, respectively.[14] As I described in the previous chapter, rare neighborhoods of stable racial integration have emerged in the past few decades. One of the keys to their success appears to be the introduction of a Latino or immigrant presence that breaks up historically polarized black-white relations.

3. *Where blacks or Latinos exist in large numbers, whites flee, especially whites with children.* Overall, our nation's largest 100 cities lost 2.3 million whites in the 1990s, shepherding in a new era of the Chocolate and Salsa City. More than half of America's largest cities became majority-minority in the 1990s. While many cities, thankfully, are being bolstered by waves of immigration that are critical to their vitality, this coloring of large urban centers is likely contributing to white flight and, hence, persistent segregation.[15] The white component of Anaheim, California's population went from 57 percent to 35 percent in the 1990s. Philadelphia's white population went from 52 percent to 42 percent in the same decade.[16] Milwaukee lost 46,471 whites, leaving it with a white population of 45 percent, down from 61 percent in 1990.[17]

The five-decade outflow of whites from cities to suburbs accounts for why the average white American's experience of diversity is so very different than that of other racial and ethnic groups in the United States. Whites, by far, are the most suburban of the major racial and ethnic groups. Nearly 71 percent of whites live in suburbs.[18] This may explain why children are more segregated than the whole population. While the national black-white segregation index is 65, the national segregation index for black and white children is 68.3.[19] Children are more segregated than adults, apparently because the movement of white families with children to predominately white suburban enclaves has left childless whites to live in more integrated settings. As I explain in detail in Chapter 6, while children are more likely than adults to be separated into racially distinct neighborhoods, segregation levels in schools are even higher.

Massive suburbanization of racial minorities has not contributed substantially to new integration. Minorities are now moving to suburbs at rates that far outpace that of whites.[20] One might think that this coloring of suburbia would reflect progress toward integration. But, as with the national trends I have presented, significant declines in the segregation of suburbs are occurring only in areas with small minority populations—areas where only a small fraction of blacks, Latinos, and Asians live.

These lessons of the census offer hope of some future progress. But the overall trajectory of race in America is still one of persistent separation of whites, particularly whites with children, from people of color. As of 2000, almost fifty years after America first began a serious struggle with the issue of integration, the average white person in America lived in a neighborhood that was 80 percent white, 7 percent black, 8 percent Latino, and 4 percent Asian.[21] And these numbers are *averages*. Millions of whites, particularly those with children,

live in neighborhoods that are much more racially homogenous, or "lily white" as we used to say in the South.

By contrast, in 2000 the average black person lived in a
neighborhood that was 33 percent white, 51 percent black, 12
percent Latino, and 3 percent Asian.[22] As a general matter,
blacks, Latinos, and Asians experience more racial diversity
than do white people. In subsequent chapters of this book I try
to make sense of these differential realities. Whites, blacks, and
other racial groups are moving through their daily lives in
often distinctly different environments—ones that afford different opportunities and evoke differing worldviews.

Class Trends

Our classist social order no longer hides below the surface of
things. It now permeates public debates and our daily existence. The Enron age of notorious corporate scandals and the
securities fraud claims swirling from Merrill Lynch to Martha
Stewart laid bare the avarice of at least some of the monied
classes and the vulnerability of everyone else. American Airlines executives pay themselves huge bonuses and set up a special trust to insure their own pensions while demanding pay
cuts from workers, ostensibly to save the company. A $6,000
shower curtain for the CEO of Tyco International, L. Dennis
Kozlowski, like the free Manhattan apartment for GE's retired
Jack Welch, provided a pointed contrast to the thousands who
lost jobs and life savings on the ash heaps of corporate implo-
sions in the early 2000s. Tax cuts for the super-affluent accompany a popular culture that celebrates people who are rich and
famous and their luxurious lifestyles.

And why not? Life is easier for the professional, six-figure-
plus class. Banks flock to you and give you preferred customer

status and sweetheart mortgage terms. The tax code heavily subsidizes your housing costs. Insider contacts and insider information—the "friends and family" networks—open doors not just to IPOs but to better private schools, to the just right internships for your children, and sometimes to jobs for which you may not be particularly qualified. The more money you have, the better investment advice you get. You can access hedge funds that protect your wealth during the down times, and lucrative private investment arrangements have a way of finding you. The more wealthy and influential you are, the more likely you are to be privy to information that saves you from tremendous loss. President George W. Bush, then a private citizen, unloaded $848,000 worth of stock just before the price plummeted; Vice President Dick Cheney sold his Haliburton shares for $20 million before the shares dropped from $60 to $13.50.[23]

But class tensions also stem from the falling behind of those at the middle and low end of the income scale. The working poor and the working classes struggle, working long hours, often at multiple jobs, with daily worries about going without health benefits or adequate child care. The rules of life work against them. It is mathematically impossible for those relegated to minimum wage work to afford most market-rate apartment rents and still have enough money left over to meet basic necessities. As a result, the challenge of getting into and staying in decent housing is a dominant worry.[24] Sometimes the trade-offs facing the working and middle classes can be brutally cruel. A waitress can't afford to put up the money for a month's rent and a security deposit, so she rents a hotel room for $60 a night. A roofer is fired because, after cutting his foot and not being able to afford the prescribed antibiotic, he has missed too much work.[25] Anxiety abounds. The working and middle class worry about the high and rising cost of health care, how they will pay for college, and simply, the impending economic crises that await them when something goes wrong.

Socioeconomic status, then, defines very different experiences and opportunities in America. It also affects where you live. Perhaps we are victims of a real estate industry and public policies that are limiting or shaping our choices. But we *have* become a classist country. It is evident in census trends. Below are three of the lessons about class separation that I have gleaned from published demographic research about the 1980, 1990, and 2000 censuses.

1. Secession of the Successful; Separation of the Poor

Beginning in the 1970s, "the affluent became progressively less likely to interact with other income classes, and the poor were increasingly likely to experience residential contact with their own class."[26] Overall, separation of the affluent and the poor increased by 30 percent between 1970 and 2000. However, I suspect that the super-affluent saw even greater increases in degrees of separation. Class segregation spiked in the 1970s, continued to rise, but less rapidly, in the 1980s, then declined slightly in the prosperous 1990s. It remains to be seen whether and how this trend will continue in the new century.[27]

Both poverty and affluence have also become more concentrated over time, meaning that they occupy more tightly compact physical space than in the past. But the overall concentration of affluence in America now exceeds the concentration of poverty. Not only are the affluent coming to inhabit their own neighborhoods, but over the last five decades of the twentieth century, they increasingly came to inhabit certain states and metropolitan areas. Affluent people are following the money. This growing concentration of the affluent into their own social and residential environments reinforces the advantages enjoyed by high-income families. By dint of their superior purchasing power, they can buy their way into superior neighborhoods, towns, and even states that offer safe, secure, and resource-rich environments.[28]

2. *Hypersegregation of the African American Poor*

The ghetto is nothing new, but few seem to realize that only the African American poor are singled out for extreme isolation from the rest of American society. Only the black poor experience "hypersegregation"—a demographer's term for segregation along several dimensions that translate into a deep wall of isolation and concentrated poverty.[29] Poor black people are highly segregated from *all* other groups, and their levels of segregation remained essentially the same in the last third of the twentieth century. By contrast, levels of segregation for poor whites are very low, and for poor Latinos levels are moderate.[30] The barrio exists, but the people who live there are not isolated to the extreme degree of ghetto residents. There is a ray of light regarding this phenomenon: The economic good times of the 1990s enabled many African Americans to escape high-poverty ghetto neighborhoods. The number of people living in high-poverty neighborhoods declined by a dramatic 24 percent in that prosperous decade.[31] It is unclear whether this hopeful trend will continue in the 2000s.

3. *Economic Segmentation for Everyone*

Our separatism extends beyond the poor and the affluent. Economic segregation increased steadily for whites, blacks, and

Latinos in the 1970s and 1980s, with the greatest increases occurring for blacks and Latinos.[32] Across the board, income segregation increased from 1970 to 1990 and then declined in the 1990s.[33]

The overall direction of census trends since 1970, then, has been one of growing economic segmentation of American life space. The prosperous 1990s offered us a respite from growing class separation, but the moderation that came with economic growth in that decade didn't effect a reversal; all it did was avoid a further deterioration of our separated condition.

Income Inequality

While we have become more separated from people outside our own economic status since 1970, income inequality also increased substantially during this period—a trend that shows no sign of abating. The span between 1950 and 1975 was a good time to be in the middle class in this country. In that period, the middle classes thrived; median family income grew by 208 percent, and income inequality fell.[34] Now, however, being middle-class is much harder. Paychecks for those in the middle of the income scale simply don't go much farther than they did in the 1970s. In the past three decades, many families maintained their middle-class status by becoming a two-income household. Those at the bottom of the income scale— the poor and the working poor—now have less income than they did twenty years ago.

Meanwhile those receiving the largest compensation packages have experienced the fastest income growth; those at the top of the economic hierarchy are being allocated ever larger shares of the profits generated by the nation's economy. While middle-income salaries stagnated and the working poor lost ground in the last quarter of the twentieth century, income for those in the top 10 percent of the income scale rose by 89 percent. The top 1 percent of earners saw their income rise by 120 percent. In other words, the income of the top 1 percent of earners more than doubled over the past thirty years, and now they earn more than one-fifth of all the income in the country.[35]

How did this happen? A new economic order or a new set of rules of the workplace has taken hold. In the new order, among the top 10 percent of earners, the higher a person ranks on the income scale, the bigger his income gains.[36] The man—and it would be a man—who ascends to the top rung of the income scale commands the largest share of the economic pie, a much bigger slice than the many women and men swelling the middle ranks. This fictional top-income earner, representing the super-affluent, also now commands a much bigger slice than his counterparts in prior generations. The top 100 CEOs received more than 1,000 times the pay of the average worker in 1999, compared to 30 times the pay of the average worker in 1970. Either society no longer can muster a sense of outrage at the excessive rewards conferred on the upper echelons of the workforce, or we have lost our ability to self-regulate.[37]

Unfortunately, the very middle classes who are losing ground are contributing to this new plutocratic order with their own classism. Those who aspire to ascend higher up the income and wealth scale may be lulled into thinking that they should not object to policies that create greater income inequality because, after all, the mythology of opportunity suggests that they, too, might one day ascend to the mountaintop of affluence. Americans tend to vote according to their aspirations rather than their actual economic status. But this way of thinking, like separatism itself, is built on false promises—the chimera or illusion that there are meaningful ladders to upward mobility for everyone. There is nothing intrinsically wrong with the notion that people of different economic classes will live separately or that those who have acquired certain skills will earn more, assuming we really do have social mobility, that is, that no one is locked out by dint of their race or class or other immutable characteristic. But as I attempt to show in the following chapters of this book, the opportunity system we have is not nearly so open. Classism and class separation, like racism and racial separation, are creating unequal opportunity along lines of race and class. Those who most benefit from this separatist system are affluent whites; those most disadvantaged are poor blacks. But between the polar realities of being rich and white in America and poor and black is an entire spectrum of differentiation based upon one's race and class.

Which Is the More Important Factor? Race or Class?

Given census trends showing stasis or modest improvement on racial integration and growing class separation since the 1970s, which factor—race or class—best explains the fact of our separatism?

Income and wealth differences are clearly having some effect. It should surprise no one that as the affluent become even more affluent, they can build larger castles and wider moats that create a degree of insulation from the masses. Consider the advent of the "McMansion" that seemed to be de rigueur in the 1990s for the big money set. Although some claim that McMansions are now passé, houses in excess of 5,000 square feet, with many bigger than 10,000 and some upward of 20,000 to 30,000 square feet, were still popping up all over New Jersey in the spring of 2002.[38] Luxury spending exploded in the 1990s, including spending on trophy homes. Higher-end homes got progressively bigger in that decade as the high-income owners—like the people who stand at a concert and force those behind them to stand—propelled others at or near their socioeconomic level to keep up.[39]

Despite the influence of class on separatism, race seems to predominate in determining where a person is likely to live. Using the demographer's index of dissimilarity—the degree to which a group would have to move in order to be evenly distributed commensurate with their overall percentage of the population—one finds that under no circumstances are there "high" levels of segregation based upon income. At the neighborhood level, class segregation edges into the moderate range. Meanwhile, black people are segregated by race at very high levels.[40] Economic separatism affects the races differently. For blacks and Latinos, a climb up the economic ladder is no guarantee that they will find themselves in neighborhoods that match their newly attained economic standing. In other words, blacks and Latinos with the same income as their white counterparts will typically find themselves living in neighborhoods with less economic status than those enjoyed by whites. Demographers have identified this phenomenon as "the neighborhood gap."[41] For example, even relatively affluent blacks and Latinos—those with annual incomes above $60,000—do not fare as well as their affluent white counterparts in the competition for "better" neighborhoods because of the racial separation that tends to pervade housing markets. Instead, for blacks and Latinos, racial separation typically equates to economic inequality.[42]

So our neighborhoods and our life experience tend to vary considerably depending on our race *and* our class. In subsequent chapters of this book I explore these divergences. For black people, race is still the predominate factor. Black people at all socioeconomic levels are highly segregated from whites. Segregation for Latinos and Asians declines appreciably with increased socioeconomic status—education, income, occupation, and so on. For blacks, segregation declines only slightly as they attain higher income.[43] America still has a serious, unique problem with Negroes. The problem of the color line seems indelible.

Nonetheless, class distinctions are emerging as a factor for everyone. In blunt terms, middle-income whites have a lot to lose in the new century if our current inclination to separate the classes and redistribute income to the affluent continues. More than any other group, middle-income whites are the ones who are being blindsided by the myth that America is the land of equal opportunity. Those racial minorities who have endured a history of repression have been served notice that America does not always live up to her promises. They have reason to be wary about existing political choices and at least some motivation to challenge them. Middle-income whites are also disserved by our separatist, increasingly classist social order, but they may be blinded by their own desires to separate from racial minorities, at least where they exist in large numbers. Yet racial separation and class separation go hand in hand. The public policy choices that fuel one also fuel the other. We are being undermined by our choices, but we have not yet figured out how to change our destructive course.

The Public and Private Choices That Separate Us

Our separatism exists, but it is not inherently natural. Through a series of public and private institutional choices, we created a separatist social order. It did not have to be this way; separation was not our preordained fate. At the dawn of the twentieth century, economic and racial *integration* was the norm. It was not at all uncommon in America to find blacks living in close proximity to other races and blue-collar workers living among the elite. This was especially the case in southern cities. As Douglass Massey and Nancy Denton, authors of the seminal *American Apartheid,* put it:

> No matter what other disadvantages urban blacks suffered in the aftermath of the Civil War, they were not residentially segregated from whites. The two racial groups moved in a common social world, spoke a common language, shared a common culture, and interacted personally on a regular basis. In the north, especially, leading African American citizens often enjoyed relations of considerable trust, respect, and friendship with whites of similar social standing.[44]

Early-twentieth-century cities could be messy and have an unhealthy juxtaposition of "dirty" industries next to residential neighborhoods. But the "clean" modern American city that ultimately ensued, indeed the founding philosophy that now pervades most land use, did not have to be premised on the separation of different types of people. Four crucial public policy choices made in the twentieth century contributed mightily to the racially and economically divided landscape, the bastions of affluence and of need, now familiar to metropolitan America. I will discuss them further in the remainder of this chapter, but here is a brief overview.

First, we adopted a system of local governance premised on a religion of local autonomy that has fueled the proliferation of new, homogenous communities. Chief among the local powers that are wielded to exclude undesired uses of land and undesired populations is the zoning power.

Second, the federal government, through its Federal Housing Administration (FHA) mortgage insurance program, adopted and propagated the orthodoxy that homogeneity was necessary to ensure stable housing values. The FHA, the largest insurance operation in the world in its heyday, essentially chose to underwrite mortgages only for new single-family homes in predominately white neighborhoods, inventing and propagating the notion of redlining and initially locking out whole races and whole classes of people from the suburban dream.

Third, the interstate highway program opened up easy avenues for escape from the city while at the same time destroying vital black, Latino, and white ethnic neighborhoods. In most cities, the new highways tore through the neighborhoods of the politically marginal—those groups that were powerless to stop the bulldozing of their homes. Worse, throughout America, newly built highways created fire walls that isolated, separated, and typically defined the "bad" and typically the "black" sides of town.

Fourth, the federal government, through a number of urban development programs, created the black ghetto. Urban renewal, famously renamed by black folks as "Negro removal," destroyed mostly black-occupied housing strategically located near the central business district, all in the name of progress and eliminating "blight." Those people who were displaced had to move somewhere, which typically meant public housing or more marginal neighborhoods. At the same time, the federal public housing program, by design and location of public housing projects, created the modern phenomenon of concentrated black poverty.

Any one of these policies, individually, would have altered the metropolitan landscape in a way that advantaged some and greatly disadvantaged others—typically blacks, Latinos, and working-class white ethnic groups. But these policies had *cumulative impacts*. Coupled with the federal government's tepid resistance to housing discrimination, these policies worked in concert to create a systemic bias in favor of racial and economic segregation rather than integration. And, as I show in later chapters, racial and economic exclusion most benefits majority-white, affluent communities and imposes the heaviest costs on black and Latino communities. Some of these policies have been abolished; others, like exclusionary local zoning and ever expanding highways and attendant sprawl, continue to this day. Whether active or moribund, the systemic effect of these seminal policy choices may be indelible.

Zoning and other Separatist Strategies of Local Government

The United States Supreme Court did as much as any institution to encourage our separatist course. In 1922, when Euclid, Ohio—then a tiny, sparsely populated suburb of Cleveland—sought to protect itself from the development that ultimately would spread from the big city, its first line of defense was to enact a zoning ordinance. The comprehensive ordinance Euclid adopted followed the lead of national proponents of zoning. The theory emanating from British author Ebenezer Howard's vision of the Garden City, was to cultivate "wholesome," soothingly homogenous neighborhoods, a vision that elevated the detached single-family home above all other uses of land.[45] This meant that industry should be excluded from residential areas. It also dictated that two-family houses—duplexes—were to be excluded from neighborhoods with single-family homes and that apartments had to be excluded from both the single-family neighborhoods and from the neighborhoods zoned for duplexes, and so on.

Euclid's ordinance was not unique. In 1916, New York City was the first city in the nation to adopt a comprehensive zoning ordinance, and by 1925, 368 municipalities had followed suit, all generally following the ideology of separation and segregation of purportedly "incompatible" uses of land. This ideology came to be know as "Euclidian zoning," because the Supreme Court sanctioned it in 1926 in a test case challenging Euclid's ordinance. The case was brought by a realty company that owned 68 acres of open land strategically located in the path of development emanating from Cleveland. With the passage of the ordinance, the Ambler Realty Company immediately experienced a 75 percent reduction in the value of its land because it could no longer develop solely for industrial uses. It now had to conform to the restrictions of the ordinance, which placed about half the company's land in residential zones that could include duplexes or apartments. None of Amber's land was zoned exclusively for single-family homes, but that did not stop the Court from invoking the symbolism of such neighborhoods to defend the ordinance.

The Court commended the reasoning of the zoning experts. Among other things, segregation of categorically different uses of land would "increase the safety and security of home life; ... decrease noise and other conditions which produce or intensify nervous disorders; [and] preserve a more favorable environment in which to rear children." An apartment house, the Court emphasized, would be "a mere parasite" on a neighborhood of smaller homes. By their height and bulk they would "interfer[e] with the free exercise of the air and monopoliz[e] the rays of the sun." Worst of all the increased traffic that would accompany apartment houses would render these neighborhoods less safe, depriving children "in more favored localities" of "the privilege of quiet and open spaces for play."[46] In other words, localities, particularly the "favored" ones, could use the zoning code to protect their citizens from external harms or "nuisances" like apartment buildings.

The Court might as well have said that the *people* that would accompany apartment buildings or duplexes would be nuisance-like invaders on the quiet seclusion of favored families. That the Court would choose to focus so heavily on a nuisance rationale and the prerogatives of the families who were destined to live "in more favored localities" when the plaintiff was not even contemplating building single-family homes underscores the powerful psychology that animates local zoning. In short, zoning is a means of social control. It plays a critical gatekeeping function. And the more critical a power is to maintaining a certain social order, the more likely it is that it will be coveted and fought for by those advantaged by the status quo. Those who shouted the clarion call of "states' rights" when their precious Jim Crow way of life was threatened, like those who have taken up the anti-growth mantra just after they have moved to a new and rapidly growing green space, were acting to preserve and protect endowed advantages.

In the end, the Court in the *Euclid* case ruled against a corporate owner that had just lost three-fourths of the value of its property at the hands of government. Ironically, the Court did this at a time when it was notoriously solicitous of the rights and expectations of private corporations and private property owners and notoriously hostile to government regulation. But exclusionary zoning was a government regulation that six typically anti-government, pro-property Supreme Court justices could relate to. Only now the interests of a particular type of property owner—single-family home owners—were being exalted over the needs and expectations of everyone else. I suspect the justices who signed on to this opinion all lived in precisely the type of favored communities that might be threatened by an onslaught of less favored people.

The federal district court judge who first heard the *Euclid* case took a different, quite prescient view of the case. The true purpose to be accomplished by the ordinance, he declared, "is to classify the population and segregate them according to their income or situation in life." The ordinance would only further "class tendencies," he correctly predicted.[47] If this concern was raised before the Supreme Court, it clearly held no sway. For the next fifty years the Court, through a series of cases, continually reinforced the right of municipalities to use local powers in pursuit of an idealized vision that tended to favor only a specific type of population. In the early 1970s, when the Village of Belle Terre, on Long Island, then home to a population of 700, wanted to clamp down on group housing arrangements, it passed a "one-family-per-house" ordinance, narrowly defining family to include only blood relatives or two-person housemate situations. The Court sanctioned the law, saying: "It is ample to lay out zones where family values, youth values, and the blessings of quiet seclusion and clean air make the area a sanctuary for people."[48] When mostly black residents in the southwest quadrant of Washington, D.C., were threatened in the early 1950s with having their homes and businesses mowed down in the name of developing a "better balanced, more attractive community," the Court upheld the use of the eminent domain powers for this urban renewal project. Deferring to local political leaders' conception of what promoted "the public welfare," the Court reasoned that this could include the "spiritual as well as physical, aesthetic as well as monetary."[49] In other words, a city legislature or zoning board is free to determine not just what is necessary to protect the public's health and safety but also to pursue the majority political consensus as to what constitutes beauty. And beauty is in the eye of the political majority that holds the power. In the case of black residents of southwest D.C., their cherished neighborhoods and homes, many of which were not "substandard," were not beautiful enough and in fact stood in the way of city leaders' alternative plans.

Once exclusion for the benefit of a favored class of property owners was sanctioned as the raison d'être of zoning, the benefits of municipal incorporation became irresistible. The opportunity to gain control of a community's economic and social destiny through the exercise of local zoning powers has been one of the reasons we have witnessed a proliferation of new suburban municipalities in the United States. Indeed, state laws—*overt policy decisions by state legislators*—have played the most significant role in granting newly formed municipalities, mainly in the suburbs, the local powers needed to achieve significant levels of homogeneity. Virtually every state in the nation has conferred upon its citizens the right to incorporate a new municipality; to be immune from annexation by the central city; to engage in exclusionary zoning that creates expensive havens of single-family homes devoid of any modest housing; to legislate, tax local property, and provide services solely in the interests of their local residents; in short, to be utterly self-interested in defining borders and policies that usually result in race and class divisions. The Supreme Court has sanctioned and encouraged this regime by consistently upholding the constitutionality of each of these planks of local autonomy.[50]

It is not surprising, given the power over socioeconomic destiny that local autonomy confers, that the United States has some 87,000 local governments, including 36,000 municipalities, 3,000 counties, 13,700 school districts, and 34,600 special districts.[51] The desire of the upper and middle classes to escape financing public services for low-income citizens of older cities and the desire for racial exclusion are the two factors most prominently identified by researchers as the operative rationale for forming a new local government.[52] The more politically fragmented a metropolitan region is, the more racially and economically segregated it tends to be. The City of Detroit, at the heart of one of the most segregated metropolitan regions in the country, is surrounded by no fewer than 338 suburban governments and 116 suburban school districts.[53] Political balkanization is much more prominent in the United States than in European and Asian countries, in part because local autonomy is enshrined in our constitutional and popular values.

To be fair, given the burdens that attach to moderate-income families or poor people, new localities are acting in an utterly rationale manner, or rather in their own economic self-interest, when they use local powers to attract only certain kinds of taxpayers and citizens. High-end homes with fewer children and attractive, job-generating commercial facilities generate more tax revenues and fewer service demands than do tracts of modest residential housing. It is no wonder that the formation of new political jurisdictions, capable of wielding their own zoning and police powers, often leads to systemic practices of exclusion. The zoning code is a convenient, race-neutral tool for realizing an idealized vision of community. Single-family homes and the lots they sit on can be required to meet a minimum, very large size. The building code can be suffused with expensive design and materials requirements. Growth controls can prohibit the development of open space, cutting off opportunities for any new housing, not to mention affordable units or even market-rate rental apartments. New towns can refuse to participate in any federal housing programs, and they often do. These and a host of other strategies create a wall of economic exclusion.[54] More importantly, only the newer, developing suburbs are truly succeeding in shaping their social and economic destinies to fit their idealized vision. They are not overburdened with a history, an existing stock of modest housing, or existing populations that tend to drain budgets. Their municipal plans, their vision, and their restrictions tend to stick. As a result, newer communities tend to be more homogenous than older ones.[55]

While newly attained local powers frequently lead to exclusion, the creation of new political boundaries also has the effect of providing crucial markers; they make it easier for people to make decisions about where to live based upon factors of race and income. Grosse Pointe borders Detroit; Palo Alto borders East Palo Alto—offering pointed contrasts of difference. Realtors and existing community members also take advantage of newly incorporated boundaries to recruit the "right" people to move in. This sorting is a nationwide phenomenon; with the formation of new localities, segregation by race, educational attainment, and occupation has come to be organized at the city, rather than the neighborhood, level.[56]

The Federal Orthodoxy of Homogeneity in Housing

While our national commitment to local autonomy has contributed mightily to socioeconomic balkanization, the seeds of homogeneity were also sown by the federal government's housing policies. The Federal Housing Administration (FHA) gave birth to the dream of home ownership for the masses when it made possible low-interest long-term financing for purchasing a home. With the passage of the National Housing Act in 1937, a family on a modest income could acquire a home with a down payment as low as 10 percent and pay the loan off at a 2–3 percent interest rate over a period of up to thirty years. Suddenly, for those who qualified for an FHA-guaranteed loan, buying a home became cheaper than renting. For its first thirty-five years, the FHA was one of the largest insurance operations in the world; it underwrote over one-third of all new housing construction in the nation and two-thirds of all single-home purchases.[57] Naturally, lenders and markets followed the FHA's lead.

Being risk averse, ignorant, and/or racist, the FHA took the view that the best or only way to ensure stable property values and to keep default rates low was to underwrite loans only for certain kinds of properties in certain kinds of neighborhoods. Early on, its underwriting manual, the bible for FHA lenders, maintained that it was "necessary that properties shall continue to be occupied by the same social and racial classes."[58] The manual instructed appraisers to predict "the probability of the location being invaded by ... incompatible racial and social groups." To "preserve" neighborhood character, FHA officials were exhorted to use racial restrictive covenants—those embarrassing clauses that surface and testify to their former prominence when presidential candidates (George W. Bush, Joseph Biden, and Ronald Reagan), Senate candidates (Diane Feinstein), and judicial nominees (William Rehnquist) have owned properties for which a covenant not to sell to blacks existed.[59] The FHA learned this practice of systemically devaluing racially and ethnically diverse neighborhoods from its predecessor, the Home Owners Loan Corporation (HOLC), which was created by Congress in 1933 to provide refinancing to existing home owners in risk of default. HOLC invented "redlining": Its manuals encoded unacceptable categories of neighborhoods in red ink, and the agency chose to lend only to residents living in areas deemed acceptable, preferably areas that were "new [and] homogenous."[60]

It was one thing to choose to underwrite loans only in homogeneous areas; it was another thing altogether to orchestrate and promote homogeneity. The FHA institutionalized the usage of racially restrictive covenants and redlining by the private sector. It explicitly recommended that lenders and the real estate industry use such covenants and often would not underwrite a loan for a house unless its deed included them. The FHA was cowed only after the Supreme Court declared in 1948 in the case of *Shelley v. Kraemer*, successfully argued by Thurgood Marshall, that it was unconstitutional for state courts to enforce racially restrictive covenants. Nevertheless, the agency made sure it gave the real estate industry a grace period; in 1949 it broadcast a warning that as of February 15, 1950, it would no longer underwrite mortgages with such covenants, giving those with pending projects plenty of notice and incentive to deploy these nefarious clauses with haste.[61] Even after the FHA ceased endorsing restrictive covenants, the agency continued to operate in a decidedly anti-black, anti–central city mode well into the 1960s.[62] And having given birth to such practices, private actors, particularly banks and insurance companies, continued redlining minority neighborhoods—practices that made federal housing and credit discrimination laws necessary. As I describe below, subtler forms of redlining endure to this day, because many private institutions have embraced the orthodoxy that homogeneity is desirable, or rather, that socioeconomically integrated neighborhoods are not.

The FHA also left another legacy. It defined through its underwriting criteria what types of homes and neighborhoods were most desirable and chose to underwrite mortgages primarily for detached, single-family homes, almost exclusively in white suburban neighborhoods. By preferring single-family homes in new suburban subdivisions to any type of property in the central city, the FHA may have precipitated America's cultural preference for a separate castle, figuratively, if not literally, fenced off from others, in a pastoral, sparsely developed setting. Worse, by withholding FHA insurance for loans in racially integrated or predominately black areas, FHA also greatly limited the home ownership options available to people of color. It prevented African Americans from participating in one of the largest wealth-producing programs in the history of our country. Early investments in single-family suburban homes have increased in value fourfold, implicating FHA in wealth inequalities between the races that are manifest to this day.[63]

Highways to Homogeneity

The federally funded interstate highway program—the largest public works program in the history of the world—also contributed to our separatism. It dramatically altered the landscape of most American cities, usually damaging and walling off black communities in the process. Begun in 1956 as President Eisenhower's gambit for enhancing commercial competitiveness and national security, in its first decade of construction the interstate highway program displaced 330,000 mostly black families.[64] It divided cities by race, often creating a firewall separating "good" white neighborhoods from "bad" black ones. It frequently mowed down vibrant black commercial corridors and neighborhoods; in fact, new highways provided an irresistible opportunity to clear out inner-city "blight"—that is, Negroes—and make room for development of the central business district. When I-95 was laid in Miami, Florida, it ripped through the heart of Overtown, a large black community. The eight-lane, four-level interchange rose as high as seven stories in some places and destroyed 87 acres of housing and commercial properties. In Nashville, Tennessee, the state highway department intentionally altered the route of I-40 such that a wide berth of concrete would cut directly through the heart of the city's black business district. In St. Paul, Minnesota, one-seventh of the city's black residents were displaced by the laying of I-94. As one critic dryly stated, "Very few blacks lived in Minnesota, but the road builders found them." Sometimes the resulting pattern of racial segregation was starkly apparent. In the Atlanta region, for example, most blacks live south of I-20, and most whites live north of it. In fact, city leaders planned I-20 as a racial barrier. According to historian Ronald H. Bayor, highways and roads in the Atlanta region were planned and built "to sustain racial ghettos and control black migration." Other cities followed a similar pattern. In Memphis, the interstates cordoned off blacks in the northern section of the city. In Los Angeles, Watts was intentionally sealed off from neighboring white communities by freeways. Black communities bore the brunt of interstate highway expansion, but in many cities, including Wilmington, St. Louis, Chicago, Boston, and Providence, politically marginalized white ethnic and working-class communities were also devastated.[65]

While the highway program was a source of pain and destruction in many minority and white ethnic neighborhoods, it was also foundational in the process of forming new, predominately white suburbs. Since 1956, the federal government has rained down more than a half trillion dollars on states to subsidize the cost of roads leading out of cities to an ever expanding suburban frontier.[66] Without such unprecedented subsidies, it has been argued, suburban development would have occurred but in denser patterns that built off existing infrastructure in central cities and older suburbs. More pointedly, massive federal outlays for roads have significantly reduced the real costs of outer suburban development for new suburbanites. If suburban developers and suburban movers had been required to fully internalize the cost of sprawled development—if markets were truly "free" in this realm—far less sprawled development and use of open space and far less physical separation would have occurred.[67]

This foundational federal investment in the current organization of our metropolitan landscape would not be so objectionable were it not for the fact that for many years some groups, especially blacks and the poor, were effectively precluded from benefiting from this public largesse. Monumental highway subsidies, government-backed low-cost mortgages made available on a discriminatory basis, and mostly unbridled exclusionary zoning by new suburban communities all worked in combination to fuel rapid suburbanization by the white middle class and to erect barriers to entry by others.

Creating the Ghetto

Policy choices gave impetus not just to racially and economically exclusive suburbs but also to the black ghetto. Concentrated black poverty—the form of segregation that has had perhaps the most enduring impact in creating inequality—was by and large a government creation. Under the urban renewal program, begun in 1949, the federal government spent about

$3 billion to help cities make the transition from the industrial era; the program resulted in the removal of almost 400,000 units of affordable, largely black-occupied housing that was strategically located in downtown centers. Blacks evicted for the purpose of renewing our nation's downtown centers were forced to move either into existing ghetto neighborhoods or into racially segregated public housing.[68] Many states also had their own programs for "slum clearance," conferring on local governments the power to condemn black neighborhoods targeted for redevelopment.[69] Overall, about 1 million people were displaced by urban renewal projects, half of whom were black.

The federally funded and locally administered public housing program helped to complete this movement of black people from strategic downtown neighborhoods. Whether by design or implementation, public housing was largely segregated by race and created pockets of intense minority poverty in American cities. Among the well-intentioned but ultimately disastrous policy choices that contributed to the phenomenon was a federal mandate requiring that at least 90 percent of all occupants of public housing earn very low incomes.[70] Local political actors were the primary authors of racial separation. City political leaders intentionally located black-occupied public housing only in poor black or transitional neighborhoods, frequently the least desirable parts of town, while white-occupied public housing was built only in white neighborhoods.[71] As a result, poverty in black areas greatly intensified.

The city of Chicago is the textbook example for how to create a ghetto while really trying. The city needed to build a large volume of public housing to make up for all the households that had been displaced by its "slum clearance" activities. Between 1950 and the mid-1960s, the city built thirty-three high-rise housing projects. All but one of them was located in neighborhoods that were more than 84 percent black, and all but seven of them were in areas that were at least 95 percent black.[72] We don't have to imagine the effect on a neighborhood of plopping down massive buildings in which at least 90 percent of the occupants are extremely poor. Cabrini-Green. Robert Taylor Homes. The names of these Chicago housing projects are familiar because they were the site of extreme destitution and violence. Chicago's worst public housing projects have frequently been the site of open gang warfare.

The federal government has sought to atone for its sins by way of the oddly titled "Hope VI" program, which is providing funds to abolish its most dystopian public housing and replace it with less dense, mixed-income developments. As well intentioned as these efforts may be, the legacy of segregation and isolation of extremely poor black people continues. Ghetto life has entered the psyche of *all* Americans, whether they are rich, poor, middle-class, black, white, or some other race. As I discuss at length in Chapter 7, perhaps the most enduring legacy of the black ghetto is fear—fear and stigmatization of black people. This legacy is so entirely established that undoing the effects of the ill-considered, unfair, and disastrous federal public housing program could take several lifetimes, even assuming there is sufficient public will to act.

Private Actors

Federal, state, and local government were not the only authors of separatism. Private actors, particularly those in the real estate industry, have contributed mightily to the racial and economic segmentation of our life space, although, as I have explained, the FHA was complicit in the widespread institutionalization of discriminatory practices. Most critically, the real estate, banking, and insurance industries embraced the federal government's orthodoxy that racial and economic homogeneity were necessary to protect property values.

Most people are familiar with at least some of the more overt tactics real estate agents used in the past to ensure homogeneity and discourage integration. Racially restrictive covenants provided a means of controlling which neighborhoods the excluded could buy into. Even after the Supreme Court declared that courts could not enforce these clauses, there was no bar to a private owner insisting on such terms with any purchaser. Another infamous tactic, "blockbusting," played on the fears of white home owners. The threat of one or a few black neighbors suddenly becoming a multitude was enough to induce many white owners to sell, enabling real estate agents to receive a nice profit by selling at a higher value to incoming blacks. The greatest irony during this era was that housing prices were often higher in black neighborhoods because of the artificially limited supply available to blacks. Realtors could demand higher prices from blacks desperate for more options.[73] Racial steering is a venerable practice that continues to this day, although usually in subtler forms.

Beyond steering, the real estate industry aggressively pursues racial and economic segmentation in another form. Technology and consumer marketing practices have enabled a systematic racial and economic profiling of neighborhoods that now dominates the processes used by real estate developers, financial institutions, insurance companies, and retailers to decide where to invest, develop, and do business. Local land-use planners also draw heavily on these profiling tools. All of these profiling databases establish a hierarchy of neighborhood types that skew investment decisions heavily in favor of predominately white suburban communities. Worse, these profiles are premised upon stereotypes that value and encourage homogeneity. They contribute to discomfort on the part of corporate America and all other institutions that have come to rely on these profiles with any neighborhood that cannot be easily categorized, that is, integrated neighborhoods.

One need only look at the marketing databases that are now available to private businesses contemplating where to invest, lend, or locate to understand the degree to which America has been segmented. One company, for example, has developed the Claritas PRIZM system of categorization—forty socioeconomic rankings of "zip quality" ranging from ZQ1, known as "Blue Blood Estates," to ZQ40, "Public Assistance." Every zip code in America has been assigned one of these forty socioeconomic rankings, with alleged characteristics of race, ethnicity, class, age, household structure, occupation, lifestyle, aspirations, consumer preferences of its residents, and so on. In the lexicon of marketers, the science underlying these databases is known as cluster analysis.

A bewildering array of specialized cluster systems is available from Claritas and competitors like CACI Marketing Systems. MicroVision, which has merged with Claritas, has a fifty-cluster market segmentation system that specializes in "homogeneous" neighborhoods for bank branch locations, fast-food franchise sites, and shopping malls. It also markets MicroVision Banking (31 segments) and MicroVision Insurance (37 segments). The CAP (Crimes Against Persons and Property) Index, offered by a Philadelphia-based company, predicts locational crime risk by correlating what it calls neighborhood "social disorder"—measured by neighborhood socioeconomic characteristics—with local crime reports. Systems like this have been used since the sixties, but Michael

Weiss's 1988 book, *The Clustering of America,* popularized neighborhood homogeneity for business decisions, and this popularity flourished in the wake of weak fair housing and civil rights enforcement.[74]

Sometimes the bias against black and Latino neighborhoods in these clustering systems is transparent. For example, under the CACI cluster system, the home ownership rate of the "Middle-Class Black Families" cluster type is actually the highest of eleven urban neighborhood types and higher than the national average, but according to CACI, such black neighborhoods rank near the bottom (only 38th out of 40) of the CACI clusters in potential loan demand.[75] When businesses make use of these databases, they are buying into such stereotyped logic.

Cluster profiles have also been used to steer prospective home buyers to zip codes with demographics similar to their own. Online home search services are building these profiles into their locator services. For example, the National Association of Realtors' "Find a Neighborhood" locator service allows home seekers to select a neighborhood "like your own" by reviewing and comparing demographic lifestyle profiles of different zip code neighborhoods.[76]

While private decisions about where to invest, lend, do business, or live are often influenced by the racial and economic profiling of neighborhoods, private real estate developers have also played a critical role in creating homogeneity. Real estate development may mirror consumer tastes, but consumers can only buy what is built and marketed. Developers have a tendency to build residential communities or subdivisions for, and market them to, a particular socioeconomic niche. Sam Fulwood, an African American journalist, tells the story of initially looking for an integrated neighborhood for

his family on his first foray into home ownership but ultimately being seduced by the siren call of marketers who knew
how to woo black professional consumers in a way that said,
"Buy here. Move in here. You are wanted here." The developers of the new subdivision in DeKalb County outside of
Atlanta had staked their fortunes on that city's burgeoning
black middle class, and their marketing techniques showed it,
right down to the model home with kente cloth and pictures of
black people.[77] Moreover, most new developments are highly
calibrated for a specific slice of the home-buying income spectrum. The sign outside a new development typically tells the
story: "New Homes from the $280s." Across the highway is a
development for a tonier class, from the "low $400s." We are
all familiar with these economic groupings because anyone
who has bought a home or rented an apartment has had to
decide where she fits in the economic spectrum that is housing
in America. We try to live in the best niche, that is, the best
neighborhood, building, or hamlet we can afford. Mixed-
income developments that throw people of very different
income brackets together are rare.

Developers also contribute to our separatism in another
critical way. Typically, developers, or some other large private
institutional interest, like a key employer in the area, are the
ones that underwrite the costs of incorporating a new town,
that is, giving the people who live in a brand-new development
the reins to their socioeconomic destiny in the form of local
municipal powers. In the 1950s and 1960s, the desire for
racial exclusion was the primary reason for the formation of
new local governments. In later decades, the predominate concern animating the formation of new towns was the desire to
avoid the higher taxes associated with central cities. In other
words, a group of newly situated suburbanites could defend

themselves from an influx of minorities or lower-income people, whose service needs might raise taxes, by incorporating a
new town. And this is exactly what many developers and powerful business interests, such as manufacturers, do, by assuming the costs and offering up the expertise necessary to create a
new municipality.[78]

Finally, developers have also been instrumental in creating
a cultural phenomenon that enables the secession of the affluent, and even the not so affluent, from the socioeconomic
"other": the gated community. Gated communities play into
the worst psychology animating our separatist tendencies: fear.
One marketing brochure for the Stonebriar gated community
in a suburb north of Dallas attests to this psychology. It calls
upon prospective residents to imagine a "perfect place to live
... outside the pandemonium of the city" where one could
"return to simpler times, when you knew you were secure
within the boundaries of your own neighborhood ... where
children could play unattended and be safe after dark."[79]
Gated communities—like their cousins, neighborhoods bound
together by a fee-collecting, covenant-enforcing home-owner's
association—are most common in new suburban communities.
Both types of communities are highly homogeneous by race
and class and are most common in those parts of the country
where foreign immigration has been highest. They have proliferated in states like Florida and California and are also emerging in some unexpected, nondiverse places. Close observers of
the gated community phenomenon report that seven states that
experienced an unprecedented wave of foreign immigrants in
the 1980s simultaneously encountered significant white out-
migration. Many of the states to which whites are fleeing have
experienced a rapid increase in gated communities. These
researchers conclude that "gated areas ... represent a concrete

metaphor for the closing of gates against immigrants and minorities and the poverty, crime and social instabilities in society at large." They offer a physical manifestation of a psychic process of differentiation and distancing from the "other." Whether a new suburban community is physically walled or just separated by distance and bound by private ties, fear is an animating impetus. One suburban resident poignantly testified to this attitude:

> See, you have to understand the fundamental feeling in suburbia is fear, let's face it. The basic emotional feeling is fear. Fear of blacks, fear of physical harm, fear of their kids being subjected to drugs, which are identified as a black problem, fear of all the urban ills. They feel by moving to the suburbs they've run away from it, in fact they haven't, in reality they haven't, but in their own mind's eye they've moved away from the problem.[80]

Was Race and Class Separation Inevitable?

In this chapter I have tried to show that our separatism was not inevitable but the result of a series of conscious choices. Individuals acting on their personal prejudices and preferences might have chosen, in the absence of exclusionary public and private policies, to cluster among their own race and economic class. But it would not have been possible for millions of individuals acting independently to create the regime of systematic stratification and exclusion that reigns today. The impact on African Americans, particularly those who are poor, has been profound. To say that black people and black neighborhoods have received a raw deal in terms of the major developmental policy choices of the twentieth century is an understatement. I personally become angry each time I reflect on this history. I see its effects everywhere. It troubles me that those who most benefit from this legacy of racial and economic exclusion seem to have no sense of the myriad ways in which public policy choices that did harm to others helped enable their own lifestyles. Instead, affluent suburbanites living in predominately white, poverty-free havens that also happen to be the site of most new job growth assume that this is just the way markets work.

In the next section of this book, I show that race and class separation are creating and accelerating inequality in American society. Any short-term gains to the advantaged social classes that benefit from separatism are undermined by the long-term consequences of living in a society in which social mobility and social cohesion may be declining.

PART 2

THE COSTS OF OUR FAILURES—
A SEPARATE AND UNEQUAL SOCIETY

CHAPTER 4

THE DILEMMA OF THE BLACK MIDDLE CLASS

THE "BELTWAY" that surrounds Washington, D.C., like the freeways that wind their way around virtually every American metropolis, serves as a rough boundary between the city and its established older suburbs on one side and the expanding suburban frontier on the other. The exits along I-495 mirror a hierarchy of communities that are worlds apart yet linked by eight lanes of perpetual motion. Prince George's County, Maryland, the highest-income majority-black county in the United States, can be accessed between exits 27 and 2a, or between one and six o'clock, if you think of the Beltway as a clock face. The Beltway slices through the county, separating its poorer neighborhoods from its elite ones. There are in fact two Prince George's Counties, one outside the Beltway that is predominately middle and upper class and the other inside the Beltway that is heavily working class and poor. Both communities are a testament to American separatism. Take an exit eastward and you will be headed outside the Beltway in the direction of black affluence. If you go westward, inside the Beltway, you will be headed toward lower-middle-class and working-class neighborhoods and pockets of black poverty.

A tour of Prince George's County would likely start at its highest end, as the phenomenon of concentrated black wealth has become part of the county's lore. If you take exit 17a, east on Route 202 toward Mitchellville, then make a left on Lottsford Road and proceed to Prospect Pleasant, suddenly you will find yourself at Woodmore, a gated, 350-acre residential development. This is a land of black-owned trophy homes that feature three-car garages, vaulted roofs, glass-encased foyers, and facades of Doric columns that suggest "money" or a seven-figure mortgage. Black people of lesser means like to drive through this area to gain inspiration; here is tangible evidence of the heights successful black people can reach. Some of its mini-palaces remind me of funeral homes, the size and pretense to stately grandeur are so overwhelming.

The black professionals that populate Mitchellville successfully lobbied the U.S. Postal Service to issue their community its very own zip code—20721—which demarcated this hamlet from its less well-heeled cousins. The median household income in Mitchellville is $85,000, compared to a countywide median of $55,000. Mitchellville boasts a high concentration of two-parent black families and college-educated residents. These are doctors, lawyers, white-collar professionals, senior-level federal employees, professional athletes, and successful entrepreneurs, many of whom moved here in the eighties when $400,000 could buy an executive-style dream home of 3,500 square feet or more on a large lot in a pastoral setting. Deals like this could not be had in the overwhelmingly white affluent communities of neighboring Montgomery County, Maryland, or those of northern Virginia. Since then, housing prices have increased dramatically, with trophy palaces going for well over $1 million, although impressive homes are available for less stratospheric prices in many of the newer developments cropping up along Route 202 and elsewhere in Prince George's County.

A Mitchellville resident—a successful doctor married to a librarian and raising three daughters—tells me that cost was his primary consideration in moving into an impressive home in the Woodmore subdivision in 1994. "Why do I live in Niggerville?" John jokes irreverently. After living in several majority-black neighborhoods in the District of Columbia, he was ready for more space for his growing family, and he was concerned about whether the streets of "the District" were the right place to raise kids. He looked at several communities in Montgomery County but settled in Mitchellville when he realized how much house he could buy for his money. Being black himself, he didn't have a problem moving to a community that was predominately black. John also admits that he liked the idea of potentially forming a black commune where he and his close-knit siblings could raise their families together at the end of a quiet cul-de-sac.

Farther south into the county, off exit 3 on the Beltway, and south on Indian Head Highway, lies the older community of Fort Washington—a less-highbrow and, I'm told by its residents, less-pretentious community than Mitchellville, but also a haven of black middle-class families. Fort Washington residents are also less insulated from their lower-income brethren. Some folks who live here are more middle class than others. A black woman, whom I will call Ruth, is the mother of three biracial daughters. She and her white husband live in Simmons Acres, a middle-class suburban development in Fort Washington, which, she claims, went from predominately white to predominately black in the space of a decade. Ruth paints a picture of a community that straddles the spectrum from affluence to working class. She conjectures that although Fort Washington is flush with middle-class professionals, about a third are "overextended." According to the most recent census data, Fort Washington is two-thirds black with a median income of $81,000. Ruth says her family chose Fort Washington because of its relative affordability compared to communities they considered in Virginia and Montgomery County.

Ask any resident of middle- and upper-middle-class Prince George's communities why they live where they do, and the answers vary from price to voluntary separatism to black pride of place. A friend of mine—I will call him Kyle—is an Ivy League–educated African American and a senior executive with a media company located in the District. He and his wife, a lawyer, recently built a four-bedroom house in Fairwood, a new development in Bowie, a predominately white town in Prince George's County. Kyle says that so far the development has attracted mostly black professionals. Although he counts a couple of Indian families among his neighbors, he has not yet encountered any white families in Fairwood. "I am comfortable with that," Kyle says. "Diversity is not as big a deal for me when it comes to where I live. I made a conscious decision to buy into a community that at least would be mixed, [meaning] I would not have gone into a community where there were very few blacks. I want the community I call home to be one that feels familiar, relaxed, and doesn't require any conscious effort to exist." Kyle admits, however, that he and his wife are in Prince George's County "in spite of the public schools." "If our number one criteria had been school quality, in reality we would have ended up in a white area. But that would have been suboptimal. We would be less happy. To spend $800,000 on a house [in order to live in a white area with high-quality schools] and risk a decline in value from over-appreciation or to be house rich and cash poor would affect our quality of life in a way that would not be worth it." In Fairwood, homes range from $300,000 to $600,000, a much more comfortable price range for a beautiful, new, custom-built home. Kyle believes he has reason for optimism, despite Prince George's County's struggling public schools. Fairwood is slated to have a new elementary school. "It is rare when you have an opportunity to build a new school. I am confident it will be a good school because I am assuming the people in this community will be sending their kids there." At bottom, Kyle says, "I wanted to make a smart investment." He says he long ago ruled out Virginia because he and his black friends perceived it as "a predominately white, conservative area where blacks are not politically involved" and because any commute to D.C. from Virginia would be "ridiculous." Having lived in Prince George's County as a renter and a bachelor, he was predisposed to building a new home there rather than in Montgomery County, the predominately white but historically inclusive county that borders Prince George's County to the north. He viewed Montgomery County as "overbuilt" and overpriced. He views Prince George's as on an upward trajectory, with plenty of room for appreciation on his investment and improvement in its circumstances. With lots of black professional families moving in and clamoring for "the good life," his home appreciated 15 percent in value before the construction was even complete. Overall, he is quite optimistic and enthusiastic about the county. As to the problems with the education system, he says, "I am confident that the investments will be made in schools because of their significance to attracting employers and more people in our income bracket."

Should the schools not meet his expectations, he says, "there are plenty of private schools in the county," and mentions Holy Trinity, a parochial school.

For others it just feels good to live in a county where black people are in control. One long-time Prince George's resident, an urban planner, plainly rejects any notion that black people should be aiming for integration. Instead, he suggested to David Dent, writing for the *New York Times,* that black people should be aiming for "the ability to control our own destiny." He proudly boasted that Prince George's County is "the most educated and affluent African-American community on the planet."[1] An acquaintance who lives in an overwhelmingly black neighborhood in the county tells me she "just loves spending an entire day in my community without having to encounter many white people."

This outspoken residential hubris and confident separatism is not uncommon among African Americans who are attracted to the black middle-class suburban enclaves that have begun to emerge outside of U.S. cities with sizeable black populations. They believe in the viability of black communities and black institutions. They believe it is possible to have the good life and the suburban dream in an overwhelmingly black setting. Marita Golden, a writer living in Mitchellville, put it this way in an essay for *Washingtonian* magazine: "Many families see themselves creating their own kind of promised land, bringing the good life with them and expecting even more. This is the classic American suburban dream, this time filtered through the lens of a history forged by inequality and the struggle to overcome." She says of her own choice to move from the District to Mitchellville: "We were sold on the area because of a great deal on a house larger than anything we could afford in D.C. and because we liked the idea of living in this kind of black community."[2]

"P.G. County,"—a moniker that some residents detest (predominately white Prince William County is never referred to as "P.W.")—has received a great deal of public attention for its transformation from majority white to majority black in the space of three decades while at the same time experiencing a substantial increase in average incomes and education levels. In the 1960s, the county's resistance to open housing laws and court-ordered busing earned it a reputation among black people as a rural backwater of rednecks, where the few pockets of blacks were subjected to a brand of justice with "good old boy" rules. Its evolution to a majority-black, buppie haven started in the 1970s when new black residents began moving in to take advantage of the large number of newly constructed garden apartments and condominiums in inner Beltway communities like Capitol Heights and Forestville. White leaders in the county inadvertently promoted a large wave of black migration in the 1980s by building upscale homes intended to entice white-collar professionals in residential developments beyond the Beltway. The county's economic developers underestimated the sizeable black middle class living in Washington, D.C., with money to spend and dreams of suburban living. As blacks reached a critical mass in new single-family subdivisions originally intended for whites, whites began to shun the area. A notable amount of white flight took place in these years of black in-migration, and this exodus was probably exacerbated by a school desegregation order forcing court-ordered busing. By 2000, the county boasted a black population of over 500,000, 63 percent of the population, up from a mere 10 percent in the 1960s and exceeding the number of black residents of the District of Columbia, the so-called "Chocolate City," by more than 150,000. Like many counties with clusters of suburban blacks, Prince George's developed a high degree of segre-

gation at the neighborhood level. Over half of its neighborhoods are at least 70 percent black or 70 percent white.

Prince George's County is part of a larger trend of black
suburbanization that began in earnest in the 1970s, after the
passage of civil rights and fair housing laws. Between 1970
and 1995, 7 million black people moved to the suburbs, a
number considerably greater than the 4.5 million blacks who
made the great migration from South to North between 1940
and 1970. While most of these black suburban movers located
in predominately white settings, a new contemporary phenomenon of predominately black, middle-class enclaves also developed.[3] More than forty U.S. metropolitan areas now boast at
least 50,000 black suburbanites. In many of the largest of
these regions, relatively affluent "buppie bubbles" have
emerged: in Brook Glen, Panola Mill, and Wyndham Park in
DeKalb County, southeast of Atlanta, Georgia; in Rolling
Oaks in Dade County, Florida; in Black Jack, Jennings, Nor-
mandy, and University City in St. Louis County; and in suburbs to the south of Chicago. In the Atlanta region, there are
at least six suburban neighborhoods where blacks are a majority and their income and education levels exceed the median
for the entire metropolitan region. These communities result
from a variety of factors: confident separatism, the pressures of
a housing market that presents stark choices, racial steering,
relative affordability compared to predominately white affluent bastions, or some complex combination of all of these factors.

A black family of a certain means faces a dilemma when
entering the housing market. They, like all Americans, desire
superior environments in which to live, work, play, and raise
their children. Their dream is the American dream. They want
equal access to all of the resources society has to offer, but they

are frequently forced to choose between a black enclave that comes with some costs but provides a spirit-reviving balm against the stress of living as a black person in America, and a community that offers a wealth of opportunities and benefits but where they would be vastly outnumbered by whites, a kind of integration they may not want. Painfully, I have come to the conclusion that external prejudice against black neighborhoods makes it virtually impossible for the black middle class to form havens of their own that approximate the economic or opportunity benefits of a white enclave. Black communities, even affluent ones, bear burdens and costs that predominately white ones do not. Most of these costs are tied either to race-laden decisions on the part of whites and predominately white institutions to avoid black communities or to the propensity (in part fueled by discriminatory attitudes) of black communities to attract low-income people. Waves of black suburbanization have been fueled by the desire to escape the social distress of "the hood," including its crime and weak schools. But within the space of a decade, most black suburban movers will find that the social distress they sought to escape has migrated to them.

Therefore, integration or living in an integrated community is practically the only route black people have to escape concentrated black poverty. Try as they might, the black middle class cannot completely escape their lower-income brethren unless they move into predominately white communities. It is a cruel truth. The black middle class carries much of society's load regarding concentrated black poverty. They usually provide the buffer from ghettoes for the rest of society. The (racist) rules of the housing market are set against them.

In a nutshell, the rules operate as follows: Blacks form enclaves by preference and because they are steered to the least controversial areas—those deemed undesirable by whites—by a discriminatory real estate industry. These enclaves are usually in the opposite direction from the centers of highest economic growth. In the booming 1990s, Prince George's County was situated (and still is) directly opposite the "white hot," technical juggernaut of Northern Virginia. In the Atlanta region, blacks suburbanized mostly south and eastward, while the fastest job growth has been in the suburbs due north, especially near the Perimeter Center. This pattern is repeated virtually everywhere black people are suburbanizing in large numbers. When migrating blacks reach a critical mass, whites flee, and demand in the local housing market falls, causing poorer blacks to move in behind middle-class blacks. Within a period as short as a decade, the black middle class finds itself once again in close proximity to social distress and often moves again, even farther away from the centers of economic growth. Meanwhile, commercial and retail investors shun these emerging black enclaves as the social distress they attract increases crime, often lowers property values, raises taxes, and reduces school quality as the student population rapidly becomes impoverished.[4]

Black separatism, even of the affluent black kind, then, comes with palpable costs. When a white person chooses to move to a middle-class suburban enclave of "her kind of people," she makes this choice, perhaps unconsciously, with certain expectations and assumptions that society tends to live up to—assumptions that a black middle-class suburbanite, living in a similar haven of "one's own," cannot make, at least not confidently. Among those assumptions are the following:

1. I can escape neighborhoods of poverty, particularly black ones.

2. My children will be able to attend good public schools. They will be prepared, maybe even well prepared, for college.
3. My neighborhood will be free from crime.
4. My property taxes will be manageable, and I will receive better government services at lower cost than I would in the city.
5. I will be able to buy all the things I want and need at stores located near where I live. I will have a wide range of options for eating out near where I live.

I'm sure I could extend this list of implicit assumptions about the benefits of suburban life; these are just the main ones. As I show below, these assumptions do not appear to be true for middle-class or even affluent black people of Prince George's County. If this county, with its relatively affluent middle-class population base, cannot transcend the racial biases set against it, if it cannot approximate the American suburban dream for its residents, then I do not see how any other black community could.

The Costs of Black Separatism

In clarifying the costs of the separation for middle-class black suburbanites, I do not mean to denigrate majority-black communities. For some residents the soul-regenerating benefits of a black enclave will be worth the costs. My point is simply that there *are* pronounced costs associated with this choice and that, unfortunately for African Americans, it appears that the suburban ideal will elude them if they wish to pursue a separatist vision. I make my case primarily by debunking the common assumptions about suburban middle-class life, showing that they do not maintain in Prince George's County.

1. I can escape neighborhoods of poverty, particularly black ones.

Although the levels of income and education have risen as Prince George's County has become blacker, the county is not immune to the brutally unfair rules of the real estate market— rules that favor majority-white communities and disfavor majority-black ones. Much to the chagrin of Prince George's County leaders, waves of low-income black people have been migrating to the county from the District of Columbia. This kind of poverty influx did not happen in the majority-white suburban counties surrounding the District. Twenty-nine of the thirty-three suburban communities in the D.C. metropolitan area that have been categorized as "at risk" because of "present and growing social needs" are in Prince George's County.[5] Prince George's and the District itself carry a higher poverty burden than their predominately white neighbors. In the 1990s, 15 percent of the metropolitan region's welfare recipients lived in Prince George's, while other surrounding suburbs were home to less than 5 percent of this population. Not surprisingly, the whiter and more affluent communities have the least poverty burden. While I am not advocating class exclusion, my point is that, to the extent that escaping poverty and attendant social distress is an aspiration of suburban movers, this aspiration is eluding the black middle class.

Most of the low-income folks who have migrated to Prince George's County have settled inside the Beltway, in the western part of the county. Despite the divided nature of the county, the affluent black residents of Prince George's are not entirely insulated. With proximity comes conflict. Evidence of classism abounds, perhaps precisely because the poor folks from the hood are a reminder of what the upwardly mobile and upper-income black residents of Prince George's thought they had escaped. There is a quiet understanding among America's relatively small population of upper-income black people. It spills out in private conversations but is not widely or publicly admitted. In truth, most upper-income black people are just as uncomfortable living in close proximity to their lower-income brethren as are white folks and indeed everyone else in America.

An infamous example of this black classism occurred in the summer of 1996 in the Prince George's community of Perrywood. When black kids from the streets of D.C. began traveling out to Perrywood to play basketball with their middle-income "brothers," the black bourgeoisie took notice. Upset with the nightly noise, recent break-ins and vandalism, and probably the mere presence of a hood element, they hired a private security company to screen nonresidents from the neighborhood. The irony of black people hiring private police to stop and check the identity of all black male youth in the neighborhood was not lost on many residents. Some expressed misgivings and anger, but not surprisingly, a consensus prevailed among the Perrywood residents on the need to protect their homes and property. A similar class dispute erupted in Prince George's in 2000 when the affluent residents of Lake Arbor objected to allowing lower-income students from neighboring Landover to attend a newly constructed high school. Prince George's County residents also displayed their classist tendencies when they built a multimillion-dollar sports and recreational facility while consciously limiting the number of basketball courts.

This classist bent has also shaped politics in the county. Wayne Curry—Prince George's first black county executive and, at the time of his first election in 1994, reportedly the *only* elected black county executive in the nation—campaigned on the assertion that housing was becoming too accessible to low-income D.C. families who would bring crime and other social problems with them. After his victory, he pressured developers to build larger and more expensive houses that inner-city working families could not afford. He also successfully sought a release from a court-ordered school busing program that brought poor students from the eastern fringes of the District into Prince George's schools. His stances were hugely popular with black and white middle-class residents. To be fair, such efforts to exclude low-income residents from the county are economically rational and consistent with the zoning and economic development policies of many other majority-white suburban communities in the nation. Given the rules of the market, Prince George's County leaders probably have to fight a little harder than most suburban locales to meet the desires of its upwardly mobile residents, that is, escaping the ills of the central city with its perceived crime and high redistributive taxes. But Prince George's is not winning this battle, certainly not to the degree that majority-white communities are.

A personal friend of mine and resident of Prince George's has worried aloud to me about the urban influx. Ron told me that he has been thinking about moving back into the District because "an element" has begun to creep into his neighborhood. It's not that these "lower-middle-class black folks" were causing an increase in crime. Instead, Ron observes that they just have different habits. They don't maintain their houses as nicely. They sit outside at night, playing their radios loudly.

Ron's property values were beginning to decline, and he thought maybe he should move back into a "Gold Coast" neighborhood in the District rather than into southern, more affluent parts of Prince George's, which would require him to endure longer commutes to his office in D.C. His family, like most black families with choices about where to live, is caught in the dilemma of the black middle class.

2. My children will be able to attend good public schools. They will be prepared, maybe even well prepared, for college.

Schools are among the prime reasons people decide to live where they do; at least that is what realtors claim. The cruelest reality about Prince George's County is that its school district typically ranks second worst in the state of Maryland on test scores, after Baltimore, a predominately black and heavily poor city. In the D.C. metropolitan area, the Prince George's County school system ranked last on the 2002 Washington Post Challenge Index, which measures public high schools' efforts to challenge its students based upon the percentage of students who take advanced placement and International Baccalaureate courses. Falls Church, an overwhelmingly white, affluent community in Northern Virginia at the opposite pole of the D.C. metropolitan universe, ranked first. Montgomery County, the highest-ranked Maryland district, came in at fifth place. The District ranked twentieth, two places ahead of Prince George's County, and one of its academic magnet schools ranked tenth among all schools. Of the 155 high schools evaluated for this ranking, the first Prince George's school to appear on the list was Eleanor Roosevelt, a magnet high school, which ranked sixtieth. In that year, only 67 percent of the seniors at Roosevelt attended a four-year college, according to the latest available reported data. Of the first ten Prince George's high schools to appear on the Challenge Index ranking, only one other, Central High, had more than half of its seniors go on to a four-year college. At the other schools, college attendance ranged from 34 percent to 46 percent for graduating seniors. Ignominiously, Prince George's and District schools heavily occupy the bottom of the Challenge Index.[6]

In the late nineties, only about a third of all of Prince George's third-, sixth-, and eighth-grade public school students scored at a satisfactory level or better on Maryland standardized tests—a level well above Baltimore's 16 percent proficiency but well below top-ranked Howard County's 60 percent. Test scores have improved of late, but apparently other school districts have improved as well. In the latest available school testing results, Prince George's third, fifth, and eighth graders still ranked second from last in the state, behind Baltimore. If one were shopping for a place to live in the D.C. metropolitan area based upon school quality, one would not put Prince George's on the list.[7]

The causes of this poor performance are not entirely clear, but residents of the county have their theories. A West Indian immigrant couple who bought their home in Fort Washington in the early 1990s—I will call them Miles and Edith—tell me that their neighborhood has changed. Initially, the neighborhood was very well integrated, but whenever a house was sold, a black family moved in. Hence, though still integrated, their neighborhood has become blacker over time. In their view, the schools are horrible. They initially put their kids in Prince George's public schools but withdrew them as the lower-income kids from families migrating from the District began to take over. The schools are bad, they say, because the middle-class parents have taken their children out, leaving them with much less parental involvement. Miles wonders aloud about why Prince George's cannot have good schools. "I am paying the same, maybe even higher property taxes than people who live in Montgomery County or Bethesda, but what do I have to show for it?" he says. He can cite examples of excellent schools in those areas but can't think of an excellent counterpart in Prince George's County.

Ruth has similar misgivings about the Prince George's schools. She offers the example of Friendly High School, which she describes as "predominately black, middle class, and low achieving." She was appalled when her daughter was excitedly praised by school counselors for receiving a 950 on the SAT. "My daughter was sick the day she took the test. I would expect her to perform much better than that. In my mind, a 950 was nothing to be excited about." She says that her kids are receiving much worse schooling than they did in Montana, where she and her family lived before moving to Prince George's County to accommodate a career move by her husband. At a PTSA meeting at her daughter's high school, Ruth claims that as few as six parents might attend, for a school that has more than 600 students. If recently reported school data are to be believed, Friendly is not an impoverished school. Only 18 percent of its students receive free or reduced-price lunch. Ruth has similar frustrations at her younger daughter's elementary school, Henry G. Ferguson, a predominately black magnet school. "The active parents of the PTSA are virtually all white," she says, suggesting that the black parents who do have their kids in public school are either overwhelmed, uninterested, or perhaps too accepting of what the school system offers their children. Alternatively, they may feel that the PTSA has become the vehicle of white parents and is not focused on issues relevant to their own children. Or maybe African Americans are simply not used to being insistent consumers of public education. A history of being locked out may have translated over time into a feeling of disempowerment and a reluctance to demand or expect changes from public institutions, even ones that blacks now ostensibly control. Or it could be that now that African American administrators are largely in charge, black parents defer to their judgment and are content to drop their children off at the schoolhouse door.

Other relatively affluent Prince George's residents also share stories of woe about the schools. An African American lawyer, working hard along with his wife to raise four black sons, removed his oldest from a public middle school in Prince George's and elected to pay about $17,000 a year to send him to an elite private school in Washington, D.C., instead. He felt the teachers at the public school simply had low expectations for his son and were not striving to teach him. I think to myself about how he will be able to afford four such tuition bills as all of his sons come of school age.

When the lawyer moves his family temporarily to the Atlanta area for a work assignment, they live in Dunwoody, a suburb north of Atlanta. "I'm ambivalent about it," he says. "This is my first time living in a white neighborhood." But in Dunwoody, he has all his kids in public schools and remarks, "Here the schools return my phone calls."

John, the affluent Mitchellville doctor and resident of the premier Woodmore development, has taken his oldest daughter out of a Prince George's public school and placed her in a parochial school. His daughter tells me that in her public school some classes had as many as forty students. "The teachers could not control the students," she says. "They were often disrespectful toward teachers." John claims that at the Ernest

Everett Just middle school, which one of his daughters attended, fewer than half of students passed an initial round of state proficiency tests in reading and math.

Stacie Banks, a Fort Washington resident, tells the *Washington Post* she faced a similar situation. She took her daughter out of Indian Queen Elementary, a local public school, and enrolled her in the private Potomac School in McLean, Virginia, which she must drive to daily in addition to her commute to work in the District. Her main concern was overcrowding; with a boundary change, Queen was slated to receive 180 more students and only three more schoolteachers.[8]

Overcrowding is not the only problem. The Prince George's public schools also appear to be under-resourced. Bridgette Tabor-Cooper, a Mitchellville resident who placed her daughter in a private Montessori school, said to the *Post*, "I would love the idea of being able to send my daughters to public school, but not the way most of them are now.... If you don't get into a good magnet program, you're sending your children to a school with uncertified teachers, not enough books, large numbers of children who don't behave."[9]

In conversation after conversation, middle- and upper-income black parents in Prince George's County indicate that they do not have faith in the public school system. There are at least two factors contributing to the problems with Prince George's schools. First, the county is hampered by a property tax cap, approved by citizen referendum, that limits school spending—an additional fiscal constraint that other suburban school districts do not have to contend with. In 2000, for example, per-pupil spending in Prince George's County was only $6,410 compared to Montgomery County's $7,584 and Fairfax County's $8,553. When County Executive Wayne Curry vigorously campaigned for the repeal of the tax cap in the fall of 1996, voters rebuffed him. Why, you might ask, would a majority-black county reject a repeal of a tax cap that would benefit majority-black schools? One possible explanation is that the people most likely to go to the polls, whites and affluent blacks in the county, were least likely to have their kids in public school.

Another potential explanation for the difference in school performance between Prince George's schools and its suburban counterparts is that there is a substantial difference in the numbers of poor children in these schools. School performance is closely tied to the family income of the student population. Indeed, the socioeconomic background of the students attending a school is probably the best predictor of the school's success. By the late nineties, more than half of the Prince George's public school system's students qualified for free or reduced-price lunches, indicating that many prosperous families in the county no longer sent their kids to the public schools. By comparison, only about 10 percent of the students in the Northern Virginia school districts of Falls Church and Loudon County—both on the opposite pole of the metropolitan region—qualified for free or reduced-price lunch. The rules of the market work against middle-class black schools. Predominately middle-class African American schools in the United States tend to impoverish rapidly because majority-black communities tend to attract lower-income populations over time, which in turn discourages middle-class parents from choosing such schools. Still, Prince George's boasts a number of predominately black, predominately middle-class schools, like Laurel, Surrattsville, Suitland, and Friendly high schools, that are decidedly under-achieving; fewer than half of the seniors at these schools attended four-year colleges in recent years.[10] Another possible explanation for this difference between black middle-class achievement and that of white suburban counterparts is wealth differences. One researcher has found that high school graduation and college attendance rates are equal for blacks and whites when you control for wealth rather than income.[11] Whether underachievement stems from an influx of poor children, a failure of the black middle class to cultivate a culture of achievement, or some other source, the end result is that many middle-class black parents who have opted to live in a "black sanctuary" are paying a premium for their separatism in the form of private school tuition. Meanwhile, their white counterparts in affluent white suburbs have the option of relying on high-quality, well-funded public schools that typically have few poor children and a host of engaged parents.

3. *My neighborhood will be free from crime.*

One of the primary reasons suburbanites leave or avoid central cities is crime. The bucolic suburbs offer the promise of freedom from fear. As with other common assumptions about suburban life, however, Prince George's County is not doing as well as its predominately white counterparts; its crime rate is higher, and its citizens are more imperiled. Even the District saw improvements in crime during the 1990s that Prince George's did not enjoy, perhaps because the District was exporting poor people to the county. Crime within the District of Columbia dropped significantly in the 1990s, while it rose slightly in Prince George's County. Although the total increase in crime in the county was marginal, the inner-Beltway communities experienced a crime explosion that was quite disproportionate to their population growth. Places like Berwyn Heights, a majority-white community of under 3,000 residents, grew by only 8 percent in population but saw crime rise

82 percent between 1990 and 1998. During the same period, the District of Columbia neighborhoods bordering inner-Beltway Prince George's communities experienced a sharp decrease in both crime and population. In fact, most of the communities with the highest crime rates in the entire D.C. metropolitan region were all located inside the Beltway, in Prince George's County.

Once again, the laws of the market are undermining the suburban dream for those living in Prince George's County. The social distress formerly tied to the District's poorer neighborhoods is migrating to the county. Such distress contributes to rates of violent crime that are dramatically higher in Prince George's County than in neighboring counties. In 2000, for example, there were six times as many murders and five times as many aggravated assaults in Prince George's County as in neighboring Montgomery County, which has about 70,000 more people.[12]

Violent crime is not limited to the lower-income communities of the county. A creep of sorts has begun. Miles and Edith tell a tale of two classes in Fort Washington. According to them, Fort Washington Drive is a socioeconomic dividing line, and everyone knows it. "The lower-income families have different values," Edith frankly observes. "They get involved with crime and drugs." Edith mentions a murder a few years ago of a well-to-do couple at the hands of two young teenagers who came from the District. In the battle to escape the hood, Fort Washington residents are not entirely successful. In fact, some affluent blacks have begun to move even farther south into predominately white and rural Charles County in part because it has "low crime."[13]

Prince Georgians have also faced another, perhaps unique,

challenge regarding crime: an enduring legacy of police brutality. In the 1990s, the Prince George's County police fatally shot more people per officer than any other of the fifty largest police departments in the nation. Ninety percent of the victims were black or Latino. Of the 122 people shot in the 1990s, including 47 that were killed, not one shooting was deemed unjustified. Almost half of those shot, 45 percent, were unarmed at the time of the shooting. Additionally, almost 20 percent of officers who shot someone had done so previously. Many were promoted and/or given raises, even while under investigation. And during that decade no officer was fired or demoted for shooting someone.[14] In 2000, for example, a black police officer shot an unarmed Howard University student, Prince Jones, six times in the back, claiming he believed Jones was a drug dealer. The police officer was exonerated based upon his claim of self-defense.

Why has police brutality against people of color endured almost a decade after African Americans gained political control of the county? Were the political leadership still white, I suspect there would have been howls of protest from black Prince Georgians. I also suspect that black classism is responsible for the tepid response of the black citizenry to this blatant brutality. Although some middle- and upper-class black residents occasionally find that their sons are the ones being stopped and roughed up, even by black county officers, most of the victims of police brutality have been poor. Meanwhile, a concern with crime that comes from proximity to a "bad element" or a desire not to embarrass the black political leadership now in charge may be fueling black middle-class complacency in the face of brutality against young black men.[15]

> 4. *My property taxes will be manageable,*
> *and I will receive better government services at*
> *lower cost than I would in the city.*

Academic studies show that the two primary motives for the formation of new suburban communities in the fifties and sixties were the desire to escape the redistributive taxes of the central cities and to escape black people.[16] For affluent and middle-class blacks with choices, as I have argued above, escaping lower-income black folks, or the crime and distress that often plagues their neighborhoods, seems to have been part of the rationale for moving to the suburbs. But black movers, like white movers, also want better services for less money. Unfortunately, this has not typically been the case for those who move to majority-black suburbs. Again, black communities tend to carry higher social service burdens than predominately white ones because of their tendency to attract lower-income people. Majority-black areas like Prince George's also tend to be discriminated against in the market for commercial investment and economic growth. As a result, black communities tend to have higher taxes *and* services that are less responsive to the demands and aspirations of the black elite. Isolation from high-growth economic corridors also means that residents of majority-black communities face longer commutes.

Prince George's County is no exception to these trends. First, as I have mentioned, the county is part of a nationwide phenomenon of steering black people to areas deemed undesirable by whites and then steering economic growth in the *opposite* direction. The affluent bastions of Prince George's are outside the Beltway to the south and east of the District of Columbia. They could not be farther away from most of the areas of highest economic growth in the metropolitan region: Tyson's Corner, the I-66 corridor, and the Dulles and Herndon areas in Northern Virginia, and Bethesda, Maryland, all of which are north and west of the District. As a result, residents of job-dense Fairfax County have shorter commute times than do Prince Georgians. Over half of Fairfax County residents who work do so in their home county, whereas only 39 percent Prince Georgians have the luxury of working where they live.

This phenomenon of the black middle class suburbanizing in one direction and jobs and economic growth suburbanizing in another is true in Washington, D.C., Atlanta, Chicago, and virtually every other metropolitan region that is home to a sizeable black middle class. Affluent, largely white suburban communities tend to attract most of a metropolitan region's economic growth. Suburban communities with large black populations, on the other hand—communities that attract *less* economic growth and *more* social service burdens—tend to have higher tax rates, higher public debt, and substantially different patterns of expenditures than do other suburbs. Residents of black/multiethnic suburbs pay tax rates that are, on average, about 65 percent higher than those of white suburbs, *even after* differences in affluence are taken into account. And black/multiethnic suburbs spend more on redistributive services than any other type of suburb, independent of levels of wealth. Prince Georgians' property tax rates ($.962 per $100 of assessed value) are considerably higher than neighboring Montgomery County ($.754 per $100 of value), yet Montgomery County spends more per pupil on public education than does Prince George's County. Montgomery County, having higher-valued—read: whiter—residential properties and a stronger commercial base, can generate more revenues for the services its citizens demand.

Overall, black suburbanites tend to reside in suburban communities characterized by lower property wealth, worse public finances, and poorer prospects for economic growth than suburbs with smaller black populations. As a result, blacks living in majority-black towns tend to receive worse government services than blacks who live elsewhere.[17] The lack of quality government services is a familiar refrain among some Prince George's residents. Bridgette Tabor-Cooper, who has lived in Prince George's County her entire life, says she contemplated leaving after becoming a parent: "It's not black people that I want to escape. It's what this county does badly that other places do well. It's quality-of-life issues that I'm concerned about. There's more to life than nice neighborhoods, nice houses, and great neighbors."[18]

The discriminatory rules of the market also mean that property values are more at risk in majority-black communities. Again, Prince George's County is no exception. The northern parts of the county that have attracted many low- and moderate-income people from the District experienced a substantial decline in property values in the 1990s. Communities like Mt. Rainier, Berwyn Heights, and Hyattsville saw property values decline by between 15 and 18 percent in the mid- to late nineties. Indeed, most of the lowest-valued property in the D.C. metropolitan area is in inner Prince George's County. This decline in property values was accompanied by a simultaneous increase in social distress, including a spike in child poverty and crime in these communities. On the other hand, the more affluent parts of the county have seen their property values increase. But the harsh reality is that Prince George's County and other majority-black communities have been faring poorly in the competition for commercial tax base, with attendant negative consequences for their residents.

*5. I will be able to buy all the things I want
and need at stores located near where I live. I will have a wide
range of options for eating out near where I live.*

Nothing seems to draw the ire of Prince George's black elite
more than the fact that the county is shunned by higher-end
retailers. The same attitude that leads a department store sales-
person to ignore a black customer fuels a propensity of many
retailers, restauranteurs, and commercial entities to ignore considerable black buying power. One affluent Prince George's resident describes this as her "civil rights" issue. Prince George's
County has a higher median income than neighboring Baltimore County, yet that county has a Nordstrom at its Towson
Town Center, while Prince George's has no Nordstrom, Lord &
Taylor, or Nieman-Marcus, much less a Macy's. The Bowie
Town Center, a 100-store, open-air mall designed to provide a
"Main Street" environment, which opened in late 2001 to
much celebration, is anchored by middle-market retailers like
Hecht's, Best Buy, and Sears. John, the doctor from Mitchellville, describes these stores as "crap." And even these so-called
"crap" stores are located in the whitest community in the
county. Bowie is 65 percent white, but its median income is
$7,000 less than that of Mitchellville; it once considered trying
to secede from predominately black Prince George's to become
a part of neighboring Montgomery County. The Boulevard at
Capital Centre, another main-street-styled retail development
that opened in the fall of 2003 closer to the center of black
affluence, is about half the size of the Bowie Town Center, with
fewer name-brand national stores. Affluent black Prince Georgians bemoan having to drive to Tyson's Corner, located just off
the Beltway in Northern Virginia—"where the stores are," as
this mall's marketing jingle ironically declares. Tyson's Corner

boasts more than 250 stores to meet every taste and budget, especially at the high end.

Marita Golden notes that the "retail equity activists" of Prince George's have "written letters to the editor, held demonstrations and news conferences, and complained to whoever would listen about the lack of respect for black buying power."[19] They want quality retail amenities that fit their tastes and budget in their own backyard. As a black resident of the District, I often experience a similar disgust. Go to the white side of town—due west and north—and you can find almost anything you want. Go farther north and west still, over the District line, and the retail options get even better. Downtown Bethesda on a Saturday night is filled to the brim with semi-suburban crowds of mostly whites enjoying a wealth of stores, restaurants, movie theaters, and no "menacing" presences like the homeless, low-income people, or many people of color, for that matter.

Another frequent complaint of Prince Georgians is that they tend to receive poor customer service from the retailers that are present in the county. Ruth complains bitterly about it. "I lived in Montgomery County for a period before moving here. In P.G. County, the service people treat everyone badly, black or white, compared to what I saw in Gaithersburg," she says. Says Andreya Richardson, a pharmacist, to the *Post:*

It's something my husband and I gripe about every day—the school system, the services. Forget shopping. Customer service here is really ridiculous.... We're seriously debating whether we'll stay. We thought about Virginia. ... Columbia [Maryland] is a consideration. I'm pretty definite that I don't want my baby going to public school here and I definitely know I don't want to shop here. We're not sure we'll leave, but we think about it a lot.[20]

If a Prince George's resident wants to experience fine dining, she also has to drive some distance outside the county to
get it. Unlike in Bethesda, Reston, Tyson's Corner, or the District, there is no Palm, no Four Seasons, not even a Houston's
in Prince George's County. The dearth of eateries, especially at
the high end, is such that when the Outback Steakhouse
announced plans to open two new restaurants in the county
and Starbucks announced plans to open a coffee shop, this was
cause for celebration. The county's official web site offers a
listing of 66 restaurants located in Prince George's. A similar
listing for Fairfax County offers over 340 eateries. In sum,
white suburbanites living in havens of their own can take for
granted the simple pleasure of eating out with their family at a
nice place in the vicinity that offers some atmosphere and
quality cuisine. Prince Georgians cannot.

One of the reasons for the dearth of restaurants may be
that national chains rely heavily on the market profiles of companies like Claritas, Inc., of San Diego, or the crime profiles of
CAP Index, Inc., of Exton, Pennsylvania—profiles that do not
convey the real positives in Prince George's County—when
they decide to open a new restaurant. The Inglewood Restaurant Park, in Largo, just off Route 202, near the Boulevard at
Capital Centre, has had difficulty attracting a critical mass of
tenants. Although crime is very low at this location and 35
percent of the households within a one-mile radius earn over
$100,000, this location does not rate well under the Claritas
and CAP profiles because it is within a six-mile radius of
lower-income neighborhoods inside the Beltway and in the
District. The executives in a national headquarters of a restaurant chain located thousands of miles away can't seem to see
past these rigid profiles.[21] Lacking any real experience with or
understanding of black markets, it is easier to rely on stereo-

types. As Marita Golden put it, "This is all part of the racial stigmatizing that education, affluence, and expensive homes can't erase."[22]

This underinvestment in Prince George's County highlights a central weakness of racially segregated communities: a concentration of racial minorities—particularly of black people—can and often does lead to a decline in access to and influence of dominant institutional actors that shape markets. This is not an apology for racist or ignorant market actors. It is a statement of fact. I have had colleagues in the academic community react angrily or skeptically when I present facts like these. They would like to explain away these unfair tendencies of markets based upon anything other than race. But I am not alone in pointing out these tendencies. Empirical studies show that commercial disinvestment in majority-black communities, even affluent ones, is commonplace.[23] I am reminded of a study commissioned by the FCC, which showed that even when minority-owned, minority-formatted radio stations were number one in terms of ratings, mainstream advertisers would send their advertising dollars elsewhere. The practice of making racist or ignorant assumptions about the buying habits of people of color in order to justify not spending advertising dollars with stations that were reaching more people than any other in their markets was widespread.[24] In short, black communities and the assets they bring are frequently devalued by nonblack institutions and people.

Prince George's County is not unique. The five common assumptions about suburban life do not seem to maintain for most other middle-class black communities. In DeKalb County, east of Atlanta, affluent blacks witnessed many stores, including Kmart and Cracker Barrel, pull up stakes and leave their community even as the influx of middle- and upper-income black movers was *raising* the income and education level of the county. A successful black lawyer who built her "dream home" in suburban DeKalb tells me she left it a few years later when she realized there were no viable public schools in DeKalb *or* public transportation routes for her son to get to a private school in Atlanta. Affluent blacks in the Atlanta suburbs face another dilemma. There are only a handful of predominately black schools in which middle-class students are a majority. And because the residential areas where these schools are located are in constant flux, the schools do not remain middle class very long. As a result, parents in the middle-class black suburban enclaves surrounding Atlanta are increasingly bypassing the public schools in favor of private schools.[25]

This pattern is replicated on the West Coast as well. An African American partner at a prominent Los Angeles law firm tells me that most of the black professionals in the City of Angels live in one of three neighborhoods—Ladeira Heights, Baldwin Hills, or View Park—unless they have opted to move to "the Valley" because it offers larger, more affordable, and newer homes. All three of these neighborhoods are overwhelmingly black and in very close proximity to low-income "inner-city" areas. Kim is a proud first-time owner of an older home in "lower Ladeira," which she says is only blocks away from a low-income neighborhood. Such proximity is okay with her. She mixes easily with all kinds of people. But it does tend to force black families with choices to opt out of the public schools. "All of the black professionals I know are either home schooling their children or they have them in private schools. I can't think of a single exception," Kim says.

I have searched the nation for a counterexample—a thriving black community with excellent public schools, an attractive and growing tax base, low crime rates, a host of stores, restaurants, and recreational amenities, in short, something approximating the advantages of majority-white communities, or the vibrancy of black communities in the era of Jim Crow. In all honesty, I have not found such a place. Obviously, black communities have their strengths, as waves of nonblack gentrifiers who have rediscovered the city and moved into black neighborhoods seem to recognize. Harlem is but one African American stronghold that is experiencing a second renaissance. Companies from Magic Johnson Theaters, to Starbucks, to IKEA are beginning to recognize the potency of minority buying power. Kim says of the Crenshaw neighborhood in South-Central L.A. where Magic Johnson has cultivated an entertainment district of movie theaters and restaurants, "I just love going there and being around other black people of all different ranges of income. At the Starbucks, the Fridays, the Fat Burger, they are hanging out, talking and playing chess. It is very vibrant, and it makes you feel so good. There are lots of self-made people there. It's ours." Kim works in a predominately white law firm but, she says, "I feel more comfortable, more secure, and better about myself" living and socializing in a black environment.

Despite their psychic benefits, there are some difficult issues that need to be addressed in order to make majority-black communities eminently viable, issues that we don't like to discuss openly. When it comes to where we live, integration may have eluded, failed, or simply been unappealing to many black people. But separation doesn't seem to be working entirely either. Because the black elite have choices about where to live, work, learn, and spend their money, blacks are no longer *forced* to depend upon one another, and interdependence was the key to the viability of black communities in the era of Jim Crow. Among the hardest of issues is how or whether we can cultivate high-performing public schools for our children. Some Prince Georgians are beginning to look in the mirror. "In the black community we have to acknowledge the politically incorrect truth that too many of our students don't take school seriously, and too many parents are conspirators," writes Golden. Some are more pointed, laying the blame for the county's shortcomings squarely on the black middle class. Ernest Quarles, a Mitchellville lawyer who is married to a physician, cites "a lack of direction and self-esteem among some of the county's young blacks resulting from a lack of parental involvement in schools and recreational activities." He argues in the *Post* that "African Americans have failed to form a strong community bond and to mobilize politically to force change in schools, government and services."[26]

To cultivate family-oriented communities that raise children well and offer "the good life" requires an insistent, organized citizenry that makes educating black children a priority and holds public institutions accountable. It also requires involved parents who join the PTA or find some other way to be involved in schools, and who turn off the television and are intimately involved with their children's development. We have to acknowledge that there is a black achievement gap and bring our resources and talents to bear to cultivate institutions and a culture where learning is taken seriously, teachers and elders are respected, and parents and the entire community are oriented toward educational achievement. I don't think this can happen in Prince George's County or elsewhere without a full, rather than a partial, embrace by the black middle class of their communities, including the low-income folks in their

midst. Black professionals who have chosen to live in separated neighborhoods but opt out of the public schools, or who
harbor a classism toward other black people, pay for it in the
long run. Their web of interconnection with the lower classes
is indelible, whether they like it or not. They can roll up their
sleeves and recruit others in their ranks to enter and stay committed to public schools, or they can pay a price in the poor
reputation of county schools and the spiraling costs of private
school tuition. If they are not prepared to send their own kids
to public school, they could at least lend time, resources, or
votes that reinforce and nurture those schools and the children
who attend them.

The Positive Benefits and Counterarguments

I expect my conclusions about the costs of black separatism to
be met with howls of dissent from some quarters. Let me be
clear: I am not some black conservative or neoconservative trying to be provocative to gain attention or career advancement.
I am a progressive Democrat who cares passionately about the
state of inequality in this nation. The facts I have presented are
inconvenient, painful, even disturbing. I struggle with them
because I am a "race" woman in many senses. I enjoy and
thrive in the company of black people.

My family had its own struggle with the black middle-class
dilemma. We started out on a black middle-class street, Lydia
Drive, in Huntsville, Alabama, but later moved to an all-white
neighborhood, my father says, in order to give my hearing-
impaired brother access to the only elementary school in the
city with a program for children with hearing loss. There was a
world of difference for a young black girl between Lydia Drive

and Owens Drive. On Owens the houses were grander, but the white neighbors, while mostly friendly and well meaning, would never be familial. The world of children's play was happy, but as we grew older the racial differences that permeated the world of adults began to seep through. Upon my entrance into the sixth grade, my parents decided to move back to the house on Lydia, which they had never sold. We moved mainly for financial reasons—my father's political activism came with a price tag—but the end result for me was a happier, more supportive social environment. Now, almost three decades later, virtually the same black middle-class families live on Lydia. I can still walk down Lydia Drive and feel the warmth, comfort, familiarity, and support network that I have never experienced anywhere else and that I doubt could be recreated for a black child in a predominately white setting.

Such community feeling is what attracts many blacks to Prince George's County. The delight and pride they take in living in spirit-renewing black neighborhoods outweighs the costs associated with racial segregation. Many a Prince Georgian would also counter my "parade of horribles" by pointing to the county's strengths. After all, the county has a richer, better-educated population, a healthier tax base, and a lower total poverty rate *because* of the influx of a sizeable black middle-class population. Black professionals have saved the county from its former reputation, at least among black people, as a white, racist, rural backwater. Prince Georgians also proudly argue that they prefer living in a county where African Americans now wield political power, providing the means to shape their own destiny. Since 1990, the school board chairman, county executive, and state and national legislative representatives have all been black. And these black officials have been particularly effective in procuring state aid for the county, particularly for transportation, although it remains to be seen how the county will fair under a newly elected Republican governor. Prince Georgians also argue that their county offers attractive, even palatial, homes at relatively affordable prices.

My Conclusion

Given the costs associated with separatism, where should African Americans who have choices elect to live? There is no universal answer to this conundrum because black people vary in their attitudes about racial solidarity, and their residential choices reflect this variety of opinion. Unfortunately, painfully, I have come to conclude that the only way for a person of color to approximate the suburban ideal is to live in a community that is both overwhelmingly white and relatively affluent. As I explain in the next chapter, the same could also be said for blue-collar and middle-income whites and residents of a variety of other types of communities that, in our current separatist system, also cannot achieve the mythic ideal. But even I, a pro-integrationist, am not recommending this choice. I would not choose to live in an overwhelmingly white community. I am merely underscoring the fact of our very different, separated realities. Between the extremes of overwhelmingly black and overwhelmingly white neighborhoods there are some admittedly rare integrated or multiethnic alternatives. My hope in writing in this book is to encourage more people of all races to make life choices that reinforce and support integrated neighborhoods and integrated institutions. With some ambivalence, I have reached the conclusion that the best—and likely the only—route to full equality for African Americans is a socioeconomically integrated one. While I support the integrationist ideal, I also understand the intrinsic value of black environments and institutions. Far from suggesting that blackness is inherently inferior, I am underscoring the discriminatory attitudes on the part of nonblacks and the impact this has on us.

As I have explained, one critical effect of racial steering and racial avoidance is the tendency for black communities to attract social distress. I am not suggesting that success in escaping from low-income people should be the standard by which a community is judged, although this seems to be precisely what buyers who have choices value. I am arguing, however, that in a system of racial and economic separation that is premised on the idea that the most-valued communities should be farthest or most insulated from the minority poor, *some community* is going to have to bear the burden of proximity to social distress, and in American society, consciously or unconsciously, middle-class black communities have been assigned that role.

The close proximity of the black middle class to poor neighborhoods makes a black middle-class existence much more precarious than a white one. Children that grow up in middle-class, predominately white communities that typically are well insulated from poverty, crime, and weak schools do not encounter the same risks that children living in black middle-class neighborhoods encounter on their passage to adulthood. In a different, socioeconomically integrated system, where low-income people of all races lived among middle- and upper-income people, we would not have the societal burden that comes with concentrated poverty and social distress. Nor would we have a situation where one group of people— African Americans—bear the disproportionate burden of concentrated poverty because they live in or near a high-poverty neighborhood. On the other hand, the black middle class pays a price for its own classism. They pay for it with private school tuition or the higher cost attached to "better" neighborhoods. And they pay a price for their neglect of or hostility toward their lower-income brethren.

If middle-class black people kept their children in the Prince George's schools and stayed involved in those schools, they would be helping to create viable socioeconomically integrated institutions that support all black children regardless of economic background. But this is a heavy burden to lay on the black middle class. It is an unfair burden. In a more integrated society, black people would not have to do so much heavy lifting. There is a different way of thinking about this, however. Some have heatedly argued with me that *only* middle- and upper-class black people are capable of providing a viable solution to the problems challenging black communities, including black underachievement and weak schools, not to mention the erosion of marriage and family formation. Only the black middle and upper classes have the possibility of having real empathy with the black poor, they argue, and therefore they should endeavor to make a difference—by fervently recommitting themselves to black institutions or by recreating socioeconomically integrated black institutions reminiscent of the pre–civil rights era. Given the classist impulse in all of us, however, I am not optimistic about this possibility. In separated America, many folks are just struggling to get by in the best community, the best school, or social track they can afford. We are all struggling not to fall through the cracks of a system that does not really attempt to bring everyone along. The black middle class experiences this dilemma more pointedly than other demographic groups because they, more than most, sit on the precipice between potential upward mobility and potential failure.

For the black middle class, then, the challenges abound. By living in a white neighborhood or sending their child to a heavily white, affluent private school, they risk acculturating their children in ways that may be discomfiting. Black baby boomers who thrived on Howard, Fisk, or Meharry educations and the black network they afforded risk having children with very few black friends. Such dilemmas give rise to organizations like Jack and Jill, that exclusive social institution for the children of the black bourgeoisie. The challenge of raising well-rounded black children who can relate to all types, including their own, while also insulating them from the specter of death, low expectations, an oversexed popular culture, or anything else that might knock a young black child off course, especially a male, is mighty. The most pointed irony is that some of the most integration-weary black parents are paying thousands to send their kids to elite private institutions where their children are the integrators. Yet, a more integrated society that did not fear black people so much might manage to deliver a quality education in an integrated setting to black professional families for free.

The dilemma of the black middle class underscores larger issues of equity. Racial and economic segregation, whether caused by discrimination or voluntary separation, leads to grave inequality. The social and economic trade-offs confronting the black middle class underscore the structural inequalities that permeate virtually every American metropolis. Blacks are hit harder because racial discrimination appears to be applied to them with unique intensity. But a similar, perhaps less stark, story of inequality also could be told for the vast majority of the metropolitan population who do not live in affluent, high-growth communities and suburbs. As I attempt to show in the next chapter, inequality is endemic to the fragmented American metropolis. The opportunity structure does not operate in the manner most Americans purport to believe in. Opportunities are much more unequal than we realize or acknowledge, despite an overwhelming consensus that equality of opportunity should be the norm. And middle-income whites may be the group that is most blind to this reality.

CHAPTER 5

WHITE SEPARATISM
The Costs and Benefits

FAIRFAX COUNTY might be labeled "most fortunate" in the D.C. metropolitan region. Though only a few degrees of separation from Prince George's County, "P.G. County" and Fairfax County are opposites. Prince George's, due east of the District, is 63 percent black. Fairfax, due west, is 70 percent white. Prince George's is the highest-income majority-black county in the nation. With a median household income of $81,000, Fairfax is the nation's second-wealthiest county and the wealthiest among counties with populations above 200,000.[1] Prince George's has almost double the poverty rate of Fairfax. Fairfax schools are high achieving. Prince George's schools are not. Fairfax is home to most of the high-growth communities in the D.C. metropolitan region, including Tyson's Corner, the I-66 corridor, and the areas surrounding Herndon and the Dulles Airport. Prince George's is without such economic engines.

Fairfax City, a separate municipality located in the heart of the county, is an "affluent suburban job center," meaning it is blessed with extensive resources and few social needs. Typically, such communities boast about five times the office space of other suburbs in the same metropolitan area. They are considered the most attractive communities in their respective regions because they enjoy a steady flow of jobs, expensive housing, and upscale retail outlets.[2] Fairfax resembles job-rich suburbs or edge cities such as Palo Alto outside of San Francisco; Stamford and Greenwich in Connecticut; Great Neck, Lake Success, and Garden City, New York; and the Perimeter Center north of Atlanta. These communities tend to attract the best of everything and the worst of nothing, except perhaps traffic. Almost universally in this country, communities that are the locus of the fastest economic growth are overwhelmingly white, affluent, and suburban. They typically have a black population of less than 3 percent.[3] In short, this type of community receives the highest immediate rewards for racial and economic separation.

The contrast between predominately black Prince George's County and predominately white Fairfax County in the Washington, D.C., metropolitan area suggests that the existence of "two societies, one black, one white—separate and unequal" that the Kerner Commission predicted in 1968 has in fact come to pass.[4] Although our nation has become enormously complex racially, overwhelmingly white and overwhelmingly black communities tend to sit at opposite extremes of the physical space that is the American metropolis. They also are very far apart along the spectrum of benefits and burdens in our society. The starkly different realities of black and white communities represent certain kernel truths about the costs and benefits of racial separation.

What is the cost of separatism to white America? For many whites, particularly affluent ones, racial and economic separatism confers certain distinct advantages, advantages that seem to fuel the insulation of white families with children. A friend of mine once asked her husband while they were walking along Pennsylvania Avenue in southeast Washington, near our nation's Capitol, "Where do you think the Capitol Hill neighborhood ends?" "Where you stop seeing white babies in strollers," her husband quipped.

He was certainly right about one thing: Parenthood contributes to white separatism. Why? Because all parents want the best possible lives for their children. I once heard Michael Harrington, the leading socialist of his time and author of the influential book *The Other America,* attest to such attitudes in a radio interview. Describing his own experience, he said, "There is no more bourgeois liberalizing force than parenthood." He might choose a shoestring, hippie existence for himself, but once he became a parent he could not impose such a lifestyle on his children.

In a rapidly diversifying America, the urge to move one's kids into "safe" neighborhoods and the best schools is acutely felt by many white parents. The most risk-free alternative in a society that is not fundamentally committed to bringing every child or every person along is to opt for those neighborhoods and schools that offer the best opportunities one can afford. Unfortunately those places tend to be the most homogeneous—indeed, the whitest and wealthiest of places. The immediate advantages of racial and economic homogeneity for affluent whites typically include better schools with more resources, stable and growing property values, lower local taxes, better government services, less crime, better commercial amenities, and proximity to job-rich growth centers—the polar opposite of the disadvantages that frequently plague black enclaves.

While our neighborhoods are stratified into various types, affluent, predominately white, suburban job centers are at the top of this hierarchy. Only about 7 percent of the people living in the nation's largest metropolitan areas reside in these most favored places. White suburbanites who cannot gain entry into these exclusive communities tend to end up in one of two other types of predominately white communities—fast growing bedroom communities or older, declining suburbs.[5] Those living in such places may identify with the affluent, job-rich suburbs, but, like residents of black communities, they actually incur high costs in our separatist system. In this chapter I first demonstrate the distinct advantages enjoyed by those who can afford to live in the affluent, high-growth suburbs. For these favored folks in American society, race and class separatism pays off handsomely. But I then show how most whites, even affluent ones, pay a price for their separatism.

The Privileges of the Favored Quarter

The "favored quarter" is a term coined by real estate developers to connote those communities that have been singled out for the kind of private investment and public largesse—infrastructure investments—that can create proverbial streets of gold.[6] Fairfax County's favored status is evident. Traverse a few exits on the Beltway from Prince George's County and you enter an altered universe, one with very different rules of the game. The five common assumptions about suburban life that

I introduced in Chapter 4 do maintain for Fairfax residents, even as they elude Prince Georgians.

1. *I can escape neighborhoods of poverty, particularly black ones.*

This is a very fair assumption for residents of Fairfax County and Fairfax City. No community in these parts experiences anything approaching the challenges that plague some inner-Beltway communities in Prince George's County. No community within Fairfax is "at risk." Nor does the county have any pockets of intense minority poverty. Its overall poverty rate is a relatively low 4.5 percent. Of the thirty-three suburban communities in the D.C. metropolitan area that have been categorized as "at risk" because of "present and growing social needs," only one, Alexandria, is in Fairfax's orbit.[7] Alexandria shares a border with Fairfax County but is outside the county. And while "at risk," Alexandria is far from destitute. It has a median household income of $56,000, far below that of Fairfax County but above Prince George's County's median income of $55,000. Alexandria's poverty rate is 9 percent, double that of Fairfax County as a whole but not approaching the double-digit poverty rates of many inner-Beltway communities in Prince George's County. Finally, Alexandria has much higher property values on which to draw for tax revenue, with a median value of $253,000 for owner-occupied units, compared to $145,600 for Prince George's County as a whole. In other words, the worst-off city in terms of its poverty load and revenue base in the vicinity of Fairfax County is better off than at least half of Prince George's communities. Meanwhile, residents of Fairfax County are well insulated from intense minority poverty.

2. My children will be able to attend good public schools. They will be prepared, maybe even well prepared, for college.

Fairfax County residents enjoy the best public schools in the D.C. metropolitan area. According to the second annual report under the federal No Child Left Behind law, 184 out of 185 Fairfax schools met the overall math achievement target and 181 out of 185 schools met the overall English achievement target. Fairfax schools consistently perform at the top of rankings based on test scores and on the degree to which they challenge their students. In a recent ranking of the top ten high schools in the D.C. metro area, based upon test scores, schools ranked 2 through 10 were in Fairfax County.[8] The most racially diverse of Fairfax's top performing schools, Herndon High, is 64 percent white, and only 13 percent of Herndon students are eligible for free or reduced-price lunch. Overall, there are only a handful of schools in Fairfax with large numbers of poor children and virtually none in which a poverty culture predominates. From a parent's perspective, Fairfax County schools are delivering best on what matters most for young people who must one day enter the workforce; the average percentage of Fairfax County high school graduates who go on to four-year colleges is 78. The average for Prince George's County is 44.[9] Fairfax County public schools are also blessed with an abundance of involved parents and volunteers. According to the school system, more than 60,000 citizens donate time and expertise to the Fairfax County schools each year. Such public support also translates into financial support for the county's public schools. In contrast to Prince Georgian voters' rejection in 1996 of the effort to repeal a property tax cap that limits school funding, in 2001 Fairfax County voters approved a $378 million school bond referendum by a ratio of 4 to 1.[10]

3. *My neighborhood will be free from crime.*

Having little in the way of social distress to contend with, Fairfax County experiences less crime than its neighbors. The suburban dream of a crime-free haven is approximated here more than in most jurisdictions in the D.C. metropolitan area. Overall, Fairfax County crime rates are considerably lower than those of neighboring Montgomery and Arlington counties. The most common crimes occur against property, not people. Violent crimes are low. In 2002, for example, there were 16 murders and 357 aggravated assaults in Fairfax County compared to 32 murders and 878 aggravated assaults in Montgomery County, which has almost 100,000 fewer residents than Fairfax County.[11] The contrast between Fairfax County and Prince George's county is more stark. In 2000, the last year for which I could find comparable statistics, there were 2 murders and 84 aggravated assaults in Fairfax County compared to 72 murders and 4,174 aggravated assaults in Prince George's County, which has about 170,000 fewer residents.[12] Fairfax County is not completely immune from social ills associated with more distressed communities; gang activity has begun to find its way into the county. Its police attribute four murders in the last three years to gang members.[13] Still, the people of Fairfax County have a lot less crime to worry about than do their Prince Georgian counterparts.

4. *My property taxes will be manageable, and I will receive better government services at lower cost than I would in the city.*

During the heady days of the tech bubble, Fairfax was at the center of this economic juggernaut for the D.C. metropolitan

area. It still enjoys the region's strongest tax base. Of the largest
twenty technology companies in the metropolitan area, thirteen
are located in Fairfax County, as are twelve of the top fifteen
federal contractors. Over half of Fairfax County residents have
the luxury of working in the county, near where they live. Their
incomes and high property values contribute to well-funded,
award-winning government services. Although property tax
rates are higher in Fairfax County ($1.16 per $100 of assessed
value) than in Prince George's County ($.962 per $100), Fairfax residents get what they pay for. In 2001, Fairfax County
was voted the "Best-Managed County" by *Governing* magazine for its excellent government services. The county boasts the
largest public library in Virginia—also the sixth-largest in the
nation—and sets the standard for E-government, enabling its
residents to conduct many activities and chores online, including, among other things, paying taxes, renewing library books,
checking school cancellations, and finding out whether a
restaurant has passed health inspections. Fairfax's fiscal health
is paramount; it is one of only fourteen counties in the nation
with a triple-A bond rating. Part of the reason for this exalted
status is the county's strong and growing revenue base; almost
every municipality in the county has enjoyed double-digit
increases in property values in each of the past three years.[14]

*5. I will be able to buy all the things I want
and need at stores located near where I live. I will have a
wide range of options for eating out near where I live.*

Nothing could be truer for residents of Fairfax County. The
county's web site proudly touts its abundance:

With more than 200 shopping centers and thousands of
restaurants offering every conceivable variety of world cui-

sine, Fairfax County offers one of the best shopping and dining experiences on the east coast.... Tyson's Corner, the
"downtown" of Fairfax County, is second only to Manhattan
in its amount of retail space on the east coast. Malls include
such retailers as Macy's, Neiman Marcus, Nordstrom, Saks
Fifth Avenue, Abercrombie and Fitch, Bloomingdale's, Urban
Outfitters and Joan and David.

It goes without saying that none of these stores have locations in Prince George's County. Fairfax County has at least
four premier malls: Tyson's Galleria, Tyson's Corner Center,
Fair Oaks, and Springfield. One can find Tiffany's, Hermès,
Gucci, and Louis Vuitton at the Fairfax Square in Vienna. The
Reston Town Center is touted as an "urban setting of boutiques and restaurants." The towns of Clifton, Fairfax, Herndon, and Vienna each boast specialty shops and boutiques in
their historic districts. In the retail or restaurant sector, no
need, desire, or taste seems to go unmet.

No one who lives in favored suburban communities would
likely admit openly, even to themselves, that feelings of separatism explain why they live where they do. It is one thing for
black residents of Prince George's County to openly share with
me, another black person, their desire for a haven of their
own. It would not be politically correct for a white person to
admit that they too harbor such feelings. But sometimes the
psychology of the bulwark spills out. The desire to demarcate
one's own separate space might explain why the overwhelmingly white suburb of East Detroit, Michigan, decided in 1992
to rename itself East Pointe.

My husband and I recently had conversations with a new
friend—I will call him Joe—that offered a rare moment of hon-

est dialogue between people of different races who ordinarily would never talk about such things. Joe, who is white, said he moved his family from Salt Lake City to Park City, Utah, precisely because he wanted to get away from lower-income people. He didn't want his kid going to school with lower-income children who might lower the standard of education. To be fair, Joe was equally dubious about sending his kid to any school with so-called rich kids. He reasoned that there are drugs at both ends of the spectrum. He defended his choice of trading up to a community with better schools and more homogeneous surroundings. He had worked hard for his money and had made good choices for himself and his family. "Why should I be penalized for that?" he argued. He made it clear that he would move his family again, if necessary, to avoid any lower-class element that might affect his family's way of life. "Everybody has their own comfort zone," he argued. He pointed out that a large number of Latino immigrants had been moving into the community. As in so many other places, immigrants in Park City were doing the laborious work that other people don't want to do, and for extremely low wages. They were nannies, construction workers, gardeners, hotel and restaurant workers, to name just a few of the occupations Joe observed them taking on. They were clustered in a particular neighborhood. In order to break up the concentration of native Spanish-speaking schoolchildren that this created, Joe's wife—I will call her Sarah—said, Park City had developed a busing plan due to be implemented the following year. Joe complained aloud that this was going to hurt the English speakers: "I know people think I am probably elitist complaining about the impact on my one white child. But it doesn't seem fair that people who make good choices to have fewer kids, to work hard and raise them well, get less attention than those people who make bad choices. If a bunch of Spanish-speaking kids are bused into a school, they are going to get all the attention and the resources. They are going to bring the standard down for everyone else. That is not fair." Joe acknowledged that many employers and citizens of Park City profited enormously from the Latino community's low-cost labor. Joe offered that this hearty band of hard-working people was being exploited, but he did not see them as I saw them: as net contributors to their local economy, as taxpayers who had every right to avail themselves of public schools. Rather than argue with Joe, I just listened, taking in the full measure of his heartfelt perspective.

Sarah's perspective differed from that of her husband. There was something of a gender gap in this home. Sarah grew up near a large city and missed its cosmopolitan atmosphere. She wanted her son to experience the kind of racial and socioeconomic diversity she did. Still, she, like Joe, was focused like a laser beam on doing the best job she could for her child and seemed unsure as to how an immigrant influx would impact their quality of life.

The dilemma and the challenge for getting beyond separatism is that many individual whites actually benefit to a great degree from racial homogeneity. Although the *costs* to whites of separation are of a more abstract nature, there are immediate payoffs to locating in a predominately white, affluent community if you can afford it. Who could blame an individual family for making this kind of choice given the payoff? A very liberal white colleague of mine acknowledged this tension when she lamented that although she would prefer to live in a well-integrated neighborhood, she wanted to send her kids to public school and felt that she would be compromising her children's education by living in a neighborhood with worse schools. Hence, this very liberal white person lives in an over-whelmingly white neighborhood in Washington, D.C.

To be fair, one could just as easily assume that residents of affluent, predominately white communities live where they do simply because they can afford the best. Why wouldn't you choose to live in a community that offers the best combination of benefits (a lot of upside) and burdens (very little downside) if you could afford to make such a choice? Katherine, the inte-grationist who lives in the District, described her sister's choice to live in an overwhelming white neighborhood of North Arlington, Virginia, this way: "She is not choosing 'white.' She is choosing comfort." Katherine notes that her sister—I'll call her Linda—spent four times what Katherine did for her house, an enormous sum in Katherine's view. But by doing so, Linda bought her way into a community and an infrastructure that serves her children's needs very well. According to Katherine, Linda is surrounded by a host of other professional families with young kids; the PTA meetings are packed with concerned parents; the public schools have a great deal of stability, with excellent experienced teachers. Linda's family has paid a steep price to live where they do. But as Katherine describes it, her sister is able to relax in the comfortable knowledge that she has given her kids educational opportunities above a certain threshold level below which she and many other white parents are not willing to go.

My point in this chapter, however, is to underscore that homogeneity—both of race and class—has a lot to do with why communities like the one Linda lives in are so advan-taged. For Prince George's County and other predominately black communities, the tendency of (discriminatory) markets to create pockets of intense minority poverty leads to distinct disadvantages. The same discriminatory forces that concentrate minority poverty, and its attendant social costs, in certain communities create the absence of it elsewhere. More than just luck is involved in this process of institutionalized advantage and disadvantage.

The pattern of entrenched advantage in favored communities and entrenched disadvantage in others is repeated in most metropolitan areas throughout the country; certainly it appears in every metropolis that has a sizeable population of black people. The phenomenon should be familiar, especially to those who live in the Midwest and on the East Coast. Affluent, overwhelmingly white, suburban communities are the bull's eye in an area of rapid growth that is occurring away from a central city that frequently is heavily populated with racial minorities. This economic boomlet has bypassed the older suburbs that, decades ago, were the new best thing. Communities in the "favored quarter" enjoy three distinct advantages: (1) they capture a disproportionate share of the public infrastructure investments being made in the metropolitan region; (2) they enjoy the strongest tax base and the highest job growth in the region; and (3) they use local powers to close their housing markets to nonaffluent regional workers.[15] I suspect it will be rather easy for you to identify the favored quarter in the region where you live.

In the Chicago region, for example, the favored quarter is made up of the affluent suburbs far northwest of the city—job centers that have cropped up along I-94, Route 14, and I-90 northwest of the Windy City. The most prestigious of these favored suburbs are the close-in "gold coast" communities due north, bounded by Lake Michigan and I-294. Like their counterparts elsewhere in the nation, places like the North Shore and Winnetka are the "best" suburban addresses because they offer both easy access to the big city and the comfort of exclusivity. In the 1980s the northwest suburbs garnered nearly 100 percent of the new job growth in the Chicago region—458,000 new jobs—while all the other suburbs gained only 90,000 new jobs and the city of Chicago lost about 90,000 jobs. In terms of job growth, the Schaumburg area, along I-90, has been the most successful edge city in the region. It includes Barrington Hills, Inverness Village, Itasca, Schaumberg Village, and South Barrington Village. Schaumberg Village alone has nine industrial parks and over 13 million square feet of industrial space, with tenants like Motorola and 3M. This job-rich quadrant is not accessible to Chicago's many low-income people. To get to an employer or retail outlet in Schaumberg one must drive a car, as a train or bus will take you only as far as the Schaumberg station. Assuming you had a car, a drive from Chicago's Southside, where many low-income black people live, would take more than an hour each way. Thus the economic might of the Chicago region's most favored communities is simply closed to many who do not live there.

Why was this northwest quadrant so blessed? It was more than just a Midas touch of economic competitiveness or so-called free markets. An area with only about 40 percent of the region's population was allocated nearly 60 percent of all the transportation infrastructure funds spent in the area. Development booms and land-use patterns have a way of following the highway spending, not the other way around.[16] Although Chicago's northwestern suburbs were garnering many of the benefits of participating in a regional economy with access to regional workers and consumers, as well as federal- and state-funded infrastructure investments, they were not sharing appreciably in regional social burdens. While enjoying virtually 100 percent of all the economic growth in the region, they housed less than 3 percent of the area's young children who lived in poverty; less than 1 percent of the elementary school-children in their schools received free or reduced-price lunch. Meanwhile, the city of Chicago, which was experiencing a decline in its job base, was home to 35 percent of poor young children. Some 70 percent of Chicago's elementary school-children received free or reduced-price lunch.

These stark patterns of advantage and disadvantage, favor and disfavor, recur in varying degrees throughout the American landscape. In the Twin Cities area, the favored quarter is to the south and west of the I-494 beltway. In the 1980s the state spent about $1 billion on new highways, and 75 percent of this largesse went to these developing suburbs. In the 1990s, virtually all of the transportation budget for the Twin Cities region was earmarked to expand roads in the southwest quadrant. The citizens of the Twin Cities paid more than $6 million annually in the early 1990s to subsidize the cost of new sewers and utility lines in the favored southwest suburbs, even though there was plenty of unused sewer capacity in established communities.[17] In Atlanta, of the $1 billion spent on highways between 1987 and 1997, about $620 million was allocated to the fast-growing, predominately white northern suburbs. Nearly 80 percent of the $1 billion spent on new highways in the Detroit area between 1986 and 1995 went to one county— Oakland County—that accounted for only 26 percent of the population and is over 80 percent white. In the San Francisco Bay area, between 1996 and 2002, the majority of the $1.8 billion in spending for new highways was allocated to a ten-mile radius primarily serving I-880 Silicon Valley commuters and the fast-growing, affluent communities of eastern Contra Costa County.[18]

All communities, including less affluent, middle-income, and older communities, would like to be chosen for valuable federal and state public investments in infrastructure. Massive federal transportation funds are not limited to spending for new highways. Federal transportation funds can go to extensions of subway or light rail lines, bicycle paths, or expansion and improvement of existing roads. The development dreams of a mayor of a new suburban town can be realized only when the necessary infrastructure—roads, sewers, utility lines, and so on—is in place. Cars and people have to have a means of getting in and out. Water and electricity have to go in; sewage and run-off have to be channeled somewhere.

How can new communities afford to pay for such expensive new infrastructure? They don't. An individual suburban community, particularly a highly residential one, typically cannot pay for all of the infrastructure that its impressive new development requires. A person who moves to a new suburban subdivision, therefore, is not fully internalizing the cost of this lifestyle choice. Other taxpayers subsidize his choice, and some would argue, to an excessive degree. A study of new development surrounding Phoenix in the 1990s provides a cogent example of this widespread phenomenon. It found that new developments occurring around the fringes of the city were subsidized at a rate of $14,000 to $15,000 per unit and that a cross-subsidization of suburban households was occurring, paid for with inner-city dollars.

So we have an ironically inequitable situation in most metropolitan areas. Our separatism enables a privileged minority to receive subsidies from tax and fee payers in less well-off communities that contribute mightily to the favored quarter's advantaged position. At the same time, with strategic use of their local zoning powers, they are able to isolate and wall themselves off from society's most pressing burdens. This is not a new thesis; empirical studies show that low-density suburban sprawl does not pay for itself and that public infrastructure subsidies are influencing which communities are blessed with economic growth of the most valuable kind.[19]

One would think that individual communities fortunate to be the beneficiaries of such public largesse and its attendant economic growth would have an obligation to share some of their increased tax base with the communities that subsidized them. But that is not the way our separatist system currently operates, save for a precious few progressive metropolitan regions that go against the grain of extreme parochialism in local governance. Instead, our separatism has created a closed loop of entrenched advantage. The wealthiest communities are the winners in the competition for high-end development—the clean commercial businesses and executive-style housing that generate the most tax revenues and the least demands for government services. Hence they are able to keep taxes low, funding a less needy populace from a broad, rich tax base. Lower tax rates attract more and more businesses, which in turn lowers the overall tax burden even more.

In contrast, the nonwealthy developing suburbs are left to fend for the remaining new development—typically lower-value homes and multifamily apartments—which adds to the tax base in the short term but creates a vicious cycle of rising service costs that come with having more schoolchildren per square mile. These costs are much more difficult to meet on a modest tax base. Working-class suburbs, then, are either forced to raise taxes to meet new service demands or provide less attractive services, both of which makes these communities less attractive in the competition for economic growth. Central cities may be somewhat better off in this metropolitan competition because they typically have a central business district that bolsters their tax base. But most central cities are also saddled with high concentrations of poverty that force them to have much higher tax rates or less attractive services than out-lying suburbs. This tax differential, coupled with the negative perceptions often attached to the demographics of the city, is a large negative factor in the competition to recruit and retain businesses and middle-class taxpayers. With these spatial rules of the game, it is very hard for central cities, older suburbs, and lower-value developing suburbs to compete, much less provide their citizens with anything approaching the idealized combination of taxes, services, and amenities available in the favored quarter.[20]

I often reflect on this separatist arrangement when I am driving around the D.C. metropolitan area, observing the stark differences among the communities I see. It bugs me. Job-rich, affluent suburban communities get to export some of the costs of their advantaged lifestyle both in the form of direct subsi-dies they receive from less-advantaged taxpayers and in the costs others bear for their exclusivity. As one astute observer of suburban development patterns put it, many new suburbs "create social costs without paying for them." By enacting exclusionary zoning ordinances that maximize home values, such communities "force low- and moderate-income workers to live far from suburban jobs and commute long distances, which increases traffic congestion and air pollution and imposes time losses on all commuters."[21] Exclusionary, low-density suburban development also causes other problems, including rapid loss of open space and waste of existing, underutilized sewers, utilities, and schools in older communi-ties.

Clearly, all of these allegations are debatable. I don't mean to suggest that wealthy suburbanites are to blame for all of the problems endured by central cities and older suburbs. There is a vast literature that chronicles a thirty-year debate about the relative costs and benefits of sprawled suburban development. One area of agreement in this debate is that sprawled development costs more in the way of capital expenditures for infrastructure than compact development.[22] Tax and fee payers, therefore, have been bearing this extra cost. Another thing that is clear, at least to me, is that affluent, job-rich suburban communities typically are devoid of affordable housing. And this exclusion of low-income people, indeed, even moderate-income people, whom other communities must house, is a critical component of their fiscal and economic success.

The Costs of Separatism to Whites

The favored quarter, like the black ghetto, represents an extreme of American separatism. It also represents the mythic American dream. But there is another dimension to the dream that is America: the shibboleth of all boats rising. Everyone who works hard and plays by the rules is supposed to be able to get ahead in this land of opportunity. American mythology has a powerful hold on us in part because there *are* real-life rags-to-riches stories. Those who are celebrated in American popular culture mirror this possibility for the masses. Likewise, our separated neighborhoods offer up the promise that one day, we too might be able to trade up to an ideal we wish for, even if we can't live that ideal today. But this separated system comes with serious costs. The costs of separatism to whites is enormous, yet they are the ones who are likely to be least conscious of separatism's insidious effects. Currently, whites are also the segment of the population that is most apt to live a separated existence. Without an altered consciousness on the part of many more whites, I fear, our nation will never be able to transcend the separate and unequal society we have created.

Racial and economic separation creates both short- and long-term costs for white people. Admittedly, these costs fall differentially depending on the type of community one lives in. They are borne most heavily by the middle and working classes.

The first cost *is* cost. Separation is pricey. Whites typically pay an expensive premium for a white neighborhood. In the Detroit metropolitan area, for example, the average cost of a home for a white person is 43 percent more than that of a black person with the same income. David Rusk, former mayor of Albuquerque, New Mexico, and nationally recognized author on cities and suburbs, calls this gap between home values in majority-white and majority-black suburbs a "segregation tax" and points out that as segregation declines, so does the gap.[23] Investigating recent bankruptcy trends, two researchers have concluded that the modern middle-class family is caught in an "income trap" because they typically must devote the entire salary of one parent to the mortgage payment. Middle-class families with children are much more likely to face financial collapse—bankruptcy—than are childless households because parents feel they have no choice but to pay the expensive premium attached to a "good" neighborhood with "good" schools. The authors acknowledge, however, that parents' subjective beliefs that only certain neighborhoods offer good, safe schools are driven by parental worries rather than objective facts.[24]

I have watched white friends struggle with the challenges of getting into an "appropriate" neighborhood in the Washington, D.C., metropolitan area. For those whites committed to living inside the District, the well-traveled path is to one of the two dozen neighborhoods "west of the park"—that coda of preference and comfort that just happens to describe an overwhelming white bastion in an otherwise majority-minority city. For many white professionals, these neighborhoods represent quality elementary schools, safety, and stability. They are appropriate neighborhoods in a way that the heavily minority and black neighborhoods east of Rock Creek Park apparently are not.

The cost of entry is steep. Take Cleveland Park, one of the "west-of-the-park" neighborhoods. Situated between the main thoroughfares of Wisconsin and Connecticut avenues, Cleveland Park offers gorgeous older homes with character on quiet, leafy streets close to a host of desired amenities. Grocery and health food stores, bagel and coffee shops, a pet superstore, and many other services can be reached on foot. Dry cleaners, drug, video, hardware, and wine stores, not to mention home furnishings, are all within easy walking distance of most homes. On any given evening, Cleveland Park's cafes, bars, and eateries overflow with patrons. The spacious historic movie theater, the Uptown, typically screens the hottest megahits. Residents of Cleveland Park can walk to a Metro stop on the most traveled Red Line, which allows them a convenient, stress-free commute to most points in the city. No driving is required. The neighborhood has beautiful parks and greenery; it is one Metro stop, or a pleasant long walk, from the world-class Smithsonian National Zoo. Cleveland Park's public schools are among the best in the city. It also happens to be walking distance to some of the city's most elite private schools, including Sidwell Friends, the National Cathedral School, and St. Albans. Like many other upper northwest Washington neighborhoods, Cleveland Park's better-equipped parks, recreation centers, and public schools result from activist, "Friends of" groups that raise money from the deep wallets of the residents who live here. Overall, this feels like a happy, idyllic place for the families with children who are privileged to live here. It seems more diverse than it really is because it is so popular; people from across the city come to enjoy its eateries and other amenities. But this community is about 85 percent white. Almost 80 percent of the families here earn six-figure incomes.

Not surprisingly, the cost of housing in Cleveland Park is prohibitively expensive. Smaller homes in the area sell in the $500,000 to $600,000 range, assuming you can find one for sale and are able to win the auction-like bidding process. Overall, in upper northwest D.C. you can easily pay $700,000 for a house that is badly in need of remodeling. The fiercest competition is for the lower end of the price range. Younger white professional couples desperate to make the transition from an apartment to a house in an upper northwest neighborhood have been engaging in frenzied bidding wars. In this environment, a house with a bad foundation and a bad roof can sell for $40,000 over the asking price.[25]

For whites in search of "good" public schools or a level of comfort that happens to coincide with overwhelming whiteness, these kind of costs can defer or interfere with the dream of home ownership and "the good life." A newly married Jewish couple, both lawyers who are highly successful in their chosen professions and quite liberal in their outlook, are not atypical in the costs they have endured. They are friends of mine. I will call them Deborah and David. For more than a year they have been pursuing an elusive, exhausting quest for a home they can afford in the District in a neighborhood that is "close to the Metro, has good public elementary schools, is in upper northwest, and is a house that will hold its value." Deborah says race has not really entered her thinking, and I believe her. To the extent that it has, she says she would prefer neighborhoods that are more diverse than those west of the park. But, like many a would-be parent—Deborah is expecting—she says that if she had to choose between a diverse neighborhood and one that has quality schools, she would go with the latter. Her husband, David, feels the same way. When I suggest to him that they consider my neighborhood, Shepherd Park, a considerably cheaper northwest Washington neighborhood situated immediately east of Rock Creek Park, he responds, "It's complicated. We want to send our kids to public school." I think I understand his meaning and even empathize with his dilemma. I don't push him to explain further, although I want to argue my neighborhood's case. This is delicate territory; nothing is more personal than choosing where to live. I decide to back off. For me this is a moment where the reality of difference is quite palpable. You should come look at some of the houses here and give it a chance, I think to myself. Shepherd Park is great; it is integrated. You would feel comfortable there. I would love to have you and Deborah as neighbors. Whites and blacks have lived here for decades. But I harbor the argument in silence. On this subject our perspectives seem quite different. Where I see opportunity, he seems to see risk. We are no less friends for me having recognized that sometimes there really is a huge gulf of perception between people of different races.

Deborah says there is nothing left in the "entry-level" ($500,000–$600,000) price range in Cleveland Park, where she and David now live in a condominium and where they would very much like to stay. Older homes that need a great deal of remodeling in Cleveland Park are going for well over

$700,000—a stretch for any young new family that might want to have something left over for other needs, like saving for college, or new furniture. Still, my friends keep trying, going out virtually every weekend to look at and sometimes bid on homes in upper northwest neighborhoods. They have concentrated their search heavily on neighborhoods that surround one of four elementary schools they have identified as good.

Deborah says the consensus among her friends, many of whom are also Jewish professionals like herself, is that "there are no good junior high schools in D.C." Among this group, she says, one starts the search for quality by "trying to get a home in an upper northwest neighborhood that has a good elementary school." Then one either plans on moving north to Bethesda or Chevy Chase to get their kids into quality middle or high schools, or one prepares to write big checks for private school. There is a concern among this professional set, she says, that Montgomery County, Maryland, schools, which are rapidly becoming more diverse, will not maintain their quality.

"The separated nature of things feeds on itself," Deborah says. Beyond the desire for good schools, she and David are drawn inexorably to upper northwest because that is where their doctors are, where all their closest friends live, where most of the amenities and services that form the stuff of their lives are located. She also observes that the competition to get into upper northwest neighborhoods has been made worse by a culture of consumerism that demands marble vanities and $10,000 Sub-Zero refrigerators. "Everyone wants a really nice house," she frets. In other words, the excesses of the burst tech bubble are showing up in overdone remodeled homes that render them far more expensive than they should be. Deborah says of the thirty- and forty-somethings closing out the baby boom: "In some ways our generation has become too spoiled in our expectations of what should be standard in a home. The appliances bought off the floor of Sears that seemed perfectly good enough for our parents now no longer do."

The phenomenon is the same in other bastions of upscale whiteness in the D.C. area, like the job-rich Maryland suburbs of Bethesda, Kensington, Glen Echo, Garrett Park, and Somerset. In Clarendon in Northern Virginia, a relatively easy commute across the Wilson Bridge from the District, tiny boxlike one-floor homes, the lower-middle-class starter homes of yesteryear, now sell for $500,000. Pottery Barn, Crate and Barrel, Whole Foods Grocery, Ann Taylor, Barnes and Noble, Origins, and Myer-Emco are just a few of the marks of privileged civilization that occupy Clarendon. On a late afternoon in July, almost no black people can be seen on the main drag, Wilson Boulevard, although a few Asian or Latino pedestrians are here. A white twenty-something rents an apartment in Clarendon and loves its wealth of shops and restaurants. She bemoans that she will never be able to afford to buy a house here and live the solid "middle-class" existence she grew up with in her parents' home.[26] Her voice is a testament to the struggles of the white middle class in a separatist world. She apparently doesn't see integrated or minority middle-class neighborhoods as an option, although nicer houses could be had in such neighborhoods for a fraction of the prices in places like Clarendon or Bethesda.

The struggle to achieve a middle-class white existence is really defined by the ethos and achievements of the white upper classes. Their neighborhoods and schools define a gold standard of quality that is difficult for others to attain. For the families attempting to gain entry into exclusive neighborhoods, it is likely that both parents must work. There are few single-parent households because the price of entry is so steep.

This phenomenon of overpriced or out-of-reach whiteness pervades real estate markets throughout the country. The problem seems magnified, however, in metropolitan areas where there is a "tale of two races," as in Washington, D.C., Atlanta, Detroit, and Chicago. Real estate markets in areas with large black populations seem to mirror white people's worst fears. Buying your way into a well-buffered, "premium" white neighborhood is the best defense against perceived crime and bad schools. My fear is that the feelings animating this phenomenon will grow even more intense as urban and suburban communities continue to rapidly diversify in the coming decades.

Some whites do decide to jump off this bandwagon, whether out of economic necessity, courage, or a seemingly rare affirmative preference for life amongst "others." Psychologically, I suppose it is easier to do this if one is not a parent or expecting to be one. But the children of those rare examples of integrationists among my white friends and colleagues—people who live in integrated neighborhoods and/or send their kids to majority-minority schools—don't seem to be any worse for the wear. I am proud of those precious few white professionals in my universe who go against the grain. Ironically, their children might even have a leg up in the competition for elite private colleges because they have a perspective and experience that, unfortunately, far too few white college applicants can offer. A student at the top of his or her class at the better public high schools in the District stands out in college admissions from the scores of applicants from Sidwell and St. Albans who populate the area.[27]

To those who think I am being unduly hard on white people who are just trying to do the best they can for their children, I will admit that public and private institutional policies that shape markets contribute to separate and often very unequal neighborhoods and schools. In this market it is hard for individuals to make choices that go against the grain, especially where the whiter neighborhoods and whiter schools confer a competitive advantage. It is also not a natural human tendency to voluntarily allow oneself or one's children to be heavily outnumbered by other races. A white colleague of mine argues that many elite private schools in the D.C. area are more racially integrated than most D.C. public schools. Admittedly, the children of the white and black elite mingle in Washington's prestigious private schools, and these schools do offer scholarships in order to include talented minorities who are not wealthy. But the validity of my colleague's statement greatly depends upon your perspective. According to its web site, Woodrow Wilson Senior High School, in northwest Washington "is one of the most diverse public high schools in the nation's capital" because over "85 countries are represented, and members of the Wilson community speak approximately 100 languages." Wilson, which has a host of AP classes, community partners, and in-school academies is 55 percent black, 19 percent white, 18 percent Latino, and 8 percent Asian/Pacific Islander. Such racial breakdowns are not disclosed by the elite private schools in the District. Sidwell Friends discloses only that students of color make up 36 percent of its student body, meaning it is 64 percent white. The Edmund Burke School claims that its student body is "20 percent African-American, Asian or Latino," rendering it 80 percent white. What my colleague is really saying to me, somewhat defensively, is that only the private schools in the District offer an integration or diversity he is comfortable with, one where upper-middle-class white children from privileged backgrounds predominate.

I wish more white people would challenge the perceptions that our separate markets create. The unwillingness of many whites to view integrated or majority-minority neighborhoods or schools as viable options fuels our separatism. It creates stratospheric costs for whiteness and concentrates public and private resources and civic energy in communities that need it the least. The smart money might in fact consider a neighborhood like mine, Shepherd Park, which also offers leafy, quiet streets and beautiful spacious homes with character at lower prices than those of the predominately white upper northwest neighborhoods. A white couple here would not be alone, just not a majority. They would find themselves among many like-minded, high-achieving professionals. In the District, this choice could save the integrationist more than $200,000 on home costs alone. If they chose to send their kids to the local Shepherd Elementary School, they would find that it is ranked near the top in test scores, performing on par with Eaton Elementary, and close behind Murch Elementary, in Cleveland Park. The difference, however, is that Shepherd Elementary is 91 percent black, 4 percent white, 4 percent Latino, and 1 percent Asian. Although the school is solidly middle class—only 23 percent of its students are poor—its overwhelming identity as a black school likely renders it a nonstarter for most parents who are not black. In the complicated, tortured relations between blacks and nonblacks in this country, only the most unusual of nonblack souls would choose this option for their children.

Unfortunately, many of the upper-income black professionals who live in Shepherd Park also do not see Shepherd Elementary as an option. They, too, are exercising the elite private options they can afford. I can't say that I blame any parent for making whatever choice they feel is best for their own child. It saddens me, however, to think of the missed opportunities. I jog past Shepherd Elementary almost daily and watch parents as they walk their kids to school, stopping to chat excitedly with each other. I see them as engaged allies in this school. They are mostly black and have the same aspirations as any other parent. But I, a black person, am relating to my own people in making this observation. Perhaps I can see potential here that others can't. I also have an empathy and concern about how we can create world-class public institutions that educate "other people's children" well. What if all the professional parents who lived in this neighborhood sent their kids to this school and supported it? The possibilities are exciting.

A new integrationist logic on the part of whites and others might turn certain, formerly overlooked neighborhoods or schools into newly viable, cost-saving options. With the hundreds of thousands of dollars saved in housing costs, a parent living in an affordable, integrated neighborhood might be able to work part-time or stay at home. He could spend more time with his children. She might be able to jump off a corporate or partner track that is not satisfying in order to pursue more rewarding, but lower-paying work. He might have a saner life than the illusion of overpriced exclusive whiteness actually offers.

Private school tuition is another cost of separatism. Parents opt for private schools for many different reasons, but one theme emerges in my conversations with upper-middle-class people who can afford expensive private schools. This choice feels like insurance against the risk of their child falling through the cracks or not succeeding in a world that seems increasingly unforgiving for those who don't "make it." A highly paid financial executive who lives in Nashville, Tennessee, and is white tells me that he paid twelve years of private school tuition for all three of his daughters "because the public schools were not good enough." He grouses at the financial burden, even as he admits that he is more prepared than most to weather the cost.

I believe that the perception that public schools are risky is heightened for white parents, especially when the local school district is full of minority and low-income children. It amazes me that friends and colleagues pay upward of $17,000 for private school kindergarten. I think about the cost of twelve years of double-digit tuition at private school—for one, two, or three kids, no less—and wonder how these admittedly upper-income folks have anything left over to pay for college or retirement.

Those middle- and upper-income whites in the District of Columbia who, at least in terms of the municipal tax base, have thrown their lot in with the city's minority poor are indirectly bearing the cost of concentrated minority poverty. In a separatist system that has dictated that the black poor must be shunted into inner-city (and sometimes older suburban neighborhoods), the social costs of concentrated distress has multiplier effects. An urban school district that must overcome enormous challenges on a constrained tax base will cost whites who live there—in higher taxes, in a lack of confidence in the school system, and in private school tuition.

White suburbanites also pay a cost for their separatism. "The desire of middle-class whites to avoid the perceived problems of integrated neighborhoods has pushed them farther from central cities across America."[28] The price of being "safe," or having good schools, or neighbors who keep up their property, or whatever characteristic just happens to be a rough proxy for a predominately white neighborhood, can be great. Those who work in the central city and can't afford to buy their way into convenient majority-white neighborhoods or private schools pay a price in commute times and, ironically given the logic of suburbs being safer than cities, in a higher risk of mortality due to traffic accidents. The average commute time in the Atlanta metropolitan region is thirty-one minutes. That means an average Atlanta suburbanite is spending an hour each day in the car, not to mention the miles traveled for the "life-in-the-car" existence of driving for everything, from groceries to soccer practices to the video store. The separatism of our suburbs by land use, by class, and by race means that the white families with children that tend to populate suburban frontier enclaves are heavily tied to the car, with an often withering impact on quality of life. The car-dependent design of most suburbs is such that one must drive for virtually every human function outside the home. Beyond creeping weight gain from a lack of walking, an insidious, unrecognized cost of this car-bound existence is a high incidence of teenage death from auto accidents caused by inexperienced drivers.[29] Worse, when one factors in the traffic deaths to which suburbanites are vulnerable, living in the outer suburbs is more dangerous than in the city, even with its higher rates of street crime.[30]

A couple living in Rockville, Maryland, complain of having to drive an hour each way to traverse the fifteen miles between their home and their place of work in the District. Those who endure the daily aggravation of driving for work, errands, and even recreation for several hours a day may not stop to think about the costs and consequences of living this way. In a different universe, one ordered such that "the other" was not excluded or feared, life might be easier. If people of different income classes could live in close proximity to each other, to their employers, and to the commercial entities that fulfill the necessities of life, suburban quality of life might just be a little saner.

Suburban sprawl, as a general matter, affects most suburban residents in various ways depending on individual values. Collectively, all residents of the metropolis endure the costs of increased air pollution that comes with increased commute times. Conservationists and environmentalists decry the loss of farmland and open space and the inefficient deployment of natural resources that come with sprawled, low-density development. Then there is the inefficient deployment of man-made resources—the older schools and hundreds of older suburban malls that are dying as the middle class moves farther out to new communities on the suburban frontier.

Some might argue that white suburban residents live quite happily in their chosen environment, despite any costs they may endure. The market has responded to a strongly felt cultural preference. A family who can live in their dream home— 3–5 bedrooms, 2 1/2 baths with a 2-car garage and full basement on a cul-de-sac in a new community in Fauquier County, two counties west of the District line, for $249,990, a deal unimaginable in more conveniently located areas—may happily accept the trade-off.[31] On the other hand, maybe they accept this deal because the market isn't offering many better alternatives. And so they endure the stress of long commutes, lost time with family, and the social isolation of suburban kids who cannot move without the aid of a driving adult. In the worst cases, suburban isolation can lead some kids, who can become overdependent on TV and the Internet, to highly destructive behavior. The secluded suburban dream does come with a price.

Other potential costs of white separatism are more intangible and perhaps remote. America is rapidly becoming more diverse. The ability to relate to the "other" will increasingly be critical to one's effective functioning in society and to our society's effective functioning. Those who experience daily city life in the Big Apple, for example, absorb some of these life skills. The ability to step onto a subway and be comfortable, even smilingly amused at the dizzying array of humanity, will be a necessary quality in the majority-minority America that is to come. Insulating oneself and one's kids from the socioeconomic rainbow is like the proverbial ostrich sticking his head in the sand, oblivious to a rich world that is full of joy and pain, distress and beauty. When the ostrich raises his head, he may be overwhelmed by the reality he has refused to see. Whites who choose a separatist course, whatever their benign or nefarious intentions may be, will pay a price for this choice. They will pay for it in the occasional experience of panic and fear when they involuntarily encounter a socioeconomic "other" rendered strange or menacing because such a person is unfamiliar; in the rising levels of fear that seem to permeate our society, despite long-term declines in crime rates; in the long-term societal cost of the inequality and social distress that our separatist system engenders; and finally, in the continued strain in race relations borne of a lack of common experience and understanding.

While many whites may willingly accept such intangible costs, given the immediate advantages of white separatism, there are additional insidious, hidden costs. I believe that many middle- and lower-income whites experience the same costs of separation as do African Americans and people of other races, but their identification with whites farther up the income scale masks this reality. In a separatist system that sets up "winner" and "loser" communities, "winner" and "loser" schools, and even "winner" and "loser" classes within schools, those in the middle of the income spectrum, of whatever race, have to work harder and harder to stay in or get to the "winner" column. In an integrationist system designed to bring everyone along, there would not be so much daily anxiety in the lives of middle-income white people.

An ironic example of how far we have fallen from the myth of "all boats rising" was the debacle of Jack Grubman, the former high-flying investment advisor at Salomon Smith Barney who made $20 million in 1999, manipulating stock investors in order to get his twin daughters into one of the best nursery schools in Manhattan.[32] In a winner-take-all system even those at the height of the income scale cannot relax. Everyone knows implicitly that some kids, some people, and some communities *will* be left behind. Otherwise they would not feel so much pressure to fight their way into the best schools with the best advantages. Because of the risk of being left behind, they buy their way into the best track, or the safe track, which in our separatist society is usually the insulated track, the one with few minorities and even fewer poor people. This is the ugly side of America. The one we all understand implicitly but are loathe to admit exists, much less talk about openly. Conservatives preempt any honest discussion with talk of "class warfare." That preemptive strike works as effectively as "playing the race card," because no one, least of all, middle-class whites, wants to believe our system is not fair and open to everyone.

For individuals who must live their lives in this separatist, winner-take-all system, it may seem too much to ask for them to think beyond their immediate circumstances. The daily struggle to make ends meet, to find time for children, friends, and family, to find a job in a jobless recovery—these are the things that preoccupy. Rethinking the costs and consequences

of our choices and rethinking integration may seem like an idealistic indulgence. Meanwhile, the specter of fear, discomfort,
unfamiliarity, and risk is ever present. As our country grows in
diversity and the numbers of racial minorities begin to overwhelm, my fear is that white America will continue to respond
with a garrison impulse rather than an integrationist one.

CHAPTER 6

SCHOOLS
Separate and Unequal

PUBLIC SCHOOLS became more segregated in the 1990s. More so than our neighborhoods, our schools are bastions of race and class privilege on the one hand and race and class disadvantage on the other. Black and Latino schoolchildren are bearing the heaviest costs. They tend to be relegated to high-poverty, overwhelmingly minority public schools that are characterized by poorer test scores, less-experienced teachers, and fewer resources than the public schools most white children attend. Everyone in America, from President Bush to the average parent of whatever race, intrinsically understands this. It is an unspoken truth that we do not own up to: America's schools are separate and unequal.

In any given metropolitan area, I could tell a tale of two schools systems, or of two different schools, a tale in which inequality closely mirrors the race and class of the students attending the school. Parents know these dichotomies all too well. Many, if not most, white parents stake their decisions about where to live and where to send their kids to school on such inequality—that is, they assiduously avoid the "bad" schools, which typically are minority and/or heavily poor, and they work overtime to get their children into the "good" schools, which typically are predominately white and middle class.

Even comparing the better public schools in a heavily minority, heavily poor school district to their suburban counterparts, one can see real differences. Woodrow Wilson High School in upper northwest Washington, D.C., is only about four miles or a ten-minute drive away from Walt Whitman High School in Bethesda, Maryland, but it differs substantially in performance, demographics, and resources. Wilson is the best-performing neighborhood public high school in the District. It is located near Tenley Park, an attractive, sought-after neighborhood west of Rock Creek Park. Like Walt Whitman, Wilson is surrounded by a predominately white, affluent neighborhood, but its similarities to Walt Whitman stop there. Many of Wilson's students are from neighborhoods much farther south in the District. The children of Tenley Park are more likely to attend private schools. According to one white parent in the neighborhood, most white parents avoid Wilson because of its "problems," by which she means issues of "safety." Two Wilson students were recently charged with gun possession when they tried to smuggle a weapon into the school, and a few years ago, two Wilson students, a couple, were shot and killed away from the school grounds.[1] To observe Wilson students, however, is to see a veritable rainbow of humanity. This is what the public common school should look like—the white, black, Latino, and Asian students that enter Wilson daily mirror America's future. They are learning to deal with one another. The striving student can thrive here by tapping Wilson's many strengths. Despite any shortcomings it may have in comparison to its better-funded and better-resourced suburban counterparts, or compared to the elite private schools, I would seriously consider Wilson were I a parent. That said, the contrasts between Wilson and Whitman are clear.

Wilson is poorer than Whitman. Only 1–2 percent of Whitman students are eligible for free or reduced-price meals, whereas nearly 40 percent of Wilson students qualify. Whitman is 78 percent white. Wilson is 55 percent black. Whitman's operating budget (without facility costs) is more than $5 million greater than Wilson's, although Whitman has only 138 more students than Wilson; the biggest difference appears to be the salaries paid to teachers and staff. The schools perform at different levels. As of 2002, Whitman students scored an average of above 1200 on the SAT, whereas Wilson students had not cracked an average above 1000. Wilson offers the largest AP program in the District, but Whitman has more offerings, and students do better on the exams. Whitman ranked 83rd in *Newsweek*'s Top 100 Public High Schools in America, published in June of 2003, based upon the number of students who take AP and International Baccalaureate tests. Wilson ranked 644th, but to its credit, it did make the expanded list. Two-thirds of Wilson seniors go on to attend four-year colleges, compared to 86 percent of Whitman seniors.

The clubs and organizations of the two schools match up quite well, although Whitman has many more honor societies and cultural programs. In athletics, Whitman fields many more teams and does so evenly between boys and girls; it offers more opportunity for the younger students to participate in junior varsity.

Whitman's facilities are also superior. Each classroom in Whitman is linked by computer. There are eight computer labs, ten science labs, a suite of technology education class-rooms, and its music rooms have up-to-date acoustical fea-tures. The athletic facilities are vastly different. Wilson has the basics—a stadium, an armory (in the basement), one gymna-sium, and a swimming pool operated by the D.C. Department of Recreation and Parks; Whitman boasts two full gyms, a new weight room, six team rooms, a whirlpool, trainer's facili-ties, an eight-lane track, softball field, baseball and field hockey field, eight tennis courts, and two basketball courts.

While Wilson is among the best that the District has to offer its high school students, I could provide much starker contrasts to an idyllic suburban high school like Whitman. At Ballou Senior High School, located in Congress Heights in the District's poorest ward, one measure of success is merely keep-ing order in the halls, which can be chaotic unless the school's formidable principal, Dr. Art Bridges, a respected authority fig-ure, is out in force. Ballou is 99.9 percent African American and 87 percent poor. In 2001, fewer than 5 percent of Ballou students performed at the level of "proficient" on Stanford achievement tests in math and reading, although the school elliptically explained that students took tests under adverse "fire-health and mental hazards."[2] Recent events suggest the kind of stress Ballou students face. The 2003–2004 school year has been hellish. Ballou was closed for a month in the fall when someone took mercury from a science classroom and spread it around the building. The day the school reopened, a gunman fired shots half a block from the premises just as classes were letting out. Since then, several fistfights have bro-ken out among students involved in loosely organized gangs. The latest fistfight turned deadly. On February 2, 2004, one student, Thomas Boykin, fatally shot another student, James Richardson, a star football player, near the school cafeteria and wounded another student in the leg. Both students were from rival communities associated with impoverished public housing complexes—Barry Farm and Condon Terrace—that reportedly have been feuding for twenty years.[3]

The black children who walk the halls of Ballou are full of potential and are every bit as deserving of the quality of educational opportunity being afforded Whitman's students. Yet their separation translates to a quite different educational experience. I argue in this chapter that public schooling has become the "great inequalizer" in America because it tends to place white children in predominately white middle-class schools and black and Latino children in predominately minority, heavily poor schools. We are rapidly retreating from the ideal of integrated schooling that animated the decision of *Brown v. Board of Education*, with costs and consequences for everyone.

Brown v. Board of Education: A Losing Battle

We conclude that in the field of public education the doctrine of "separate but equal" has no place. Separate educational facilities are inherently unequal.

—*Brown v. Board of Education,* May 17, 1954

On May 17, 1954, in a mere four pages, a unanimous Supreme Court decision overturned a nearly sixty-year-old standard, established in *Plessy v. Ferguson* in 1896, that "separate but equal" was legal under the U.S. Constitution's equal protection clause. *Plessy*'s insidious edict ultimately legitimated Jim Crow segregation, from the "whites-only" train coaches at issue in *Plessy* to other public accommodations, housing, voting, and of course, public education.

The *Brown* Court stopped short of saying that "separate but equal" was illegitimate in all spheres. It would take another decade-plus of civil rights struggle and federal legislation to establish integration as the appropriate response to "the Negro problem." *Brown* did, however, ignite a spark that enabled civil rights revolutionaries to envision and fight for a different America. The nine justices, or at least, Chief Justice Warren, the opinion's author, seemed most concerned with the effect of state-mandated segregation on the psyches of "Negro" children. It did not matter that their schools' physical facilities and other "tangible" factors such as school transportation or teacher qualifications might at least in theory be made equal. "To separate them from others of similar age and qualifications solely because of their race generates a feeling of inferiority as to their status in the community that may affect their hearts and minds in a way unlikely ever to be undone," Chief Justice Warren wrote. Therefore, in public education, according to the *Brown* Court, "separate educational facilities are inherently unequal" because of the feelings of inferiority they engender. The Court seemed swayed by the social science research of Dr. Kenneth Clark and others, which suggested that such feelings of inferiority were being cultivated in black children. A year later, in *Brown II,* the Court made clear that it would defer to school authorities in deciding how to accomplish desegregation but famously admonished them to proceed "with all deliberate speed." It would take a decade more before federal district courts, with the encouragement of the Supreme Court, began to vigorously enforce school desegregation orders. Across the South especially, federal judges oversaw local school desegregation efforts—the most massive federal intervention in the name of racial justice since Reconstruction.

Implicitly, the Court in *Brown I* seemed to be saying that

state-sanctioned separation, even into ostensibly equal facilities, is what sends a message of inferiority to black children. This seems to be a point of general agreement in American society and the reason the decision is afforded near-sacred status in the annals of Supreme Court jurisprudence. It is now accepted common wisdom that state-sanctioned racial apartheid of schoolchildren or of adults is both morally repugnant and inconsistent with the equality principles embodied in our Constitution, specifically the Fourteenth Amendment clause that guarantees "equal protection of the laws" to all citizens. *Brown* is a decision that makes us proud of ourselves. It represents an idea that is fundamental to our democratic values. It recaptured or reimagined the vision of common schools, embraced and advanced by a broad coalition of late-eighteenth-century reformers, including Thomas Jefferson: the idea that there should be at least one institution in American society that provides a common experience of citizenship and equal opportunity, regardless of the lottery of birth. *Brown v. Board of Education* has entered the psyche and lexicon of average Americans everywhere. It is the one Supreme Court decision that most schoolchildren can easily identify. The other might be *Roe v. Wade* or, more ignominiously, *Dred Scott*. As I write this chapter, a national commission, created by the Bush administration, is planning a series of events to celebrate the fiftieth anniversary of the Court's decision. Everyone, save certain radical political factions or fringe elements of American society, now venerates or at least pretends to venerate the opinion that repudiated the principle of "separate but equal." And yet the idea and vision animating *Brown* could not be farther from the reality of American public education today. Indeed, we are not even living up to the repugnant principle established in *Plessy v. Ferguson*. Our schools are separate, but hardly equal.

Any sincere celebration of *Brown v. Board of Education* could not occur without acknowledging our collective failure to live up to the promise and vision that animated the decision. No one, in my view, felt such disappointment more that Thurgood Marshall, the chief oral advocate for the *Brown* case. I had the great privilege of working as a law clerk for Justice Marshall in his last year as an active member of the Supreme Court—the Court's 1990–1991 term. In that year, I witnessed Justice Marshall's personal devastation at the erosion of fundamental protections he had dedicated his life to creating and upholding. He was at the end of a nearly sixty-year career that had been devoted to legal justice for all Americans.

Justice Marshall was probably the only Supreme Court justice whose accomplishments before reaching the high court equaled or maybe even exceeded what he accomplished on the bench. Before becoming a justice, he had argued thirty-two cases before the Supreme Court—and had won twenty-nine of them. Most of these victories were won while he was the lead lawyer for the NAACP Legal Defense and Education Fund, and thus Marshall became known as "Mr. Civil Rights." In a series of cases leading up to *Brown,* Justice Marshall made the best of the separate but equal doctrine; at that time, it was a core constitutional commitment of American apartheid. Marshall, working under the tutelage of Charles Hamilton Houston, the dean of the Howard University law school and the father of the civil rights bar, turned it on its head.

Houston and Marshall first exploited the "equality" principle of *Plessy* in a case against the University of Maryland School of Law. Together they argued that Maryland's policy of offering Donald Murray, a black man who had been denied admission, a scholarship to attend an out-of-state school did not offer him an "equal" education.[4] This was poetic justice for Marshall, as he had been denied admission to the very same law school a mere five years earlier. Knowing that states could not possibly completely replicate their premier graduate schools, Marshall went on to drive this strategy into the heart of segregated higher education. In 1950, the Supreme Court agreed with Marshall that the reputation of the University of Texas School of Law could not be duplicated in a basement law school hastily created by the state for Herman Sweatt, a thirty-three-year-old African American who had attended medical school for two semesters at the University of Michigan before seeking to become a lawyer.[5] The Court also agreed with Marshall that the State of Oklahoma was not providing an "equal" education to George McLaurin in a Ph.D. program in education when it consigned him to a desk in an anteroom to the classroom and to separate reading rooms in the library, or when it forced him to eat at a different time from other students in the school cafeteria.[6]

These cases laid the groundwork for the much more difficult battleground of primary and secondary public schools. They planted the seeds for the Supreme Court's acceptance of the idea that only an "integrated" education would meet the vision and requirements of the equal protection clause.

The education cases were but one strand of Marshall's legacy in making the Constitution truly meaningful and effective, particularly for black people. The State of Texas had limited its Democratic Party primary elections to whites only, at a time when the Republican Party in the South was a mere shadow of what it is today. Marshall put a stop to that, too, winning over the Court in *Smith v. Allwright,* which he often said was his proudest victory.[7] He had several more civil rights victories, making inroads in housing and public transportation and other realms.[8] All of these cases were premised on the same integrationist, open-society vision that animated *Brown.*

Yet, there we sat, in his chambers in 1991, anticipating the erasure of his achievements. The case I remember most vividly from my year working for Justice Marshall is *Board of Education of Oklahoma City v. Dowell.* That case reflected the history of the post-*Brown* struggle to make integrated public education a reality in the United States. In the words of Justice Marshall:

> Oklahoma gained statehood in 1907. For the next 65 years, the Oklahoma City School Board (Board) maintained segregated schools—initially relying on laws requiring dual school systems; thereafter, by exploiting residential segregation that had been created by legally enforced restrictive covenants. In 1972—18 years after this Court [in *Brown*] first found segregated schools unconstitutional—a federal court finally interrupted this cycle, enjoining the Board to implement a specific plan for achieving actual desegregation of its schools.
>
> The practical question now before us is whether, 13 years after that injunction was imposed, the same Board should have been allowed to return many of its elementary schools to their former one-race status. The majority today suggests that 13 years of desegregation was enough.[9]

In short, although a federal court–ordered desegregation plan did in fact produce integration in Oklahoma City Schools, after the federal court retreated from supervising desegregation, local autonomy resulted in a neighborhood schools plan for elementary students that recreated several separate "black" and "white" elementary schools.

In helping Justice Marshall craft his dissent for this case, I read every school desegregation case the Supreme Court had ever decided. The justice and I spent a good deal of time talking about this history. The worst, we concluded, was the 1974 *Milliken v. Bradley* case, in which the Court decided that suburban school districts surrounding Detroit could not be included in any desegregation plan unless predominately white school districts were shown to have engaged in discriminatory practices—a case in which Marshall vigorously dissented. *Milliken* proved disastrous for the cause of integration. The decision essentially insulated predominately white suburban school districts from the constitutional imperatives of *Brown,* gave suburban citizens more incentive to create their own separate school districts, and offered white parents in urban districts fearful of school desegregation havens of predominately white public schools to which they could flee. It is not surprising, then, that Detroit is surrounded by some 116 suburban school districts or that the city's school system has gone from a black-white ratio of 60/40 in 1967 to 91/4 in 2000.[10]

The Court did not help with the equality battle between urban and suburban school districts when it declared in 1973 that education was not a fundamental right under the U.S. Constitution and that therefore the State of Texas was not required to provide equal funding to all school districts. Marshall dissented in that case, too.[11] The battle for equal or adequate funding in public education would be left to a later generation of civil rights lawyers, and it would be fought in state courts based upon state constitutions. To date, litigation has been brought in forty-five states, and about twenty state supreme courts have ordered funding equalization remedies based upon a state constitutional requirement of an adequate education.[12] But this battle has focused almost exclusively on closing disparities in financing between poor and wealthy school districts. Even so, there is little evidence that such litigation has improved outcomes for minority and/or poor children.[13] It has been argued that urban school districts require greater funding, not just equal funding, to meet the significant challenges of educating large numbers of poor students.[14] Despite litigation, funding disparities between rich and poor school districts persist.[15]

The quest for integration, however, has been even more elusive than the quest for equal funding. In the fifty years since *Brown v. Board,* the civil rights bar has fought a losing battle for the soul of *Brown* in public schools. Justice Marshall was well aware of this, and it pained him deeply. He struggled to find the words and the arguments to persuade his colleagues not to use the 1991 case of *Board of Education of Oklahoma City v. Dowell* to mark the end of federal court intervention on behalf of integrated public schooling. It did not matter to him that racial segregation in schools now mirrored racial segregation in neighborhoods. "I believe a desegregation decree cannot be lifted so long as conditions likely to inflict the stigmatic injury condemned in *Brown I* persist and there remain feasible methods of eliminating such conditions," he argued in his dissent. For Marshall, no condition perpetuated stigmatic injury more than racially identifiable schools. He knew all too well that "all-Afro-American schools"—he had made the transition from "Negro" but not to "black" or "African American"—risked "the relative indifference of school boards." He cited empirical evidence that many black schools "suffer from high student-faculty ratios, lower quality teachers, inferior facilities and physical conditions, and lower quality course offerings and extracurricular programs." He identified racially identifiable schools as "one of the primary vestiges of state-imposed segregation," reiterating the Supreme Court's prior edict that the central goal of desegregation was "to ensure that it is no longer possible to identify a 'white school' or a 'Negro school.'"[16]

For Marshall there was no basis for his conservative colleagues' apparent suggestion that the result should be different if residential segregation is now perpetuated by "private decisionmaking." Marshall was well aware that the all-black racial identity of the northeast quadrant of Oklahoma City did not subsist solely because of personal private preferences. The school district had been instrumental in shaping those preferences. Its prior manipulations of school locations had been designed to create all-black schools "clouded by the stigma of segregation—schools to which white parents would not opt to send their children." "That such negative 'personal preferences' exist should not absolve a school district that played a role in creating such 'preferences' from its obligation to desegregate the schools to the maximum extent possible," Justice Marshall wrote.[17]

These arguments did not persuade his colleagues. They would amount to yet another powerfully argued dissent that Justice Marshall had grown used to writing. In his chambers he worried aloud about what he would say to a poor black kid about his life chances, given the schools and neighborhoods such kids were relegated to. This normally humorous man, so full of joy, despite his gruff exterior, was at a loss as to how to stop the inevitable. He was partially effective, however. Justice Marshall's colleagues waited until after he had died to strike a clear blow to the imperative of *Brown*. In *Dowell* the Court merely hinted at what would be necessary to declare a final retreat: "a finding by the District Court—that the school district was being operated in compliance with the commands of the Fourteenth Amendment's equal protection clause and that it was unlikely that the school board would return to its former ways—would be a finding that the purposes of the desegregation litigation had been fully achieved." Before *Dowell*, the Supreme Court's position had been that school districts with a history of discrimination were in violation of the Constitution if they took actions that would forseeably re-create segregated schools. The *Dowell* case signaled that lower courts engaged in overseeing school desegregation would now enjoy more discretion. I don't think his colleagues could have gone any farther with Justice Marshall sitting in the room. Although many of his colleagues were ideologically opposed to him, they revered him and had great affection for him.

Although the retreat from *Brown* started with the *Dowell* decision, our schools became even more separate and unequal after Justice Marshall stepped down from the bench in 1991. In 1992, in a case arising from DeKalb, Georgia, the Court painstakingly laid out the demographic changes in DeKalb and the good-faith efforts by the school district to address the demographic effects on the racial mix of its schools. The Court ultimately held that the lower courts could find a school district has complied with the Constitution where racial imbalance is not traceable to constitutional violations but to demographic changes.[18] By 1995, in a case involving the Kansas City school district, *Missouri v. Jenkins*, the Supreme Court essentially decided that it was time for federal courts to retreat altogether from the business of policing school desegregation orders.

In a world where black and brown kids were largely separated into their own neighborhoods and parents of all races had rejected busing, magnet schools were seen as the answer. In the *Jenkins* case, the district court's desegregation plan required every high school, every middle school, and half of the elementary schools in the school system to become magnet schools. The cost of making schools attractive enough to retain white students had exceeded $200 million annually, and the state legislature that had been ordered to pay the bill was crying out for relief. The Supreme Court emphasized that the goal of district courts is to remedy desegregation to the "extent practicable" and to restore local authority over the school system. The Supreme Court signaled to lower courts that their primary role was to apply a remedy that decreased the effects of *de jure* segregation to the extent practicable, not to ensure meaningful integration, and certainly not to spend millions to increase the "desegregative attractiveness" of urban schools to their suburban neighbors.[19]

After the Court's decision in *Missouri v. Jenkins*, school districts everywhere clearly understood the Court's meaning: It was time to let school districts off the hook. Eliminating the vestiges of *de jure* segregation was either too difficult, too expensive, or both. Within a year of the *Jenkins* decision, school districts across the nation were scrambling to get the benefit of the case's relaxed standard; it was now much easier for school districts to get out from under desegregation orders and to weaken their integration efforts. In Denver, a federal judge found its schools sufficiently desegregated and released them from federal supervision. In Arizona, the Republican governor launched a campaign to release all of the state's school districts from federal court orders. In Pittsburgh, the mayor lobbied the school board for an end to court-ordered busing, and two state lawmakers introduced a bill to stop state officials from requiring busing to achieve desegregation. In Seattle, several school board members pushed for a return to neighborhood schools. In Indianapolis, the school board voted to spend $40,000 to assess citizens' views of the schools in anticipation of seeking an end to a fourteen-year-old busing order.[20] Empirical research concluded that the nation's schools were resegregating at the fastest rate since 1954. Researchers found that as the federal courts eased oversight of school desegregation programs in the early 1990s, the percentage of minority students in schools with a substantial white enrollment fell appreciably.[21]

Take Charlotte-Mecklenburg, North Carolina, for example. By the early 1980s, the school district had come close to fulfilling a court order to eliminate its system of dual education, with only a handful of schools that remained racially identifiable as minority or white. By the late 1980s, with very small increases in the proportion of black students in the system, the number of racially identifiable schools began to grow and then in the early 1990s began to accelerate. By 1999, the school system was resegregating rapidly, even though the district's demographics were relatively stable, the Charlotte-Mecklenburg area was still majority-white, and Mecklenburg County as a whole was more residentially integrated than it had been thirty years earlier. Whereas roughly 19 percent of black students had attended racially identifiable black schools in 1991, by 1996, the count had risen to 23 percent; by 2000, that percentage had risen to 29 percent, and by 2001, the number jumped to 37 percent. In the 2002–2003 school year, fully 48 percent of the black students in the Charlotte-Mecklenburg school system attended racially identifiable black schools.[22]

A similar fate befell many, if not most, school districts throughout the country that serve significant numbers of minority children. Black and Latino public school students are now more separated into racially identifiable schools than at any time in the past thirty years. Nowhere are the effects of this retreat more palpable than in the South. Court-ordered desegregation of African American students in the late 1960s and 1970s resulted in the South becoming the region with the most integrated schools. By 1988, the South reached a high point of 43.5 percent of black students attending majority-white schools, up from a mere 0.001 percent in 1954. But by 2000, marking a twelve-year and continuing process of resegregation, only 31 percent of black students in the South attended majority-white schools.[23] Although the South remains our nation's most integrated region in terms of public schooling, it is also undergoing resegregation at the fastest rate. The rest of the country is following suit, however. Overall, the trend of increasing integration of black students between the 1950s and the late 1980s has been reversed, and we are slowly marching backward toward greater segregation of black children. The situation is similar for Latino kids. Latinos, who were rarely the direct focus of federal school desegregation orders, have been on a continual trajectory of increasing segregation in U.S. public schools since the 1960s.

The 2000s: Separation and Inequality

As a result of this resegregation trend, seven out of ten black and Latino students attended predominately minority schools in 2000.[24] But white students are the most racially segregated group in public schools. On average, a white student attends a school that is 80 percent white. Asian public school students enjoy the most integrated existence; they come closest to living Dr. King's multicultural dream and realizing the ideals of *Brown*.[25]

With the loss of racial integration in schools, we are also witnessing economic segregation, which in turn is creating separate educational tracks that vary greatly in quality. White elementary school students, on average, are in schools that are 30 percent poor. Asians children are in schools that are 43 percent poor. By contrast, black and Latino elementary children are in schools where two-thirds of their classmates are poor.[26] Older students have similar experiences. Across all ages, the average black or Latino student attends classes where almost half of his peers receive free or reduced-price lunch, meaning they are poor. The average white student, on the other hand, attends a school where less than one in five of his peers are classified as poor.[27]

The urban-suburban divide explains much of this class dichotomy. Urban schools are attended primarily by black and Latino students. The middle classes of all races have been moving to suburbs, leaving behind large numbers of minority poor students, especially in the school districts of America's largest cities. As of 2000, between 85 and 90 percent of the students in New York, Los Angeles, Chicago, Miami-Dade, and Houston—the five largest central-city school districts—were minorities. In Detroit, New Orleans, and Santa Ana, 96 percent of the students were minorities, as were 95 percent in Washington, D.C., 92 percent in Dallas, and 88 percent in Baltimore. Overall, the twenty-seven largest school districts, which serve almost one-quarter of all black and Latino public school students, have lost the vast majority of their white enrollment.[28] Not surprisingly, a large percentage of the students remaining in urban school systems were poor. For example, in the five largest urban school systems, typically more than 70 percent of the students are eligible to receive free or reduced-price lunch.[29]

Such segregated schooling comes with serious costs. The Executive Director for Education at the Gates Foundation,

Tom Vander Ark, put it to me this way: "Unless you are affluent, auditory, compliant, and well supported, you are screwed in American public schools."[30] Actually, his indictment of public high schools is more searing. "American high schools are racist," he argues. "It's not that most teachers are; it's the institution—the basic architecture." According to Vander Ark, American public schools reflect and propagate the class structure of our society. The tracking system that permeates virtually all schools reflects precisely our socioeconomic strata. The honors classes are filled primarily with white and/or affluent kids, and if not affluent kids, the most affluent of those that attend that particular school. The basic or lowest-level classes are filled with black and Latino and/or poor kids. Those kids with the most aggressive, educated, and informed parents will find themselves in the better classes with the better schoolteachers, culling the best resources that a school has to offer. Tracking is subtle and starts very early on. As early as the fifth grade, students begin a process of segmentation based upon test performance that can mark them for life. Says Vander Ark, "Rather than addressing particular challenges, struggling students are 'remediated,' ignored, or retained. In the middle grades, tracking becomes more visible—algebra is made available to urban 'honor' students and 'college prep' students in the suburbs." Segregating children based upon their performance on standardized assessments may be well intentioned. But it tends to have a self-fulfilling prophecy. Students rarely ascend from the tracks they are initially assigned to, and their initial assessments are virtually certain to reflect the socioeconomic backgrounds of the families and environments they come from.

Thus, the school system ultimately is premised upon the idea that children will be divided into classes of winners and losers. Vander Ark concludes: "Affluent, auditory, compliant students from families that have experienced educational success are propelled into the nation's best colleges. With great but subtle precision, [public] schools sort by zip code, income, and race—poor and minority students fall to the academic bottom and drop out at twice the rate of white students." Overall, our school system is quite pernicious, devaluing low-income and minority kids virtually from the start.[31]

A parallel, hopeful trend, however, also took hold in the 1990s. While public schools were rapidly resegregating, charter schools also proliferated. In the 1990s, educational entrepreneurs formed small public schools largely independent of the school district bureaucracy. Such independent public schools tend to focus on individual differences between children, including styles of learning, in order to develop the potential and achievement of each child. They also disproportionately serve poor, struggling minority students at risk of dropping out and rely heavily on less-experienced, uncredentialed teachers. The number of charter schools grew from a handful in the early 1990s to more than 2,700 today. As a result of this burgeoning of alternatives, between 1993 to 1999, the number of families choosing options other than a neighborhood public school, whether public, private, or home-schooling, increased by a third, with most of that increase coming from parents placing their children in public schools of choice—magnet or charter schools.[32]

Although charter schools are not necessarily any less segregated that neighborhood schools, where they exist, they offer alternatives to children who might otherwise be trapped in low-performing inner-city schools. They are more able to dismiss disruptive students, and because parents must navigate a selection process in order to get their children admitted, charter schools are more apt to have the support of motivated parents. The first national portrait of charter school performance, conducted by the Manhattan Institute in 2003, showed that charter schools in the eleven states studied produced slightly higher gains in reading and math over a one-year period compared to other public schools with similar demographics. In addition to the flexibility afforded by being free of school district regulations, one possible explanation for this relatively better performance is that parents voluntarily choose these small schools, and hence they are more accountable to the demands of parents than most local public schools.[33] Meanwhile, magnet schools—public schools that admit students on an application basis—have also proliferated. Currently, there are over 1,400 public magnet schools in the United States. And some school districts, including Cleveland, Milwaukee, and, most recently, Washington, D.C., have also adopted school voucher experiments that enable a relatively small number of students to receive publicly funded vouchers that help pay for private or parochial school tuition. Many African American parents support vouchers because they want better options for their children. Indeed, conservative Republicans who support vouchers are essentially admitting that most urban inner-city schools fall far short of the standards we say we demand for public education. Whether the burgeoning school choice movement—charter and magnet schools and vouchers—can counter the effects of growing race and class segregation in public schools remains an open question.

The Achievement Gap

The costs to black and Latino kids of segregated education are palpable. When you place most black and Latino kids in majority-minority and heavily poor schools, as American society *has* done, there are two main consequences, both of which contribute to an achievement gap that we all pay for in ways we may not recognize. As one scholar of the problem of majority-minority and majority-poor schools has argued, "The first cost is purely financial: Because poor students typically have greater needs, schools composed of poor students are costlier to run than schools composed of middle- and upper-income students. The second cost arises from peer influence: A growing body of research confirms that peers generally exert strong influence on student performance and that students from lower socioeconomic backgrounds in particular suffer from being surrounded solely or primarily by students of similarly impoverished backgrounds."[34]

It should not be surprising that there are large achievement gaps between black and Latino students and their white and Asian counterparts, given that black and Latino children tend to be in schools where large numbers, if not a majority, of their peers come from low- and moderate-income backgrounds. This has been clear ever since James Coleman issued his seminal report in 1966 that, among other things, identified an individual student's socioeconomic background as the greatest determinant of his likely success in school. More importantly, Coleman found that when a student body is composed of large numbers of poor students, this has a significant negative influence on student achievement, especially for students from disadvantaged backgrounds. Numerous studies have since backed up these claims.[35]

Students in high-poverty schools do not have a host of models for success. They do not enjoy a wealth of activist parents who know how to work the educational system and succeed in it. As one white parent who has her children in integrated public schools once put it to me, "you have to understand that for some inner-city parents getting their kids to school on time and in clean clothes is a miracle given all that they have to negotiate in their daily lives." In high-poverty environments, students risk falling prey to an oppositional culture that often denigrates learning—one where pursuit of academic excellence is perceived as "acting white." We may not like to own up it, but social scientists have documented that this oppositional culture does in fact exist.[36] In my view, it is the worst consequence of concentrated poverty. And it is not limited to poor black students. On average, poor whites also denigrate achievement; they just happen to have the advantage of being more likely to live and be schooled in middle-class environments than in predominately poor ones. Overall, researchers have demonstrated that "factors that make for a difficult learning environment—peers who are disruptive, who cut class, watch excessive TV, and drop out of high school; parents who are inactive in the school—all track much more by class than race."[37] Yet if you are a black or Latino child in America, you are more likely to go to school in just such a high-poverty, difficult learning environment.

White students, on the other hand, largely attend school in predominately middle-class environments and therefore experience a very different culture—one oriented toward achievement. Indeed, a rat race of competitiveness emerges in the bastions of suburban white affluence. In this environment, most students are propelled toward college. A host of institutional supports and expectations point in that direction, starting very early in life. White middle- and upper-class anxiety means parents feel compelled to pay for enrichment classes, career counselors, and PSAT and SAT prep courses. In a world that is black, brown, and heavily poor, different cultural standards, expectations, and supports point to a very different path. The same goes for the black and Latino students who tend to populate the lower tracks of integrated schools. These children suffer from the low expectations that are set for them. Yet, black and Latino students who are given the same expectations and supports as their white middle-class counterparts can perform competitively. When low-income black students from the worst public housing projects of Chicago were taken out of these environments—as a result of an anti-discrimination order against the Chicago Housing Authority in the *Gautreaux* case—and placed in middle-income suburban schools with small student-teacher ratios and high expectations, within a few years of the move they were outpacing their peers who had been left behind in Chicago schools.[38]

The story of Laura and her mother, Noelle, who were one of many *Gautreaux* families followed by researchers, is illustrative. Laura spent her first years of elementary school in the Chicago public school system. Though her grades were good, she did not have a positive experience in the city schools. As Noelle said of the Chicago school system in the early 1980s, in an interview with researchers, "Chicago schools are raggedy. . . . The teachers complain that there wasn't enough room in the classroom. It was so crowded . . . nobody is learning anything. She comes home with headaches. . . . The whole attitude [of the teachers was] . . . I don't care I've got mine. Either you learn it or you don't because I'm going to give you a passing grade anyway." Laura had her own complaints. "They really didn't try to teach you anything." The teachers were "mean" and did not listen, and broken glass covered the playground. Laura was also afraid to go to school because of fights. In 1982, when Laura was eight, Noelle was able to move her family to the suburbs because the *Gautreaux* court order gave Chicago public housing tenants this option. One of the major reasons she gave for moving was for "schools to better my children." After the move, Laura's grades went down a little, but her mother was pleased: "The workout here is much harder than what the kids are doing in the city. Yes, her grades have changed because the work is harder now. Because the little math she was doing in the city, it counted for her to get that 'A' in it. Now for her to come out here and just jump into geometry and trigonometry in sixth grade and still be getting B's and C's is good. The reason I feel she is doing better is because the teachers are different."

When they had first moved to the suburbs Laura had to take a battery of tests to prove that she was not "slow" and that her problem was merely that she had not been exposed to the material the suburban children had already learned. Laura passed these tests and did not have to repeat a grade, but the experience was difficult. And even though she passed, she still had to deal with the fact that the city schools had not taught her as much as the suburban schools expected of sixth-grade students. The suburban school offered Laura new educational opportunities. In addition to the more advanced curriculum, the school provided the kind of extra attention that impressed both Noelle and Laura. As Noelle said in a 1982 interview:

> The schools ... are not overcrowded. They had time to give them the help they needed. The teachers out here, they seem to care more.... They will call you everyday to let you know how your child is doing in school. And send work home and tell you to help your child with this. Put them on special projects and different things. It makes me happy because [the teacher] really doesn't have to call me and let me know these things. But she does. I just like talking to her. She calls me in

the evenings. If you are not satisfied with your child's progress, you can always call the school and make a meeting.

Laura said that her suburban teachers "help you more." One teacher arranged for her to make up a missed exam; another, Laura's track coach, made a special effort to keep her from quitting the team. Laura had a B average in high school and was in honors English and math classes. She was planning a career in computers or word processing. By 1989, she had finished high school and was enrolled in, but had not yet started, the local community college for a two-year degree. She also saw herself going on to a four-year program.

Her mother cited "living around whites" as a positive influence. She appreciated the better amenities and schoolteachers that came with such proximity. "The three years that I've been out here I've seen that white people want the best, and they're going to get it." There was also prejudice, but the prejudice in the suburbs was much less threatening than the physical dangers they faced in the city.[39]

Laura's experience underscores an important benefit of socioeconomically integrated schooling. Students of any race or class will perform in an environment of high expectations, with high-quality teachers and low student-to-teacher ratios that afford individualized support. Creating such learning environments in a context of high poverty, however, is a Herculean task. The two main approaches to improving public education that have been pursued of late have been raising academic standards and reducing class size. It is all well and good to raise standards, to require accountability for meeting those standards through testing, and to reduce class size, which has been shown in some studies to raise student achievement. But these approaches require not only more teachers but strong teachers—the kind that are least likely to be willing to teach in high-poverty school districts or high-poverty schools. With a national teacher shortage, why would a strong teacher opt to teach in a challenging, sometimes even dangerous, work environment, often for less pay than in more advantaged school districts? In most cases they do not. As a result, high-poverty schools tend to attract less-qualified teachers, who are four times as likely to teach outside their field of expertise than teachers in middle-class schools.[40]

Even when extra resources are made available to high-poverty school districts to hire additional teachers and address the unique challenges that come with poverty—students who suffer from malnutrition, poor health care, lack of parental involvement, frequent changes of residence, and exposure to violence and drug use—the entrenched bureaucracies that tend to run large urban schools systems often fail to allocate the new resources effectively. History does not offer much hope. Despite more than three decades of federal Title I compensatory funding for low-income schools and an equity financing movement that has increased the resources available to many poor school districts, as of the late 1990s, two-thirds of students in schools where a majority of the students were poor did not perform at even the basic level on national tests.[41] In my own research I could not find a single example of a school district with large numbers of poor children that had closed the achievement gap between high-poverty schools and their middle-class suburban counterparts.

The latest federal approach is not helping much. The Bush administration's No Child Left Behind Act responds to the achievement dilemma in part by requiring standards testing and accountability for all racial groups and mandating penalties for failing schools. It also requires that children attending public schools needing improvement be given the option of attending better-performing schools.[42] But despite grand promises, the act provides more in the way of mandates for testing than it does resources for the most challenged schools to meet the new standards. In fact, the Bush administration reneged on its promise to provide an additional $5.8 billion in funding for the poorest schools to meet the act's tough performance requirements.[43] Even assuming that all of the extra dollars needed to improve high-poverty schools were forthcoming, overcoming the oppositional culture that tends to permeate such environments cannot be accomplished with mere dollars. Rhetoric and mandates are easy. Transforming urban education in school districts saddled with concentrated poverty and few resources is not.

The Costs and Consequences

We all pay a price for this separation and the attendant achievement gap. Society picks up the tab directly or indirectly when a school system fails to provide all children with a quality education. Society pays, for example, when a black male drops out of high school. There is a direct correlation between each year a black male spends in high school and his likelihood of avoiding participation in crime.[44] A high school diploma is a cheap, effective crime prevention strategy. Yet most suburban voters resist when it comes to fiscal fights about giving urban school systems more resources, even as they support more expensive, "tough on crime" funding of the prison industrial complex. Young black males are now statistically more likely to end up in the criminal justice system than in institutions of higher learning. There are now more black males behind bars, in prisons or jails, than enrolled in colleges and universities. In 1980, black men enrolled in institutions of higher learning out-numbered black men behind bars by three to one.[45] We pay an opportunity cost for this trend in the lost value of potentially productive citizens. We pay a direct cost as taxpayers. It costs much more to house a young person in prison than it does to send him to college.[46] Between 1985 and 2000, state spending on corrections grew at six times the rate as state spending on higher education.[47] This is not a sustainable trend nor a sensible one.

Another potent long-term societal cost of our separate, unequal schooling is our continually strained race relations. One of the consistent problems with race relations in the United States is that whites generally believe that blacks have reached parity with them and that there really are no remaining issues with regard to racial inequality, whereas blacks still experience very real discrimination and inequality.[48] In fact there are considerable gaps of opportunity along race and class lines—the disparity in educational opportunity being one of the more profound contributors to such inequality. How to bridge this divide is America's unique conundrum. It will be very hard to close gaps of opportunity when white advantage is a direct result of racial and economic homogeneity. Any direct threat to that homogeneity, like fair-share affordable housing proposals in the 1990s or busing proposals in the 1970s, is usually met with virulent resistance. Yet, we are resegregating public schools even as the student population, like American society, is becoming more racially diverse. The numbers of Latino and Asian students are increasing dramatically in public schools. Nationwide, minority students now make up about 40 percent of enrollment; in the West and South, almost half of public school students are nonwhite. The

Latino student population will soon exceed the number of black students.[49] This explosion of color is being greeted with more separation, not less. Like the rainbow itself, we are breaking up our rays of light into separate streams of color and separate realities. America is not seeing how beautiful these kids are. We do not see them as an asset; we see them as a problem. Many of us are afraid of black and brown kids, especially if they are poor. But children of color are our fastest-growing resource. We are not prepared for the multicultural, multiethnic society we are becoming. Black, yellow, and red children of today will be the backbone of multicultural, majority-minority America after midcentury, yet we relegate most of these children to separate schools with high numbers of poor children. It amazes me that those who oppose affirmative action do not take into account a history of affirmative choices that have conferred on most whites a separate middle-class peace. In my view, the separated architecture—or rather, geography—of opportunity in America holds more explanatory power for these achievement gaps than does any theory of race inferiority.

If the answer to the problem of concentrated poverty in schools is breaking up those concentrations and sending more inner-city kids to suburban schools or attracting more middle-class kids to public schools through magnet programs, it is not clear that the great suburban majority—70 percent of voters now live in suburbs—will support this. Many white people are tired of hearing about "black complaints." They know ghettos exist. They know urban schools are often quite bad. The majority of whites are suburbanites who have escaped these problems. Few feel any sense of responsibility for solving them. The marked differences in where blacks and whites tend to live contributes to this social tension. Suburban voters living in their own racial and economic havens are not exposed to communities or schools with dire needs, so for them these needs do not exist. Finally, the growing separation of minority and white children into highly different educational realms and social milieus suggests that this strain of difference will continue to haunt us in future generations.

One way to build support for more innovative responses to race and class separation in schooling is to educate the vast majority about the costs they directly bear under this system. Black and Latino children and families bear the brunt of race and class separation in schools, but white children and families also pay a price in this separatist system. Historically, we have accepted inequality in our nation when it appeared that it was racial minorities, particularly black people, who were receiving unequal treatment. Middle-income whites who cannot afford private school tuition also suffer in this system. In a public school system that is essentially premised upon the notion that some children will fall behind, middle-class parents must be ever vigilant to make sure that their kids get into the right classes with the best teachers. If the system were fundamentally committed to bringing every child along, regardless of race or class, parents would not have to fight so hard to ensure that their child is not one of the ones who falls through the cracks. There would be less anxiety for everyone, particularly the white middle-income parent who may be more aware than most of what their child is missing compared to the experience of children in more affluent enclaves or in private schools. White middle-class anxiety will only increase as public school systems become more and more populated with disadvantaged minority kids. Those who cannot escape to private schools or "safe" havens of white affluence will pay a price, just as the minority kids do, in school systems that have failed to figure out how to educate all kids.

In my conversation with white South Arlington school moms, recounted in Chapter 2, they attested to this anxiety. Said Jan, "Our schools teach to the top and the bottom. You are either gifted or in special education. There are no programs geared at middle-level kids." In this context, argued Melinda, "Parents must choose the best programs and intensified classes for their kids." The anxieties over making sure one's child does not fall through the cracks spills over into the college application process. Kari lamented: "The system is set up so that you must accomplish certain feats by certain stages if you want [your child] to go to college. It starts in the sixth grade. I constantly struggle with this. If you are not in the advanced class, then how do you get there from here? You really do have to get in there and demand it. I feel so much pressure. They send [my kid] home with lists of what he must have, like algebra by the eighth grade." Said Donna, "There are parents who put their kids in summer intensified math class so that when they arrive at school in the sixth grade they will test better. I know of third graders who are put in special math classes in addition to their regular schooling to keep ahead. This is what people with resources do." One mother admitted to paying a private college counselor $1,000 to help one of her older children build a successful college application after he "took 5 AP courses and flunked all five of them." Fortunately, it worked; her son was admitted to a public four-year university. The same mother said her younger son is "severely depressed by this grind of everything he has to do." His psychiatrist said the only trauma he has in his life is related to school. "My son says he is not there to learn. He is just there to jump through hoops to get to the next level. We used to tell him education was important, not grades. Now we say we lied. [We tell him,] 'Stop complaining. Just get the grades so you can have the options.'" She said of the academic pressure being put on kids: "We are not asking what we want our kids to be like in ten years. We are only trying to get them into the best college, period."

The rat race, then, tends to feed on itself. Parents are too busy worrying about how their own children will fare in a pockmarked opportunity structure to have the luxury of worrying about other people's children. They reach for "insurance" for their child in the form of an elite set of colleges. With the pressures that attend the race to get their children into this elite strata of schools, it is hard for them to be empathetic about affirmative action or the problems that plague inner-city schools or public school systems generally. American life is hard. Both parents, if there are two of them, feel compelled to work. Raising children well seems to be a challenge. Affording the safest path to a middle-class existence for your child seems particularly daunting, with the average tuition for a private four-year college now approaching $23,000 and those of the elitist schools at $30,000 or more annually. Where is this rat race taking us? Who will worry about the collective? Where will the political will to solve the "hard" problems come from? It will come, I hope, from an ethos of togetherness that we need to cultivate, lest the public, common good be completely sacrificed and those disadvantaged at birth be left to falter in inadequate public schools.

In a well-integrated school system, one where every school has a majority middle-class population and no school is overwhelmed by poverty, parents of all races would not have to worry so much about the quality of education their child is receiving. In an economically integrated system, white parents would have much less to fear about the risks of public schools. They might be more willing to live in multicultural settings or send their kids to public schools. In the din of debate about what can work to ensure a quality educational experience for all children, a small movement for socioeconomic integration has been emerging. The school systems in Cambridge, Massachusetts; Wake County and Charlotte-Mecklenburg, North Carolina; South Orange–Maplewood, New Jersey; Manchester, Connecticut; St. Lucie County, Florida; and San Francisco have all adopted economic integration plans in recent years.[50] I think this is the right focus of the debate, although I am aware that these strategies swim against a tide of parental skepticism. Parents of all racial and socioeconomic backgrounds would like to believe in neighborhood schools. They are not much interested in integration; they are interested in quality. But the growing public support for vouchers, particularly among black parents, is an implicit nod to the concern that existing public school systems are not delivering for minority kids.

There is one glimmer of hope in demographic trends in public schooling. In the 1990s there was a rapid rise in the number of multiracial schools where at least one-tenth of the students were from three different racial groups. Of course, as with our neighborhoods, few whites experience this multiracial mix. Although only 14 percent of whites attended multiracial schools as of 2000, about 25 percent of Native Americans, 30 percent of blacks, 40 percent of Latinos, and 75 percent of Asians did.[51] From the standpoint of the civil rights lawyers who tried the *Brown* case and the Warren Court that decided it, the only students who now come close to approximating the vision of that decision are Asian students. They are most apt to experience racial diversity and middle-class norms in public school. Unless and until we can approximate this experience for black, Latino, and Native American children, I do not believe we will successfully close gaps of inequality in education in any systemic way. Herein lies the rub. Unless more middle-class students, including white students, enter into this multicultural fray, we are doomed to a status quo of increasing segregation and inequality.

CHAPTER 7

THE COST OF THE GHETTO

Sometimes, a crime is so offensive, it turns a city's stomach and leads to great change. So far, the killing of Jasmine Jackson is not one of them. On Sunday night, the 16-year-old Ms. Jackson, a slender, copper-skinned girl called Jazz, was walking home from a block party when she was jumped by two other girls. Her cousin said she tried to fight them off but was stabbed in the arm with a steak knife. One of the girls then plunged the knife into Jazz's chest. Ms. Jackson could not run because she had been shot in the leg last year, randomly, and still walked with a limp. She collapsed on a nearby stoop, holding her hand over her heart. "I remember saying, 'Stay with me, Jazz, stay with me,'" said Keila Smith, 15, who tried to help. "Then she closed her eyes." Jazz died barely a week after two teenage girls were sent to prison for fatally stabbing another 16-year-old girl with a steak knife. But besides a few news accounts, there was little outrage beyond Christopher Homes, the broken-dreams public housing neighborhood where Jazz fell.

—Jeffrey Gettleman, "New Orleans Struggles with a Homicide Rate
That Belies Its Size," *New York Times,* July 11, 2003

A SIXTEEN-YEAR-OLD African American girl is killed on the streets of New Orleans and no one notices. It is not an unusual scenario. We read, or overlook, stories like these in the metro section of the newspaper every day. They are so commonplace that we have become inured to them. But they are pieces of the reality that make up daily life for the millions of people living American ghetto life. Our separation limits us from acknowledging, much less entering into, this pain. We do not personally experience it, so for us it does not exist in any real sense. Our separation from this environment also makes it easier for us to absolve ourselves of any responsibility for doing something about it. Most of us would not trade one day with the people who live in the severe economic and racial isolation of the inner-city ghetto. Not with the mothers living on Elvans Road—a cul-de-sac in southeast Washington, D.C., that has had fourteen slayings since 1988.[1] Not with the retiree who has had nearly every window in her Chicago Southside apartment shot through by gangs engaged in a turf war.[2] Not with the Harlem eighth-grader struggling to succeed in a school where fully 90 percent of his classmates failed the state's annual reading exam.[3] Not with the young black males trapped in ghetto neighborhoods for whom escape to better surroundings or just holding down a job is a major victory against the odds.[4]

Society rarely asks people who are relegated to the ghetto what their life is like or what they think. These are not stupid people. Most of them must survive very challenging daily circumstances. The post-traumatic stress of having lived "thug life" weighs heavily. "I have a lot of mental distress," says Ozzie E. Garcia, a twenty-one-year-old former gang member tells columnist Bob Herbert. "I think about the things that have happened and I get chills. I start shaking. People get shot around here. I got shot in the neck and it broke my jaw. That's why my teeth are crooked. My friend that got shot with me, the bullet was just three inches from his spinal cord. Some guys came up to us and I said, 'What's crackin?' And they just started shooting. That's the way it is out here. A lot of my homies have passed away. Six or seven of them.... How many times have I cried? I feel sorry for the young kids who are killed. We call them the little angels."[5] Juanita Moody, 52, describes to writer Helen Epstein what it was like living in a low-income housing complex on Nepperhan Avenue in an inner-city neighborhood of Yonkers, New York, where she lived for thirty years with her husband until they were able, with the help of a special program, to move to a middle-class area of the city: "[I]t was stressful just to walk out of that place. You were always scared for the kids.... You wake up stressed, go to sleep stressed, you see all the garbage and dealers. That is depressing. In a bad environment like that you say, 'What's the use of doing anything?'" After she moved, her blood pressure fell from high to near normal. Her liver no longer shows signs of hepatitis, which had been rapidly progressing. Removed from the withering daily grind of worry about person and property, she stopped eating at McDonald's and became health conscious in her food choices. In her new, decidedly nonluxurious but safe environs—an apartment with leafy views on a busy street near two gas stations and a mall— she has a new attitude: "It inspires you to do all you can—spiritually, health-wise, any kind of way."[6] Other families who were lucky beneficiaries of the Enhanced Section 8 Outreach Program, or ESOP, a locally run effort to help poor families living in dangerous ghetto neighborhoods of Yonkers to move into middle-class areas, display similar transformations. The so-called ghetto mentality does not move with the resident. It is not inherent in the resident. It stays back where it thrives—a foul, mysterious miasma that falls on the ghetto and its inhabitants, making them literally sick.[7]

The Peculiar Institution

The black ghetto, like slavery in earlier centuries, is a peculiar American institution. Poor black people pay the highest price for racial separatism. They are the only demographic group in the United States that is "hypersegregated." As Douglass Massey and Nancy Denton explained in their seminal book, *American Apartheid,* a neighborhood is hypersegregated when it experiences a high level of separation along at least four of five possible measures. The technical explanations of these terms are not as important as the fact that large numbers of black people live in extremely isolated ghetto conditions, whereas no whites, no Latinos, and no Asians—not even the poorest among these groups—live in such environments.[8] Hypersegregation, or extreme isolation among disadvantaged blacks, is a stubborn, ongoing reality for many blacks. While the overall trend for African Americans going into the twenty-first century is one of slightly more integration, the number of census tracts that are over 80 percent black remained constant in the 1990s.[9] When it comes to true ghettos, the most favorable development is that fewer black people now live in such conditions than in the past. After increasing steadily in the 1970s and 1980s, concentrated poverty—the share of poor people living in neighborhoods where at least 40 percent of their neighbors are also poor—declined by a dramatic 24 percent nationwide between 1990 and 2000, with especially large declines among African Americans. It remains to be seen whether this positive trend continued in the 2000s. We do know, however, that concentrated poverty falls heaviest on poor blacks and poor Native Americans. Poor whites are much less isolated; only 5.9 percent of poor whites live in concentrated poverty.[10]

Not surprisingly, given the racial segregation they are subjected to, "blacks remain the single largest racial/ethnic group living in high poverty neighborhoods."[11] These neighborhoods are becoming less populated as blacks with choices move elsewhere, but that only worsens the isolated condition for those black folks left behind. I cannot describe their situation any better than Massey and Denton did in *American Apartheid:*

> Typical inhabitants of one of these ghettos are not only unlikely to come into contact with whites within the particular neighborhood where they live; even if they traveled to the adjacent neighborhood they would still be unlikely to see a white face; and if they went to the next neighborhood beyond that, no whites would be there either. People growing up in such an environment have little direct experience with the culture, norms, and behaviors of the rest of American society and few social contacts with members [of] other racial groups. Ironically, within a large, diverse, and highly mobile post-industrial society such as the United States, blacks living in the heart of the ghetto are among the most isolated people on earth.[12]

It is not an accident that only black people have been relegated to such extremely isolated ghetto conditions in the United States. As I discussed in Chapter 3, the black inner-city ghetto is the product of intentional public policy choices—a history that few Americans of any race are familiar with. In the 1930s, the discrimination of individuals was augmented by government-encouraged institutional discrimination and redlining. Racially restrictive covenants, which the Federal Housing Administration (FHA) required and encouraged to create "neighborhood stability" in the 1940s and 1950s, ensured that even black people of means were denied the option of procuring an FHA-backed mortgage, with the result that in those decades when home ownership was a new opportunity for the masses, blacks were stymied from pursuing the

American dream. Beyond the FHA, black people as a general matter were discouraged by violence and discrimination from living beyond neighborhoods deemed appropriate for them. The ghetto, with its intense concentration of low-income black people, emerged from the synergistic forces of institutional discrimination and three specific public policies that dramatically shaped the physical and socioeconomic destiny of the American metropolis. First, the urban renewal program, begun in 1949, removed black populations from desirable areas, in the name of "progress," to more marginal neighborhoods. Second, the interstate highway program, begun in 1956, decimated mostly black neighborhoods and erected physical barriers of isolation, which ensured that the people who were the weakest political actors would be even more marginalized and separated. And third, the federally sponsored but locally administered public housing program of the 1950s and 1960s ensured that black public housing residents would be placed in buildings and neighborhoods where virtually everyone else around them was also poor. White public housing residents were much less likely to meet such a fate.

I would argue that the creation of black ghetto communities was no less intentional than other official public policies designed to subordinate African Americans. Racial discrimination fueled these choices. Although affirmative action programs in education and employment were initiated to rectify past injustices, America has never undertaken any serious effort to reverse its nefarious role in creating such residential misery. The Department of Housing and Urban Development's Hope VI program of the 1990s, designed to replace its most decrepit public housing with mixed-income development, and a small demonstration program called "Moving to Opportunities," which was funded briefly in the mid-1990s, are exceptions, although it could be argued that the Hope VI program is unfair to the powerless public housing tenants who are not invited to return to newly "nice," gentrified developments. The few programs that make some headway against the tide of inertia and indifference toward high-poverty minority neighborhoods pale in comparison to the systemic forces that encourage the isolation of impoverished people of color. Those low-income minorities lucky enough to procure a HUD "Section 8" housing voucher, which helps pay the rent for a market-rate apartment, are challenged to find an apartment they can afford, and if they do find one, it tends to be located in a low-income neighborhood. The "urban development" and "war on poverty" programs of the 1960s and 1970s, however well intentioned, were not efforts to change the location of people relegated to ghetto islands; they were aimed at making those communities more livable or enhancing opportunities to escape poverty generally. In other words, the precious few federal programs that could possibly counteract the massive institutional forces that created and sustain ghetto segregation amount to a trickle.

Our modern response to the ghetto is mostly reactionary. We respond to the distress and violence that such concentrated poverty incubates with a "war on drugs" that locks up and stores away "the problem" of thousands of unemployed and undereducated black men. We respond to the problem of concentrated poverty in schools with a "No Child Left Behind" law that is long on educational testing requirements and short on funding for overcoming a critical shortage of quality teachers in such communities. Books about the conditions of the ghetto come and go: *The Truly Disadvantaged. Savage Inequalities. There Are No Children Here.*[13] The occasional riot borne of an outpouring of frustration, typically in response to police brutality, comes and goes: the Liberty City and Overtown sections of Miami in 1980, South Central L.A. in 1992, the Over-the-Rhine section of Cincinnati, Ohio, and Benton Harbor, Michigan, in the 2000s. It doesn't matter. Nothing seems to change for those left behind in such communities. The hood endures, although gentrification or demographic tides may cause it to migrate to new territory. The ghetto, a creature of America's own making, continues to exact costs for which we do not assume much, if any, responsibility.

The Costs to Ghetto Residents

The daily toll for those relegated to ghetto neighborhoods is steeper than most of us can imagine: greater risk for disease and death, exposure to violence, poor schools, limited access to jobs, higher risk for teen pregnancy, less likelihood of marriage, higher likelihood to be a participant or a victim of crime, and so on. The list is endless. No one who has alternatives would choose this existence for themselves or their children.

People who live in high-poverty ghetto communities live a very different reality than folks who live, say, in a community that is merely working poor. William Julius Wilson has interpreted this environment for us. He defines a ghetto as a neighborhood where at least 40 percent of the residents are poor. These are communities where more adults are likely to be not working than working. He offers the example of fifteen black communities in the Chicago area where only 37 percent of all adults were gainfully employed in a typical week. There is a serious difference between a "working poor" community and one where unemployment is the norm. With the loss of the organizing structure of work comes a host of destructive behaviors. The social networks that are the lifeblood of a healthy community are eroded. The natural supervision that residents tend to exercise and the degree of personal responsibility they assume in addressing neighborhood problems are lowered. Residents participate in far fewer voluntary and formal organizations. In such environments, when there are no other jobs, drug dealing becomes more attractive. Drug trafficking in turn brings in people attracted to lawlessness and violence. Because informal controls are weakened, social processes that regulate behavior change. As a result, even those who don't sell drugs are affected, for example, by buying a gun for protection, which then sends the message to kids that the possession of guns is acceptable or even necessary. Conversely, where people are working, alternatives to drugs are apparent, and lawlessness doesn't gain a foothold. There is more neighborhood stability since residents are not fleeing a bad situation, and employed people have the informal contacts necessary to help others find work.[14]

Obviously, poverty is not limited to black people or black children. The Native American poor endure similarly high rates of concentrated poverty, although not in an urban ghetto context. The Latino poor also tend to be concentrated in urban neighborhoods, although they are not isolated to the extreme degree that the black poor are; they are not hypersegregated. In the birth lottery, the degree to which one is at risk of living in concentrated poverty and segregation varies depending upon one's race. The black poor are the most isolated, the Latino poor less so, the Asian poor less still. The white poor are the least isolated among the impoverished. They are more likely to live in middle-class, suburban surroundings. The differences in life chances between those who grow up "ghetto poor" and those who grow up poor but in a mostly middle-class neighborhood are considerable.[15]

By allowing them to live in more socioeconomically integrated settings, American society tends to afford the white poor a chance at upward mobility that it denies many of its poor black and Latino citizens. This consequence of racism is immoral, in my view. Ghetto inequality is a subject for which certain absolute truths apply. The accident of birth, the happenstance of being relegated to a highly impoverished, isolated neighborhood, clearly determines a reality that is quite the opposite of the American dream. Concentrated poverty incubates social distress in a way that dispersed poverty does not. As one research team put it, "There is growing evidence that when poverty rates exceed 30 percent, neighborhoods have great difficulty sustaining the economic and civic institutions essential for a healthy community. Poor education, joblessness, teen parenthood, discrimination, and crime all reinforce one another ... creating a vicious cycle of poverty, inequality, isolation and distress."[16] Inner-city residents of highly segregated neighborhoods suffer higher rates of infant mortality, elevated blood pressure, heart disease, crime, and unemployment than inner-city residents of less segregated neighborhoods. One researcher has directly correlated racial segregation with quality-of-life indicators, predicting that if segregation levels in metropolitan Detroit were cut in half, median income for black families would rise 24 percent; black homicide would fall 30 percent, the level of black high school dropouts would fall by 75 percent; and black poverty would fall by 17 percent.[17] Ghetto isolation clearly is dangerous to one's health and well-being.

Ironically, society isolates ghetto residents even as these communities morbidly fascinate. The ways of the ghetto are legendary. They are the stuff of movies, TV, and hip-hop culture. In many ways they are familiar to even the most distant and affluent because ghetto culture has permeated American popular culture. To their parents' horror, suburban white kids can appropriate the clothing and swagger of urban hip-hop, becoming full-fledged "wiggers" from a safe, insulated, middle-class distance. We all have some vague sense of what "thug life" is about—its signatures, its style, values, and mores. We recoil at it, but it is familiar. The real irony, in my view, is that we shunt low-income black kids into isolated neighborhoods where certain types of behaviors can be essential to personal survival, and then we expect these kids somehow to reject those behaviors and adopt the norms of mainstream society. We vilify and glamorize them for doing what is natural, maybe even essential, in their home environment.

Our hypocrisy is most apparent in our penal policies. Almost one in three young black males is incarcerated or under some other form of supervision by the criminal justice system. One out of three black males born in 2001 will be imprisoned at some point in their lifetime if current trends continue, compared to about one out of eight in 1974.[18] In a black ghetto, frequently more young black males are under criminal supervision than not.[19] In such an environment, prison becomes its own right of passage. It is the way to become a man. Doing time brings a certain status. As former inmates return to the hood and share the lessons and mores of prison life, the community itself begins to take on a culture of incarceration. The modern American ghetto and the modern American prison, where nearly half the population is black and male, become more and more alike.[20] In Maryland in 2001, 60 percent of all released prisoners, excluding those released from local jails, were returned to the city of Baltimore. Six of the city's fifty-five neighborhoods were home to 30 percent of these repatriates.[21] No wonder TV shows like *The Wire* and *Homicide* are set in the gritty neighborhoods of this city on the water. In these hardscrabble places, the prison system plays a greater role than the education system in shaping the lives of young black men. Once a young man has made the passage, he is unlikely to be able to rehabilitate himself. A recent test of the discrimination endured by young black men showed that even those who have never had a brush with the law fare poorly in the competition for employment. Potential employers favor a white male with a criminal record over a black one with no record.[22] The pervasive negative stereotypes of ghetto neighborhoods and their residents limit the job opportunities available even to those black males who have never been imprisoned.[23] Imagine what it must be like for a brother who does have a record when *he* looks for work.

The Costs to Society

America simply does not know what to do with her poor black boys. Researchers argue that she has adopted a "'new penology' that seeks not to deter or rehabilitate individual offenders but merely to warehouse the riskiest segment of the so-called urban underclass."[24] Because it is easier to inflict harsh "get tough" punishments on marginalized lower-income people in a stratified society, the hypersegregation of black urban communities enables the pursuit of policies that disproportionately impact their residents.[25] It is not surprising, given the levels of segregation of African Americans, that in June 2002, 12 percent of all black men aged 20 to 39 in United States were in prison or in jail, the highest rate ever measured. In contrast, only 4 percent of Latino and 1.6 percent of white males in this age group were incarcerated.[26]

We think that we have evolved as a country on issues of race in part because our retrograde tendencies are buried. There is a complicated nexus between the desire for racial exclusion and public commitment to harsh penal policies. Those states with large minority populations are more apt to try to exclude these groups and to pursue punitive law enforcement, while states with small minority populations are more apt to be inclusive of these groups and to favor social welfare over harsh anti-crime policies.[27] If geographic isolation does not entirely succeed, then removing certain people from society altogether is the next best alternative, albeit an expensive one.

There is a steep cost to this policy. The American prison population now exceeds 2 million. The current incarceration rate in the United States is by far the highest of any industrialized Western nation and more than triple that of U.S. incarceration rates in the late 1970s. The prison population increased tenfold between 1972 and 2002, with two-thirds of that increase consisting of racial minorities. A clear cost of America failing to figure out how to include and develop all of her people is a burgeoning prison population that is busting budgets. The current growth rate of the prison industrial complex is simply not sustainable. The federal prison population grew by 5.7 percent between 2001 and 2002. Locking up "the problem" not only multiplies prison spending but also undermines possibilities for devoting scarce public resources to wise investments, like hiring more quality teachers, and ensures that a culture of incarceration gains a permanent foothold in high-poverty minority neighborhoods.

The costs to society for shunting poor minorities into isolated neighborhoods do not stop with prison budgets. The aggregate costs that society carries directly and indirectly start with the social distress that concentrated poverty incubates.

Extreme segregation obviously harms those who are segregated, but it also has multiplier effects. Increased health risks, for example, translate to more emergency room visits to hospitals on the part of the poor and uninsured. When governments are unable or unwilling to pick up the full cost of this uncompensated care, inner-city hospitals decline and suffer. In the city of Detroit, because of cuts in Medicaid and Medicare, three hospitals closed in a five-year span, laying off more than 8,000 hospital workers. More than 50 percent of Detroit's primary care physicians moved to the better-insured suburbs.[28] There are also the obvious costs of increased taxes for those who live in proximity to the ghetto and even for suburban taxpayers who must contribute to state and federal spending to cover added health care, law enforcement, and welfare costs. Beyond higher taxes and the indirect costs of lost human capital, the social distress of concentrated poverty creates a perception of danger that middle-class people, particularly whites with children, view as untenable—something to be avoided at all costs.

The social ills associated with ghetto or inner-city neighborhoods, real or imagined, have become associated with cities in general. Historians and social science researchers have documented the impulses that fueled the five-decade mass exodus of whites and other races from cities to suburbs. The desire to escape the redistributive tax burdens of the cities and the desire for racial homogeneity—escape from black people— were the strongest of those impulses, especially in the '50s and '60s when whites were first confronted with the specter of integration of schools and neighborhoods.[29] The exodus has continued unabated. The middle classes of all races exit or avoid urban and older suburban environments with pockets of intense poverty because these neighborhoods and all that they represent—poverty, violence, crime—are simply not acceptable, especially for families with children and choices. Those who feel compelled to escape such "scary" environs likely do not think of their stultifying commutes or high housing costs as a consequence of the existence of the urban ghetto.

Then there are the invisible costs. The crime and violence of ghetto neighborhoods contributes to a devaluation of black life. I am reminded of an article in the *Washington Post* that ran during the Washington, D.C., area sniper scare. During three weeks of October 2002, suburbanites experienced the stress of living with the daily menace of gun violence. A total of ten people died at the hands of the snipers; during that month alone the District of Columbia's violent crimes unit was investigating eighteen other homicides. The ordinary body count received little public attention.[30]

Perhaps the most enduring "invisible" cost is the gulf of perceptions between Americans who live far from the reality of the ghetto and those who live in it. The impact of the ghetto on American race and class relations is hiding in plain view. Beyond its contribution to white and middle-class flight, the ghetto animates current race relations, although we may not fully realize it. White America is largely a suburban nation—71 percent of whites call a suburb home—while black America is still mainly an urban nation. Although the black middle class is suburbanizing rapidly, only 39 percent of blacks lived in suburbia, according to the 2000 census.[31] In the code of our unspoken understandings, "urban" means black. For many, it also means more crime and bad schools. "Suburban" may have a less definite connotation, but generally it means the opposite of urban or an escape from all things urban—a bucolic haven of single-family homes, a place where parents need not fear for their children, who can run free in the streets, a place that is not overwhelmingly black. A person who tells you she "grew up in the suburbs" is telling you she lived a certain homogeneous existence. I hear it from my students all the time, suburban kids of all races who experienced diversity for the first time upon attending college or law school.

This separation into starkly different figurative and actual "life spaces" contributes mightily to a social gulf—in opportunities as well as the ability of the races to connect. It fuels misunderstanding in several ways. Ghetto life and culture contribute to racial stereotyping and fear of black people. It allows the white suburbanite to rationalize a move to a homogeneous neighborhood, although the mover may not consciously admit this to herself. The stark physical separation from concentrated poverty also contributes to a gap of understanding. For those who do not see, regularly or ever, the effects of concentrated poverty, such effects do not exist.

This stark separation also contributes to the seemingly eternal challenge of creating social and economic parity between whites and blacks—to the extent this even remains an agenda item. White voters, for example, typically show great antipathy to any spending that is perceived as helping the "welfare poor," which in their lexicon means poor black people.[32] Usually they are well buffered from "those people." Indeed, as I argue in the next chapter, the welfare reform policies of the 1990s were fueled in part by the need of a Democratic president, Bill Clinton, to appeal to white suburban voters.

Black Classism

The black middle and upper classes have their own issues with their lower-income brethren. We do not like to own up to it publicly, but there is a serious class division in black America, and ghetto culture contributes to the schism. There are really three realms of blackness in our nation. First, there is the elite, "talented" 1 percent who have annual incomes of $100,000 or more—a total of about 200,000 people. Many of these folks went to elite colleges. Among black people, they are the ones who have benefited most from affirmative action in schools and in the workplace. The brothers and sisters who make up this tribe enjoy the full privileges of American citizenship, except perhaps when caught "driving while black." They are most able to overcome the slings and arrows of racial discrimination. They have options; they face few constraints in choosing where to live. And like their white counterparts, they have no desire to live next door to "Shaniqua," nor do they. Second, there is the black middle and working class. These are the information technology technicians, the machinists, the sales people, the military, police, and fire fighters, the school teachers, the postal workers, the civil servants who have proudly obtained a high "GS" scale. They prosper in good economic times and are among the first fired in a recession. Many are college educated. All are strivers. A definitive issue for many of them is insulating themselves and their families from the hood. Finally, there are those African Americans who are poor, working or otherwise. Fully 24 percent of black people and 30 percent of black children fit into this category. Many of them live in the ghetto.

There are really only one or two degrees of separation between the first and third rung of black America. Even the most affluent of African Americans would be hard-pressed not to know someone personally—a childhood friend, a loved one, a cousin—who has fallen on hard times or who never rose above his or her meager circumstances of birth. If they don't know someone personally in such circumstances, they probably know someone who does. A friend of mine, an Ivy-educated black professional, has a sister lost to crack addiction who lives, as far as he knows, on the streets. A black Harvard Law School classmate of mine, an accomplished professor, has a half-brother in jail for committing murder. In many black families there is a sibling who prospered and another who struggled to maintain a middle-class existence. The forty-something black banking executive with degrees from Stanford and the London School of Economics, who grew up in a black neighborhood in Houston, is familiar with the ways of the street. He has childhood friends who escaped the hood and those who did not. He chuckles and worries aloud that his kids, who have been brought up in affluent, predominately white surroundings and elite private schools, will not have the street wits they may need in an unexpected encounter with a hood element. His son might not know instinctively, he laughs, to hit the floor if shots go off at a party.

Those black professionals, like myself, who grew up with friends from the projects, as well as the sons and daughters of doctors, lawyers, and entrepreneurs, exercise a great deal of dexterity when moving between the three rungs of black America. We play the dozens or bid whist and are steeped in the black popular culture of our generation. We know who "Shine" is and can recite at least parts of "the signifying monkey," the rap lyric of our fathers' day. We like the familiarity of a black barber or beauty shop and a rocking black church, places where the black classes tend to intersect and share a common culture. It seems as if black people of all ages and classes can do the Electric Slide, the Booty Call, or the cha-cha step. These are the common threads of blackness we hold on to and hold dear. But there is a distinct schism among us.

In contrast to the Jim Crow era, when blacks of all economic circumstances were thrown together in economically integrated communities, the class separation that has emerged since the civil rights revolution has cultivated differing cultures. In some black neighborhoods "Ebonics" prevails, while in others the idiom is standard English, or rather, one masters both dialects and switches back and forth as context requires. Among the black elite, discomfort with or hostility toward low-income black people is often palpable. The class tension can extend from the serious to the ridiculous. At our worst, we work at keeping low-income people—our people—out of our schools and our neighborhoods.

But hostilities work both ways. A senior program officer at a foundation, who is a black Ivy League graduate, told writer Lise Funderburg that when he moved his family onto a predominately black street in Montclair, New Jersey, he expected to be welcomed. "But we weren't just black people, we were the outsiders driving up property values and forcing the old folks out." He recognizes, however, that the class tension in Montclair cuts both ways. "Most people are willing to talk about the folks with resources coming in and supplanting those who've been here a long time.... What isn't talked about are the new black folks coming in who aren't well off, trying to get their kids into better schools. That would send the wrong message about Montclair. A lot of people—white and black, but maybe more white folks—want Montclair to be less diverse than it is. They want it to be middle class."[33]

My friend Audrey experiences similar tensions in the LeDroit Park neighborhood of Washington, D.C. The beautiful brownstones with the conical rooftops that line these streets near Howard University are populated with middle-class blacks, affluent white and gay couples, and low-income black families. Audrey says the occasional class conflict spills out, for example, when a low-income neighbor responded with choicely expressed anger when a middle-class parent attempted to intervene to correct the bad behavior of her children. We are loathe to admit it, but yes, sometimes a lower-income milieu produces "Bebe's kids."

Sometimes the class schism is lighthearted, as when Chris Rock incants, "I hate niggahs," making it clear he means the people who steel your TV or rob you at an ATM. Or when the black bourgeoisie bandies about terms like "ghetto fabulous," "ghettogenous," or, my personal favorite, the "Niggeoisie," pronounced "nigwahzie." A good friend coined the last term, which she says refers to that class of black people who are above ghetto but have not yet entered the ranks of the solidly middle class.

Sometimes the class schism turns dangerous. A black forty-something business lawyer laments that there is no club he can go to in Washington, D.C., to enjoy hip-hop without the risk of accidently bumping into a ghetto brother who may respond violently. I feel he is exaggerating the dangers, but I understand his reluctance. I recall my friend David's encounter in a bathroom of a nightclub; an ostensibly low-income black man took one look at David, who rose from very modest beginnings in L.A. to become a successful lawyer with a telecommunications company, and saw not another brother but a guy who was living large and a world apart compared to his own circumstances. He confronted David with menacing bravado and unprovoked hostility.

Why did he exhibit such aggression toward David? I think those relegated to a ghetto existence, especially men, feel the need to express their frustration at the raw deal they were dealt by American society. It shows up in hip-hop and rap culture. An expletive-filled, often misogynistic vernacular, a doo-rag under an oversized baseball cap tipped sideways or back-wards, big chains with real or fake "bling-bling," baggy pants, a scowl—all of these signatures are borrowed from the ghetto. These in-your-face statements of difference intend to convey the message "No, we are not like you and we don't want to be like you." Suffused in this swagger of opposition is a tacit acknowledgment that society does not really embrace or include ghetto kids. A poor black kid, especially a black male, frequently feels the recoil that "others" display in his presence. Jesse Jackson Sr., that champion of the left out, tacitly admits what far too many of us think about when we encounter a young black male on the street: "There is nothing more painful to me at this stage in my life than to walk down the street and hear footsteps and start thinking about robbery—then look around and see somebody white and feel relieved."[34]

Some ghetto kids retaliate against this treatment. They become modern-day Bigger Thomases. They will show an America that locks them out just how scary they can be. A law student of mine told me of a conversation she overheard on the Metro in Washington, D.C. Three black teenage girls were speaking loudly, seemingly intentionally so all around them could hear, of whether or not to kill another girl they had a beef with. Is this the bravado of teenagers intent on shocking adults or is it real? My student says she will probably be haunted by this conversation for years, trying to make sense of how three young girls could speak so cavalierly about killing another human being, even if in jest. Yet the death of Jazz Jackson at the hands of other teenage girls is real. Her murder was the product of a violent alternative culture with patently different rules and mores for settling scores or merely express-ing jealousy. To recognize how America has incubated such an alternative universe is not to absolve the individual perpetrators. Understanding the depth of the difference between this world and the one most of us inhabit is critical to comprehending the costs of our extreme separatism.

The Path Not Taken

Had we chosen a different path in the twentieth century and not created high-poverty black ghettos, I do not believe we would have such stark divisions of figurative and actual life space in the United States. Perhaps African Americans are the group all other races are most resistant to integrating with *because* they are the ones most confined to and associated with ghetto neighborhoods and everything they represent. There was and is an alternative course. As I mentioned in the previous chapter, the *Gautreaux* case in metropolitan Chicago bears witness to the alternative possibilities. When the Chicago Housing Authority and the Federal Department of Housing and Urban Development (HUD) were found by a federal court to have intentionally discriminated against black people in the location of public housing, plaintiffs in the *Gautreaux* case were given an option. They could take an affordable housing voucher and use it in more integrated communities, including predominately white suburbs. HUD was charged with helping these residents of the worst of Chicago public housing—the "mother of all ghettos"—to find affordable, market-rate units elsewhere. Social science researchers followed these families for many years, comparing the outcomes of the suburban movers to those of families that chose to remain in Chicago public housing.

By every indicia of well-being, the lives of suburban movers improved. The parents, mostly single, former welfare mothers, found jobs. The children, who initially struggled in suburban schools with higher standards, had dramatically higher rates of high school graduation and college attendance. The children spoke of suburban teachers who took more time to help them with their work and set higher expectations for them. The parents spoke of being motivated to go out and work and no longer being worried about their children being caught up in street violence. The children said they initially struggled but ultimately made friends in the new suburban environments.[35]

When poor people are empowered to get out of the ghetto, small miracles occur. They feel better. Severe asthma attacks give way to boundless energy. Children do not want to go to sleep, because for the first time in their young lives they are free to play outside, surrounded by grass, trees, and fresh air that does not make them sick. They can play without fear of bullets. Parents feel calmer; they have a new sense of peace. They eat better. They feel exuberant at having escaped the constant daily grind of "us versus them." The police are no longer there to harass them. These lucky movers have experienced a transforming personal makeover without winning the lottery of a reality television show. They simply were given the chance to live somewhere that offers a modicum of peace, dignity, and opportunity. It is not much to ask for, yet a modest apartment on a busy street with a view of trees and no menacing presences is a queen's castle for those who have endured ghetto conditions.[36] Still, the opportunities most whites have in this country—to live outside a high-poverty milieu—will continue to elude millions of people of color if we continue with our present course of accepting ghetto poverty as inevitable, rather than enabling all who are poor to live in a low- or even moderate-poverty context.

We are all losing under the status quo. My fear is that it will take more direct, concrete losses to the white masses to scare us into action or at least a willingness to consider a more enlightened course. The *Gautreaux* experiment offers a hopeful vision of what race and class integration could achieve were we to have the courage to pursue an integrationist course. I discuss policy alternatives in more depth in the final chapter of this book. The critical prerequisite for pursuing an alternative vision, however, is a change of mind-set and an opening of the heart.

PART 3

OUR FUTURE

CHAPTER 8

THE 50–50 NATION
Loggerhead Politics

As our nation grows more diverse it also grows more polarized. Is it coincidental that 1964 was a watershed both for civil rights and arch-conservatives? In that year, Lyndon Johnson signed landmark civil rights legislation and trounced Barry Goldwater in the presidential election. Conservative purists did more than lick their wounds. They set about building the foundations for a conservative ideological movement in which ideas that were then out of the mainstream of even their own party would ultimately take center stage. It took less than twenty years for a revitalized conservative movement to bear fruit in the election of Ronald Reagan in 1980.

The "Reagan Revolution" was buoyed in part by the phenomenon of Reagan Democrats. In the eighties, there was much more of a so-called vital center; swing voters would split tickets and vote for candidates they liked, regardless of party affiliation. In the nineties the center narrowed. Culture wars or wedge issues became more critical in shaping party identity and affiliation. Republicans were for "family values" and against abortion. Democrats were pro-choice and supportive on issues like gays in the military, civil rights, and affirmative action. Politics in Washington and elsewhere corroded as negative attacks and exploitation of hot-button symbols that might play to each party's base became de rigueur in campaigns and policy battles. From the Robert Bork nomination in 1987, to the Clarence Thomas–Anita Hill spectacle, to the Clinton impeachment proceedings, to the Bush-Gore election debacle of 2000, each national political moment seemed more heated. By 2003, after the midterm elections, Democrats were both out of the White House and in the minority in both houses of Congress for the first time in fifty years.

Meanwhile, party affiliation has hit a low; today about one-third of voters identify themselves as Democrat, and one-third as Republican. The other third identifies as independent. But partisan differences among registered Democrats and Republicans are at an all-time high. And only a very narrow slice of registered voters, independents included, truly swing between voting Republican and Democratic. The "swing vote" now constitutes less than 10 percent of voters, according to pollsters. In recent presidential elections about 40 percent of the electorate—registered voters and unregistered citizens—did not vote at all. That leaves both major parties in a quandary about how to shore up their respective bases, while also appealing to the narrow slice of "persuadables" in the center. Demographics and geographic separation explain some of this polarization. It is as if the folks in the opposing Democratic and Republican camps live in two different countries. And in a sense they do.

Our tendency to create separated communities of abundance and of need contributes to a divisive, loggerhead politics. With homogeneity comes parochialism, or a reduced capacity for empathy with those who live beyond the gate—figuratively or literally. Homogeneity of any kind has a way of breeding an inward-looking self-interest. Once achieved, homogeneity can become its own entitlement—a fortress of advantage that must be defended—whether the invaders are low-income Latino workers or "average" students entering the ranks of AP classes.

Parochialism—or worse, selfishness—is inevitable when we create entrenched communities of abundance and communities of need. Citizens in their individual localities are motivated to maximize benefits for their own community and to limit fiscal burdens by denying access to populations and land uses that they perceive as undesirable. This fiscal and social defensiveness is heightened when the bulwark is being raised against a heavily poor and heavily black community that may be miles away but can still loom large as a potential threat to the status quo. In one opinion survey, for example, residents of upper- and middle-class suburbs of Philadelphia ranked "maintenance of their community's social characteristics"—defined as "keeping out 'undesirables' and maintaining the 'quality of residents'"—as a more important objective for their local governments than providing public services or maintaining low tax rates.[1] New suburbia holds dear the tools of exclusion. Those devices that control social access and quality of life "become the issues over which suburbanites fight most vehemently"—issues that challenge most directly the citizens' perceived way of life, such as busing, public housing, zoning, and efforts to require a sharing of tax-base wealth.[2]

The bulwark mentality explains why the black middle-class residents of Mitchellville and Lake Arbor in Prince George's County do not want lower-income kids from nearby Landover attending their new high school. It explains why a state court had to intervene and order a complete moratorium on any new development in the city of Folsom, California—an affluent suburb of Sacramento where the famous Folsom prison also happens to be located—before the city would comply with a state law that required the city to plan for its fair share of affordable housing units. It explains why it took twenty-six years of legal struggle and a landmark state supreme court decision before Ethel Lawrence and the NAACP in Mount Laurel, New Jersey, were permitted to build a modest apartment complex for low- and moderate-income black people, even though Ms. Lawrence's roots in the community spanned seven generations.[3] In sum, no group that benefits from exclusion is going to give up that advantage without a fight. Homogeneous communities are also relatively unwilling to enter into cooperative arrangements with other communities that differ socioeconomically.[4]

In order to understand how separatism corrodes political discourse and limits our capacity for shared sacrifice, we should examine how race and class separation has colored state politics, national elections, and policy debates.

State Politics and the Dominance of the White Suburban Voter

At the state level, the horizontal competition for limited resources that goes on between communities of abundance and communities of need has distinct political consequences. As Richard Child Hill, a political scientist and close observer of metropolitan inequality, once aptly argued, embedded in our political culture is a bias—a set of institutional rules of the game—that frequently benefits middle-class suburbanites at the expense of others. "Residential segregation by class and race shapes interaction patterns, friendship ties, marital selection, and social consciousness. The distribution of income and residential location shapes political relationships between collectivities with discordant interests and creates differential access to public goods and services."[5] Or as Margaret Weir, another scholar of metropolitan politics, has argued, we have a "new political geography of growing suburban strength and declining urban power" in state legislatures, which now respond to an "increasingly entrenched and narrow" set of suburban interests. As a result, Democrats in the Illinois legislature who were once sympathetic to the concerns of urban residents "now agree to push costs back down" to the city of Chicago in order to win suburban votes. At the same time, legislators act to the detriment of inner-ring "collar counties," the suburban communities of yesteryear, which struggle to raise revenue to serve fast-growing school-age populations.[6] "State politics," then, "are increasingly driven by a suburban-based politics of 'defensive localism' that seeks to limit State action in addressing urban economic and social problems."[7] In this scenario, cities and many older suburbs are in the same boat. They both suffer in a state political economy that increasingly responds to more affluent suburban interests.

When it comes to allocating education aid, for example, middle- and upper-class suburban communities often have decisive influence. Our separated condition seems to play out most frequently in state budget fights about education. All fifty states have faced the issue of unequal funding of rich and poor school districts. In about forty-five states, citizens of poor school districts have brought class actions in state courts seeking more funding. In all states, legislatures have struggled over the issue. Ostensibly, these fights pit "suburban whites" against "poor urban blacks" or other racial minorities. The affluent suburban bastions fight to avoid higher state income taxes and to spend their local funds on their schools, whereas urban school districts fight for as much as they can get from state taxpayers. Voters perceive these fights in such raw terms, and therefore many state legislators view the push to equalize school funding as a political nonstarter. Political jurisdictions separated by race and class reflect this schism, and elected officials often must respond to specific niches with seemingly antithetical interests. When state legislatures have tried to resolve inequities in school funding in the absence of a court order, they have not succeeded; their school finance reforms have not equalized funding between affluent and poor districts. In fact, some legislatures, under the guise of school finance reform, have actually left poor school districts worse off by effecting a net reduction in their funding.[8]

State legislatures have repeatedly shown themselves to be incapable of developing an effective *political* solution to the problem of school inequality, and suburban voters are the chief obstacle.[9] Even when state courts order state legislators to "fix the problem" of unequal public education, as has happened in about twenty states, the legislators have difficulty meeting the mark because of political resistance by suburban voters. At least one researcher has argued that equalization efforts, even court-ordered ones, have often left poor districts worse off than before.[10]

New Jersey provides a good example of this intractable politics. In 1973, the New Jersey Supreme Court first declared in the case of *Robinson v. Cahill* that the state's system of school funding was unconstitutional because it violated the state constitution's requirement that each child be afforded a "thorough

and efficient education." Thirty years and some twelve lawsuits later, the state and its citizens are still struggling to give
meaning to this edict for all of its children, especially those in
poorer school districts.

Constitutions are interesting, often inconvenient social con-
tracts. They set out in very broad terms a society's basic, invio-
lable commitments. Were it not for the fact that most state
constitutions include education clauses that require "efficient"
or "adequate" public education, state legislators would not be
on the hook for dealing with the problem of frequently stark
inequality and inadequacy in education. Unfortunately that
does not mean that the problem will be resolved effectively; it
just means that it will never completely go away, no matter
how strongly political forces are set against dealing with it.
New Jersey's elusive struggles have meant that generations of
disadvantaged children have suffered from an unequal education while the adults have squabbled. New Jersey is not any
different than other states in this regard; it has simply been
dealing with these issues longer than most.

The latest of the New Jersey Supreme Court's dozen-plus
decisions concerning school finance in the state was issued in
May of 2002, in a case called *Abbott v. Burke*. The decision is
known as *"Abbott VII"* because the plaintiffs in the case have
returned repeatedly to the courts since first filing the lawsuit
and receiving a ruling from the state Supreme Court in 1985,
known as *"Abbott I."* (Students attending schools in New Jersey's thirty poorest school districts—about 25 percent of all
public school students—are the *Abbott* plaintiffs.) In *Abbott
II,* the court established in 1990 that the legislature was obli-
gated to "assure that poorer urban districts' education funding
is substantially equal to that of property-rich districts."

The legislature responded by passing the Quality Education

Act (QEA), which contemplated immediate increases in state aid for all districts, special supplements for the poorest districts, and a slow phasing out of state aid for the wealthiest districts. The legislature also passed a $2.8 billion tax increase to pay for this new largesse. Even before the act was implemented, politics derailed it. Widespread public opposition to the QEA, the tax increases, and the prospect of increased spending for urban districts led the legislature to amend the law to reduce the tax burden and the level of education aid by $360 million.

New Jersey voters penalized those mostly Democratic politicians who tried to comply with the *Abbott* court orders. In 1990, when Democratic Governor Jim Florio proposed to increase taxes on those earning over $100,000 in order to pay for the increased state education aid for poor school districts, his popularity ratings promptly crashed by 19 percent. By 1991, many of the Democratic legislators who had supported the QEA were defeated, and Republicans gained a majority in the state legislature. Two years later, the pugnacious Florio lost his reelection bid to Republican Christine Todd Whitman, who won over most voters—and as much as a quarter of Florio's former supporters—by attacking Florio's tax increases for equalizing education spending and by promising to cut state income taxes by 30 percent. No doubt Florio suffered from an intense, transparent personal style. He boldly said to affluent people that their state could not succeed fiscally and socially if they did not pay their fair share of taxes. But this goes deeply against the grain of voter expectations.

As the new governor, Christine Todd Whitman also had to contend with the constitutional mandate. In 1994, in *Abbott III,* the court declared that the weakened QEA was not constitutionally adequate. Governor Whitman responded by proposing to increase spending for poorer districts and cut state aid to wealthier districts. Robin Hood, however, is a universally unpopular fairy tale, even when a Republican is playing the lead. Whitman's support among Republican legislative allies and wealthy suburban constituents immediately began to erode, causing her to back away from her own equity proposal. Instead she endorsed an "adequacy" measure that guaranteed a basic level of funding for all districts but ignored the court's order to equalize spending. The court declared this approach unconstitutional in 1997 in *Abbott IV*. It subsequently approved a new Whitman administration proposal (*Abbott V* in 1998), only to be dragged back into the battle when the plaintiffs claimed that the state had failed to live up to certain commitments in its own proposal. The court agreed, issuing yet another order in *Abbott VI* in 2000. Things looked particularly promising in 2002, when the new governor, Democrat Jim McGreevey, established the Abbott Implementation and Compliance Coordinating Council to implement the reforms required by the court. The council included top state officials as well as a representative of the Abbott plaintiffs, who applauded the move at the time. However, in the face of revenue shortfalls and the state's reluctance to raise taxes, the council split, and the plaintiffs are now arguing that current state plans will eliminate and weaken programs that are critical to the poor school districts. The saga continues—only with hard economic times the tensions and challenges are even more difficult. In 2002, New Jersey experienced its largest revenue shortfall since World War II—a $5 billion deficit—with similar deficits projected for 2003.[11]

Similar political resistance and backsliding occurs in other states. Voters in advantaged school districts will almost always fight to repeal or weaken any effort that has the effect of raising their taxes or reducing funding for their own schools. In Vermont, equity funding reforms were enacted in 1997 pursuant to a Vermont Supreme Court mandate. One of those reforms required affluent school districts to contribute some of their tax revenue to a "sharing pool," which would in turn be distributed to poorer school districts. It quickly became known as the "shark pool" among its opponents. Among the strategies opponents undertook to evade it were lawsuits, civil disobedience, and the establishment of private foundations. Governor Howard Dean saw his approval ratings drop dramatically as a result of signing the equity funding law. Although Dean survived a 2000 election challenge from a Republican who made equity funding a central issue, Dean was moved to propose eliminating the sharing pool, and Republicans, who gained a majority in the Vermont House, promptly introduced legislation to eliminate it. The Democratic Senate proposed to give wealthy districts more time to phase in the sharing pool, and the failure to reach a compromise meant that the provision was not scuttled and the battle for its repeal would be put off until another day.[12]

A similar law popularly known as "Robin Hood" has come under assault in Texas. The law requires the sharing of the tax revenues of wealthier districts with poorer districts. Citizens in wealthy school districts have filed lawsuits challenging the law, and state legislators have introduced bills to repeal it. In Ohio, even the state supreme court seemed to be cowed by public opinion against resolving the problem of unequal education funding. Three years after announcing in 1997 that the state's education finance system was unconstitutional due to "[v]ast wealth-based disparities among Ohio's schools [that] deprive many of Ohio's public school students of high quality educational opportunities," the court retreated, citing "the necessity of sacrificing our opinions sometimes to the opinions of others for the sake of harmony."[13] It revived its concern about the constitutional adequacy of the legislature's response in 2002, only to declare the case closed in May of 2003. The *Columbus Dispatch,* whose editorial pages were very outspoken against the plaintiffs, proudly noted that "in the standoff between the legislature and the court over school funding, public opinion has been solidly on the side of the legislature." The *Dispatch* pointed out that voters didn't vote out "recalcitrant lawmakers for failing to obey the court's demand for a systematic overhaul of school funding," didn't vote for the gubernatorial candidate who promised to follow the court's prescriptions for school funding, and that they instead voted in a new state supreme court justice who would likely form a new majority on this issue.[14]

Such back and forth between courts and recalcitrant legislatures and voters has led one researcher who has analyzed school finance reforms in all fifty states to conclude that the state portion of school funding "is primarily a function of the distribution of political power in the state." An "inequitable equilibrium" tends to prevail in which wealthy school districts are permitted, even at lower tax rates, to spend more money per pupil than poor districts. An outside event such as a court ruling may upset this equilibrium for a brief period, but over time, the inequitable equilibrium is likely to return.[15]

A cynic might point out to the citizens of advantaged school districts that tax-base sharing or the milder redistribution of diverting state, as opposed to local, revenue toward needy school districts and away from wealthy ones is a small price to pay for the advantage of homogeneity. Were such voters and citizens offered the choice of opening up their schools or their neighborhoods to poor minorities as opposed to sharing the tax burden of paying for the high costs of trying to make all schools equal, I suspect many would choose the latter. And yet that, too, is an elusive goal. As I have attempted to show in earlier chapters, the costs and consequences of concentrated minority poverty are such that integration is actually our best, if not our only, hope of developing a cohesive society with equal opportunity for all. Parochialism inhibits us from seeing that possibility, however.

Race and class divisions also divert us from pursuing a common, greater good. Although poor minorities are most in need of strong public schools that will improve their skills and life opportunities, they are most likely to get the opposite: weak, underfunded schools with fewer strong teachers. As William Julius Wilson has argued, a vicious circle inhibits effective solutions. Because of poor schools, the relative skills of minority kids relegated to poor urban neighborhoods do not improve, which exacerbates the problems of unemployment and decay associated with the neighborhoods they live in. This result, in turn, heightens race and class conflict because it reinforces white voters' stereotypes about racial minorities.[16] Whites are more apt to blame black people for the inequality they experience, citing their "lack of motivation." Latinos, on the other hand, are considered by whites as less well off because they have "no chance for education."[17] Apparently, many whites are blind to the gaps of opportunity that exist for black people, seeing only the end result that such gaps of opportunity create. And they are most likely to ascribe this end result to "a lack of motivation." In their eyes, such "unmotivated" folks are not worthy of taxpayers' money.

In sum, race and class segregation alters not just opportunity in America; it alters politics. Among the races in America, whites on average live the most insular existence, and they tend to dominate the outcome of most policy debates in a way that reflects their insulated perspective. Blacks, Latinos, and Asians experience a more diverse America, but their political voices are not being marshaled or heard in a way that can counter white suburban hegemony. To the extent that our settlement patterns lean heavily toward separate enclaves, it is difficult to form political coalitions across boundaries of race, class, and culture. Our separated life circumstances and perspectives also contribute to class conflict—a social gulf that is increasingly reflected in electoral politics.

National Politics and the Fragmented Electorate

The 2000 election illustrated just how divided the American electorate is. We are a "50–50 nation." The red and blue of the electoral map mirrors our division. Geography and demographics can be close predictors of electoral leanings. Predominately white, high-growth communities have tended toward the Republican column, although this bias may be changing in the Northeast where affluent suburbanites alienated by Republican social conservatism have migrated away from the party.[18] Predominately black or minority communities lean heavily Democratic. Such polarization is exacerbated by the political gerrymandering that occurs whenever state and federal legislative districts are redrawn. Both Republicans and Democrats tend to produce overwhelmingly "safe" seats for their own incumbents when their parties have control over the redistricting process. There are now about 400 such safe seats in Congress. With such targeted districting, the main threat to any incumbent is typically during a political primary rather than a general election. Incumbents are more apt to play to the activist wings of their respective parties, producing ideological extremes and little incentive to compromise on the part of those who must govern.[19]

The geographic and ideological drifting apart of the right and left flanks of the major parties means that national political aspirants must look to an ever narrowing slice of undecided voters to expand their base—voters who tend to populate older, struggling, or developing bedroom suburbs. Most of these voters are middle-income whites who, like other Americans, have bought into the psychology of the bulwark. The blue-collar working-class or striving middle-class communities that constitute "swing districts" may identify culturally with their wealthier suburban cousins, but they actually have more in common with reliably Democratic communities. These communities face the challenges of a stagnant tax base, overcrowded schools, or a poverty creep that comes with an influx of lower-income people hoping for a better life and greater opportunities.[20] Since the mid-nineties, however, white working-class voters have been migrating to the Republican Party.[21]

These voters hold the balance in national elections. In the 1990s it was all too easy for presidential candidates to woo them with rhetoric and policies that played heavily, if not solely, to their interests. Today, the geographic separation of American voters makes it increasingly difficult for a candidate to pursue an inclusive politics that speaks to the needs of everyone. The end result is "niche" or "entitlement" politics. The same companies that offer market profiles of neighborhoods, like Claritas, now offer ever more sophisticated data on the elusive swing voter to political campaigns.

If the logic of the marketers is to be believed, the Nascar and office park dads have replaced the soccer moms of the 1990s as the most cherished undecided voter to woo. The "swing voter" is a white suburban guy who is middle class, home centered, and without strong ties to either party. The Democratic Party has been losing its grip on this group because these voters pay attention to social issues and values— like guns, God, and (no) gays. The Republicans have done a better job of exploiting the social issues these swing voters care about.

Facing such a fragmented electorate, the national political aspirant must choose or vacillate between shoring up the base and wooing independents. Doing both is increasingly difficult as messages and policies tailored to excite the base can conflict with those that might appeal to uncommitted independent voters. Both Bill Clinton in the 1990s and George W. Bush in the 2000s became masters at "triangulation"—a term invented by Bill Clinton's chief political strategist, Dick Morris, in the wake of the 1994 Republican takeover of the House of Representatives. Morris advised Clinton to distinguish himself from both congressional Republicans and Democrats by pursuing an aggressively centrist political agenda that would emphasize values and resonate with mostly suburban swing voters. Clinton succeeded in getting reelected in 1996 by focusing on symbolic, centrist measures like school uniforms, V-chips to enable parents to control television content, and welfare reform. The Republicans, however, have traditionally *embraced* their hard-core activists, especially religious conservatives who care deeply about social issues like fighting abortion and gay marriage. The Democrats, especially in the 1990s, have been more apt to take their activists for granted and focus on wooing moderate suburban voters. The disturbing result of both tactics is that neither party has attempted to forge a politics premised on true inclusion and the common interests of all Americans. Nor have Republicans or Democrats given dominant suburban voters any reason to feel that they need to contribute to or be a part of larger society.

The Triangulation of Bill Clinton

Bill Clinton certainly felt pressure to attract the suburban white vote. One way he accomplished this was to pursue punitive policies toward the most disenfranchised. As a candidate in 1992, he established his bona fides with suburban voters by supporting the death penalty and promising to "end welfare as we know it." In anticipation of his 1996 bid for reelection, he signed a welfare reform law that many of his own policy advisors believed was unnecessarily punitive toward the poor. During his eight years in office, he oversaw the addition of fifty new death penalties to the federal penal code and the largest expansion of the prison population in American history. Although Clinton was touted by Toni Morrison in the *New Yorker* as "the first black President," a disproportionate number of these new prisoners were African Americans.[22]

Without question, poor Americans and racial minorities benefited from numerous policies of the Clinton administration. My point is that Clinton felt compelled to pursue other, more punitive policies in an effort to convince suburban white voters that he was a Democrat who could be trusted to govern. My first personal encounter with Clinton's racial triangulation was in the first month of his presidency. I had been working in the White House only a few weeks, assigned as an elbow person to Gene Sperling, the peripatetic, brilliant economic policy advisor who would eventually head Clinton's economic policy team. I was new to this crowd. I had not earned my stripes in Little Rock working on the campaign, and I struggled to absorb and understand the culture and vocabulary the Clintonites had developed to manage the delicate Democratic coalition.

Those first few months were a roller-coaster ride. The first week of Clinton's presidency, the issue of gays in the military hit the fan. Within days of that controversy, Clinton made a speech reasserting his intention to "end welfare as we know it." The timing was useful, if not intentional. It helped to assuage swing voters who might have been upset by Clinton's embrace of gay rights. I recall the deep ambivalence I felt when, at George Stephanopoulos's daily communication meeting, the press office announced that Clinton's speech on welfare reform had been very well received. The heavily thirty-something crowd cheered. Everyone praised Bruce Reed for the job he had done on the speech. Reed, a master of political rhetoric and centrist policy, would ultimately become Clinton's chief domestic policy advisor.

For me, one of the relatively few black people in the room, it was a minor "Sister Souljah moment." I did not doubt the sincerity of Reed's or Clinton's view that welfare dependency was harmful to low-income families. But the speech and its timing resonated with me the same way the Sister Souljah incident had. In that incident, candidate Clinton attacked as racially divisive statements made by Souljah, an African American writer, activist, and rapper who tends to offer opinions that spark controversy. In a May 1992 interview conducted in the wake of the L.A. riots, Souljah was quoted in the *Washington Post* as saying: "If black people kill black people every day, why not have a week and kill white people?" The quote was later reproduced out of context and widely criticized in the media. When Clinton appeared in June 1992 before the Rainbow Coalition National Convention, the day after Souljah had also appeared before this forum, he used this highly publicized moment, rather than a private one, to chastise his hosts, including Jesse Jackson Sr., for playing host to Souljah. It felt like a sucker punch, calculated expressly for white voters. At the time, reporters, Representative Charles Rangel of New York, and even Republicans perceived it as such. The term "Sister Souljah moment" subsequently entered the political lexicon to connote an instance where a politician publicly repudiates an "extremist" in order to appear "centrist," especially in the minds of white voters.

Even as I revered Clinton, I would have more moments of deep ambivalence about his pandering during his presidency. When Clinton failed to stick by his nominee for the Department of Justice's Civil Rights Division, Lani Guinier, after this accomplished African American law professor and civil rights lawyer was unfairly and inaccurately labeled a "quota queen" by right-wing conservatives, all I could think of was how resolutely President George H. W. Bush had stuck by Clarence Thomas. But black people identified with Bill Clinton, and the president likely understood that he had a great deal of capital to expend with this community and that symbolic politics was sometimes necessary to get elected and to get things done. He even admitted as much once in a meeting with black ministers. During his second term, when a crime bill that added many new death penalties for federal crimes was being hotly debated, Clinton was challenged in a meeting with prominent black clergy to defend his support for the bill. According to one minister present, Clinton responded by saying that where the death penalty had been available in the past for federal crimes, rarely had anyone committing such crimes actually been executed. And he complained aloud that if he did not sign the bill, he would be painted as soft on crime, "which would undermine everything I am trying to do for African Americans." His audience was placated.[23]

In some ways I "felt Clinton's pain," to borrow his campaign rhetoric. After three years of working as a policy staffer in the White House, I came to understand intimately the challenge of "speaking American," with a political rhetoric that resonates broadly, while also pursuing policies that could make a difference in the lives of people who were very marginalized.[24] Clinton did it mainly by stealth. It was not until he was leaving his presidency that he broadly advertised his progressive record, one that included expanding the earned income tax credit for low-income working families, a new health care program for poor children, the doubling of Head Start and school aid for the disadvantaged, and an increase in college tuition assistance for low- and moderate-income students, all of which amounted to $64 billion in new aid being channeled annually to working-class and poor families.[25] And as Democrats who actually gave a damn about the plight of places like South Central L.A., we also pursued community revitalization and community development programs designed to help local citizens create jobs and hope. Yet these relatively modest efforts could not counter the tide of other federal policies that encouraged and even subsidized greater suburbanization and separation. Not surprisingly, any serious, forthright discussion or efforts to go against that tide were often stymied or whittled down enough so that no real change would occur. I recall the derision with which HUD Secretary Henry Cisneros's efforts to break up concentrations of race and poverty were met by some within the White House. That, too, was part of the struggle to appeal to suburban voters.

In the 2000s, the Democratic Party continues to struggle with the dilemma of a fragmented electorate. It is uncomfortable with its traditional base. The party establishment and the "centrists" of the Democratic Leadership Council fear progressive politics and fight with the "insurgents" about the best strategy for winning elections. Every election cycle, a Democratic presidential candidate must straddle a widening social gulf created by our separatism. More than ever, the party's traditional base needs to coalesce and fight to counter a political dynamic that responds to a small slice of the electorate—in the case of the Bush administration, an increasingly affluent slice. Nothing will change, however, without a renewed activism, indeed a movement, on the part of those who suffer under our current plutocratic course. To be a party that consistently wins elections and governs effectively, we need a rhetoric and policies that appeal to the vast middle class of all hues. We need a coherent agenda of inclusion, articulated passionately and forthrightly, aimed at bringing all people and all races along.

The Triangulation of George W. Bush

An inclusive agenda is decidedly not the politics we have today. In fact, the policy decisions of the current Republican administration amount to class warfare. They harm the great swath of people in the middle, most of whom are also suburban and white, for the benefit of the affluent. The Republican leadership, both in the White House and in Congress, increasingly pursues policies that reflect the desires of the GOP's affluent fund-raisers. But even George W. Bush cannot afford to ignore moderates or emerging minority groups. Bush triangulates as well, maybe even better than Clinton did. To the consternation of some Republican activists, Bush offers up "compassionate conservatism" to moderates and independents. He successfully championed a Medicare prescription drug benefit in 2003 with a price tag of $400 billion and conceded in 2004 that it will actually cost over $530 billion. But his "compassion" is limited. His pledge to fight AIDS in Africa is not fully funded. His worker visas for illegal immigrants are temporary. And the prescription drug benefit has been highly criticized for not helping the neediest seniors.

At the same time, Bush serves up red meat conservatism to the right wing of his party, offering them extreme ideological judicial appointees, consistent opposition to abortion, a proposed constitutional amendment to ban gay marriage, and large tax cuts. Bush, like other adherents of a "southern strategy," exploits racial symbols. As a presidential candidate in 2000, when asked whether the Confederate flag should continue to fly over the South Carolina capitol dome, Bush said it was a "right of the state" to decide what to do, or to use the historical code for Republican nods to southern racial relativism, it was a matter of "states' rights." (On the question whether same sex couples should be allowed to marry, clearly Bush is not content to let the states decide, showing that claimed concerns with "states rights" often mask other substantive ends.) As president, he opposed affirmative action at the University of Michigan, calling it a "quota system"— another code word that has historically been used by conservative politicians to exploit racial divisions and cultivate white voters. In January 2004, Bush laid a wreath at Dr. Martin Luther King's grave to honor his birthday, and the very next day he used his recess-appointment powers to place the highly controversial district judge Charles W. Pickering Sr. on the federal appeals court. Pickering, you may recall, once advocated from the bench for the reduction of the sentence of a man convicted of burning a cross near an interracial couple's home.[26]

In my view, President George W. Bush's successful pursuit of tax policies that greatly favor affluent voters is part of the same niche politics of catering heavily to an insulated suburban electorate. What is shocking, however, is how extreme this agenda has become. The party that long ago was associated with fiscal responsibility is now most profligate, pursuing an "un-tax and spend" course that has resulted in more class inequality, less opportunity, and sprawling budget deficits that risk the security of future generations. The class divisions reflected in these policies, which Republicans assiduously attempt to hide, are reminiscent of the gilded age of plutocracy.

The mendacity surrounding the tax cut debates was especially wretched. When George W. Bush was running for president, he campaigned on a platform of cutting taxes. Those who had the temerity to point out that the cuts he proposed would put us back on a course of deficit spending were accused by Bush of using "fuzzy math." Since taking office, Bush pushed through tax cuts in 2001, 2002, and 2003, all of which mostly benefit the wealthy. In the process, he took us from a position of a healthy $127 billion budget surplus in 2001 to a deficit of $521 billion for fiscal year 2004, according to his own budget projections—the largest deficit in U.S. history in absolute terms. Bush achieved this startling reversal of our fiscal fortunes in part by positing several faulty fiscal assumptions. With the first round of tax cuts he projected budget surpluses that never materialized to help pay for the cuts. And he projected deep spending cuts that the administration could not realistically expect Congress to enact. He has also made all the tax cuts temporary in order to minimize their projected costs, though the administration fully expects that future Congresses will make them permanent.

The opportunity to use the actual budget surpluses available in January 2001 to begin to solve the looming long-term fiscal problems haunting Social Security and Medicare was frittered away. (The projected unfinanced liabilities hanging over both of these programs now total $25 trillion, but that doesn't seem to matter. Today's children, or maybe their children, will be the ones paying this gigantic bill.) Then came September 11, a weak economy that followed the bursting of the tech bubble, and the costs and consequences of an Iraq war of our own making. The total costs of the tax cuts enacted since 2001 are projected to exceed $2 trillion over the decade, assuming they remain temporary. If they are made permanent, the ten-year budgetary costs of these tax cuts will rise to $4 trillion.[27] These three successive tax cuts are projected to leave middle-income taxpayers paying a greater share of all federal taxes by the end of the decade. The very wealthiest Americans—those earning $337,000 or more per year—will be the greatest beneficiaries of these cuts.[28] By way of example, "Bloomberg News calculated that under the Bush-Cheney tax cut proposal, President [Bush] would have gotten about a $44,500 tax cut, based on his last year's income, while Vice President Cheney would have saved $107,000 in taxes."[29] For more than half of all taxpayers, however, the cuts translate to less than $120 per year over the next two years. More than a third of taxpayers will receive no benefit. Meanwhile, payroll taxes, which pose the heaviest tax burden for most working families have been left untouched even as the top marginal income tax rate, the capital-gains tax, and the dividend tax have been reduced.[30]

The saddest part about this total of $2 trillion in tax cuts enacted in two and a half years is not that they wiped out budget surpluses and brought us the largest budget deficits in American history. The saddest part is that we missed opportunities to address our long-term fiscal liabilities, to give real attention to job creation, and to address serious domestic security challenges while also unnecessarily exacerbating wealth and income inequality in the process. To what end? The old-line logic of conservatives is that tax cuts and budget deficits are necessary to choke off revenues to a bloated government bureaucracy. This was certainly the theory animating the Reagan tax cuts of the early 1980s. By the time George W. Bush took office, however, the Clinton administration had already reduced the federal bureaucracy to its smallest size in a generation. Something more seems to animate the logic of this Bush White House. To this outsider, it seems like an unrepentant fealty to the friends and family that financed the election. Certainly that is the picture that former Treasury Secretary Paul O'Neill paints; he claims that when he challenged the wisdom of large tax cuts that would produce fiscally irresponsible budget deficits, the answer from political advisor Karl Rove was that the Bush administration should "stick to principle" or as Vice President Cheney reportedly put it: "Reagan proved deficits don't matter. We won the midterms. This is our due."[31]

The Bush administration's playing to narrow niches—primarily corporations and the very wealthy—is evident in a kind of bait-and-switch politics and rhetoric. Farm subsidies that overwhelmingly benefit large agribusiness are painted as necessary to prop up the small farmer. Repealing the estate tax, conveniently renamed the "death tax" by Republican pollsters, is painted as saving the family farm, even as only about 2 percent of people who die—the super-wealthy—actually pay the tax.[32] In a plutocratic nation, the interests of the wealthy and the large private corporations and institutions that shape markets are pursued to the detriment of everyone else. We are essentially there. In the early 2000s, there was very little in the way of government action as news of corporate malfeasance filled the airways. The Sarbanes-Oxley Act, which holds management accountable for fraudulent corporate accounting, was a notable exception. Corporate tax loopholes go unclosed, even as corporations benefit from a repeal of a tax on dividends.

Meanwhile, the pressures of globalization are now bearing down on professional and information workers as well as blue-collar ones. And as a professor of economics at Yale University recently observed, "As Americans increasingly compete in a world market, there is a serious risk that their jobs will be given to people overseas and their incomes will drop precipitously—producing sudden profit opportunities for other Americans and creating sharp increases in inequality here."[33]

In the latest recession, it was white-collar workers who seriously felt the pinch of long-term unemployment. In this environment, government has a role to play in expanding opportunity to everyone, in making the dream of a college education possible for the poor, working, and middle classes, in cultivating a tone of mutual respect and civility, and in promoting an inclusive ethos of a nation where we really are "all in this together." But as inequality becomes more pronounced, changing course becomes ever more difficult. Wealth and political influence go hand in hand, be it of the corporate or the individual kind.

In the current political environment, we have an increasingly shrill debate between the so-called left and right, or between so-called liberals and conservatives. I don't think it is an accident that this gulf closely mirrors race divisions. It is a fact that the conservative camp is more populated with whites and wealth and that the liberal camp is infinitely more diverse racially, if not economically.

The labels of right and left are unhelpful and do not truly represent the reality of America. Most Americans are not ideological. They get up every day, go to work, and try to do the best they can for themselves and their family. In the wake of 9/11 there was a huge opportunity for bringing together the various factions of our nation based upon our shared identity

as Americans. In the weeks following that tragedy, race relations were as good as they get in this country, unless you happened to be a Muslim or looked like an Arab. But instead of
appealing to a higher notion of shared sacrifice in the face of
enormous homeland security challenges and a weak economy,
the Republicans played to a very narrow niche.

Race and class separation prevents us from recognizing our
common destiny. Niche or entitlement politics works precisely
because those disadvantaged by such policy choices identify
with the affluent who benefit most from such choices. But to
change course we need a rhetoric that resonates with all the
folks on the negative end of such choices. At the same time, we
need to begin to acknowledge not just that our separatism is
contributing to inequality but also that it is contributing to a
loggerhead politics that makes it very difficult to do anything
about inequality.

CHAPTER 9

WHAT TO DO ABOUT IT

THIS BOOK was written for people of good will who care about how and why our society has come to be ordered on a separatist premise. I now return to why integration matters and address what we should be doing to bring about more of it. As I have explained, if we do not find ways to close the gaps of opportunity that result from race and class segregation, we risk becoming a permanently divided society of haves and have-nots—a state that is antithetical to the very core of our national values. And yet, as one social critic recently put it, "Our integration machinery is broken."[1]

In the twenty-first century, we will face a number of challenges as an emerging majority-minority nation. As I recount in the early chapters of this book, in the closing decades of the twentieth century, the primary response to exploding diversity in this nation has been one of separation along lines of race, ethnicity, and class. More pointedly, the primary response on the part of the haves—those who benefit most from homogeneous local autonomy—has been a defensive posture. They want to be shielded both from poverty and from "others" and from paying higher taxes to help address social problems elsewhere. Our tortured racial past has colored much of the public and private institutional decision making that has shaped our separated communities and schools. Since African slaves were first brought to this country in 1619, the tension between an overwhelmingly white nation and a small black minority struggling for full personhood has dominated American race relations. That black-white duality now seems anachronistic in light of the new, multihued complexion of the United States. Though the black-white racial paradigm no longer accurately reflects our demographics, the separatist tendencies of our real estate markets, and the institutional policies that gave birth to them, were created in that black-white context. The exclusionary impulse was and continues to be borne of an antipathy by many nonblacks to living among or near large numbers of black people. This holdover from a less enlightened period of race relations leaves us with an ossified, impoverished vision for American society. I submit that had we the luxury of a Rawlsian original position, or a chance to formulate anew how our neighborhoods and schools would be arranged, knowing just how diverse American society now is and will be, we would not choose our current separated way of being.

So how can we begin to put our nation on a course toward a more inclusive future? Only by forming grassroots coalitions—by doing the hard work of building relationships across boundaries of difference—will we jettison the existing institutional tendencies that pull us apart. There *are* revolutionary possibilities, policy directions, and concrete strategies that have transformative potential and that would offer all Americans more choices. But they all depend upon Americans under-

standing and embracing the need for race and class inclusion—
an education process that should be an integral part of our
efforts to form grassroots coalitions.

Why Integration? Why Inclusion?

We could give up on integration altogether. Some would argue
that living among people of different races, ethnicities, or
classes is antithetical to human nature, that we all simply prefer to stick with our own kind. And yet people do it, some
eagerly, when given a viable option and a degree of comfort,
that is, a context where their identity group is present in
enough numbers that they have a say in how the community is
run. Despite the enormous challenges, I have come to the conclusion that cultivating race and class integration, especially of
the institutions that define social mobility—like schools, universities, and the workplace—and building coalitions of
enlightened self-interest across boundaries of homogeneity are
the only route to creating the kind of fully democratic society
we imagine our very diverse country to be. Integration is critical to the enduring strength of our democracy. The majority-
minority America that is to come cannot prosper with a system
of public education that relegates most minority public school
children to schools disadvantaged by high degrees of poverty
and often inadequate resources. Ordinary Americans who cannot afford to pay for the exclusive track, or the private one,
also will not prosper in a separated society that is not fundamentally committed to bringing all communities and all people
along. This is especially so with an economy that is increasingly unforgiving of those who do not acquire "knowledge-
job" skills, skills that will not become obsolete.

Our critical challenge is to transcend a system where protection of the interests we individually hold most dear—family and property—seems to require choosing homogeneity or separation from the risks associated with the racial and economic "other." We live our lives in a system that forces separation, and yet we hunger for a saner existence and a better quality of life. Most of us recognize, at least intellectually, our mutual interdependence with people and communities that differ from our own, yet we are at a loss as to how we, as individuals, can do anything differently without making personal sacrifices that seem too great. Our greatest loss in a separated nation is a sense of shared community. We are all in the same national boat, but in a separatist nation we are forced to focus on making sure the individual boat we are sailing in doesn't sink.

Our nation's founders intuited that any successful ordering of society must be premised upon the individual pursuit of self-interest. Integration is in the enlightened self-interest of all Americans, for two reasons. First, only a relatively small minority of affluent people who face no barriers regarding where to live or where to go to school are benefiting from separatism. As one critic of our current, exclusionary system of public education recently argued, it is hard to imagine how any publicly financed system of schools can any longer be called democratic if it limits the opportunity to choose a good school only to families with the means to pay the high cost of buying a new home in an exclusive neighborhood.[2] Second, for the remaining majority of Americans, our separatism results in stratospheric costs and rampant inequality. In other words, to eradicate the root causes of the heavy costs we all bear, we must necessarily attack the "hard" issue of race and class segregation. Separation is not in our collective self-interest, and integration—efforts to reduce such separation—will benefit everyone. We must stop operating at the margins if we are to realize our full potential as a nation. Let's take one last, close look at both the costs and the hard issue underlying our segregated society.

Stratospheric Costs: A Recap

In Part II of this book I attempted to elucidate the costs of race and class separation. I chose to do this primarily by comparing the opposing realities of middle-class white and middle-class black suburban communities in order to highlight the surprising ways in which separation of African Americans into their own communities, even those who ostensibly have "made it," creates inequality. I also underscored the considerable costs to whites, especially those who are not affluent, of race and class separation. This pointed focus on the costs to whites was intentional. Whites, on average, live the most racially insulated lives. They are the segment of society most prone, in my view, to misapprehending the consequences of our separatist course; they are more likely to fail to perceive the palpable costs *to themselves* of separation, even as they accept and contribute to a separatist logic. I do not mean to suggest, however, that Asians, Latinos, Native Americans, or any other racial or ethnic group do not also bear the costs of separation. We all do. Finally, in Part II, I addressed the costs to individuals and to society as a whole of separate schools and of the black ghetto. My conclusions, summarized here, demonstrate that everyone suffers in a system where job growth, property wealth, excellent public schools, and attractive commercial amenities are concentrated in the few favored quadrants of the American metropolis:

People who cannot afford to buy their way into favored communities and/or are steered elsewhere because of their race

or ethnicity suffer the costs of exclusion, including longer commutes, fewer job prospects, and narrower life chances that
result from weaker schools and hence poorer job preparation.
They also endure the costs that favored communities foist
upon less-advantaged tax and fee payers in the form of subsidies for new, outer suburban development and in the social
costs of carrying more than their fair share of affordable housing and poor people. Racial minorities, who suffer doubly
from racial discrimination and class exclusion, bear the heaviest burdens. The black middle class, in particular, faces a
dilemma in choosing between advantaged majority-white communities and majority-black communities that offer psychic
benefits but carry a heavy burden of proximity to the minority
poor.

Society as a whole endures the consequences of creating
separated communities of abundance and communities of
need. By concentrating public and private resources and civic
energy in communities that need it the least, we create large
gaps of inequality *and* undermine the possibilities for amelio-
rating its effects.

Those who can afford it pay a steep premium in the form of
housing costs for predominately white, affluent neighborhoods, which equate to a gold standard of quality that is difficult for others to attain. In metropolitan areas with large black
populations, like Washington, D.C., this premium can be as
much as $300,000. For many whites and others in search of
"good" public schools, these costs are prohibitive, requiring
both parents to work full-time, and limiting them from choosing alternative, saner lifestyles. Such expensive neighborhoods
are also out of reach for most single parents.

People who lack confidence in public schools, primarily
because they are heavily minority, heavily poor, and/or lack

quality teachers and sufficient resources, endure the cost of private school tuition, if they can afford it. In large urban school systems populated with large numbers of poor children, many parents feel they have no choice but to pay this cost as insurance against the risk of their child being left behind. Those who live in large urban school districts also indirectly bear the cost of concentrated minority poverty in schools and neighborhoods, in the form of the higher taxes that come with higher educational challenges and social service burdens.

People of all races and classes suffer the anxieties of living in a society premised upon there being "winners" and "losers." In a rapidly diversifying America, the obsession with securing housing in "safe" communities and gaining access to the best public schools is felt so acutely precisely because society is not fundamentally committed to bringing all children and all communities along. In a separatist system that sets up winner and loser communities, winner and loser schools, and even winner and loser classes within schools, those in the middle of the income spectrum, especially, have to work harder and harder to get into or stay in the winner column.

Separation of people into different socioeconomic environments also has a withering impact on our daily quality of life. Especially for those who are advancing the suburban frontier, it results in more traffic congestion, air pollution, environmental degradation, loss of open space, deaths from auto accidents, as well as waste of existing, underutilized sewers, utilities, and schools in central cities and older suburbs. Because of our insistence on separating different types of people and differing uses of land, many spend anywhere from one to three hours each day driving to and from work, not to mention constant driving for other daily needs and desires—school, shopping, entertainment—in our car-dependent, inefficiently designed suburbs.

The ultimate cost of this car-dependent existence may be the loss of time with friends or family. We also lose the sense of community and social contact that comes with denser development, in which people of all kinds live close together.

Our separated schools also impose heavy social costs. Seven out of ten black and Latino public school students attend schools that are predominately minority. Eight out of ten white children attend schools that are predominately white. The growing resegregation of American schools means that the average experience for white public school students is a middle-class one, whereas the average experience for black and Latino children is one of high or concentrated poverty. In addition to the increased financial and social costs that come with educating minority children in a high-poverty context, this separatism contributes to an achievement gap on the part of black and Latino students that society also ultimately pays for. Children of color are our fastest-growing resource. In their lifetimes, they will become a majority or a large plurality of the adult workforce. By failing to provide them with a meaningful shot at a world-class education, we lose not just their full human potential but also bear the social costs of these children falling behind, especially in the case of young black males, who are now statistically more likely to end up in the criminal justice system than in higher education.

Poor blacks are the only demographic group in the United States that are subjected to "hypersegregation." Those poor blacks who are relegated to extremely isolated black communities, often characterized by intense poverty, bear the heaviest costs of separatism. They typically endure a violent alternative culture and a social distress that even the most ambitious would find hard to overcome. More pointedly, society also pays dearly for creating and maintaining black ghettos.

Beyond the direct financial costs of such social distress, beyond higher tax rates and crime and lowered school performance, ghetto neighborhoods create a perception of danger that middle-class people, particularly those with children, view as untenable. The ghetto has given impetus to white and middle-class flight, inhibiting the viability and stability of cities and some older suburbs. Worse, ghetto life contributes mightily to racial stereotyping and fear of black people and to class conflicts within the black community that inhibit collective action. Had we not intentionally created high-poverty black ghettos, I believe we would not have such stark divisions of figurative and actual life space in the United States.

Separatism also wreaks havoc on our ability to relate to the "other." Those who avoid an inclusive milieu will pay a price in the bewilderingly diverse future: the panic and fear experienced with involuntary encounters with difference. The specter of fear, discomfort, unfamiliarity, and risk—real or imagined—will be ever present for those who have not learned to relate to people who actually may not be that different from themselves.

Finally, race and class separation has contributed to a divisive, loggerhead politics, one where geographic advantage and disadvantage heavily correlate with one's partisan tendencies. State politics, in particular, is increasingly driven by suburban-based interests that seek to limit any action that might redress urban social problems, such as school inequality. Cities and older suburbs alike suffer in a state political economy that increasingly responds to the needs of affluent suburban communities. Because we tend to live in political jurisdictions that differ by race and class, elected officials often respond to specific niches with seemingly antithetical interests. As a result, it is very difficult to form a broad political consensus for anything approaching mutual responsibility or pursuit of a common, greater good.

I hope that this detailed recitation of the costs to individuals and society of race and class separation will help contribute to a new debate about the consequences of separatism. Everyone's quality of life is degraded by separatism. Worse, through separation and segregation we are institutionalizing and perpetuating inequality, to our national detriment.

Attacking the Hard Issue

The stratospheric costs we are enduring, individually and collectively, as a result of race and class separation reflect our failure to deal with the truly hard questions left over from the civil rights movement. The civil rights movement largely stopped once the barriers of formal Jim Crow segregation were dismantled. With the passage of the Civil Rights Act of 1964, the Voting Rights Act of 1965, and the Fair Housing Act of 1968, governments, government-funded institutions, and private actors in certain circumstances (those who affect interstate commerce) were barred, in theory, from discriminating on the basis of race, ethnicity, national origin, or religion (later, the classifications of age, sex, and disability were added as well). Discrimination in housing, education, employment, public accommodations, transportation, and voting was declared illegal. Although this delegitimation of discrimination was the chief success of the civil rights movement, we never reached any national consensus on barring *economic* segregation. In fact, economic segregation is perfectly legal in most states, and there are no federal laws barring economic discrimination in housing. At the same time, we also never reached any social consensus about whether integration of the races and classes—that is, the sharing of neighborhoods, schools, and life space—

was an important objective to be affirmatively pursued. Indeed, it seems the accepted social consensus is precisely the opposite. In the early 2000s, if the races and classes agree on anything, it is the proposition that it is acceptable to retreat to havens of one's own kind.

Myron Orfield and David Rusk, two close observers of fiscal and social inequity in American metropolitan regions, have both argued for taking "the hard path" not yet chosen, in order to tackle segregation frontally. Orfield explains:

> David Rusk has often told me that in dealing with issues of race in our society, there have always been two approaches—the soft path and the hard path. The soft path is less direct and hits issues more obliquely. It is more race neutral in its focus, generates less controversy, and generally gains more early support from philanthropies and the elite. Over time, however, the hard path—the more direct path—wins the day and converts many of the soft-path advocates to more substantive reform. The hard path takes direct aim at the core of these issues.[3]

The "hard path" abolitionists ultimately won out over "soft path" advocates of recolonization of slaves. The "hard path" of racial equality advocated by W.E.B. DuBois ultimately won out over the "soft path" of separatism and uplift advocated by Booker T. Washington; it became the intellectual basis for the civil rights movement and ultimately the mainstream social consensus.[4]

Currently, very few organizations are frontally attacking race and class segregation or concentrated minority poverty. Most large national civil rights organizations focus on preserving the gains of the civil rights movement, for example, supporting affirmative action or combating racial profiling. While this is important work, very few groups are attacking the housing discrimination and segregation that underlie our fundamental challenges.[5] Indirect approaches are no substitute for a frontal attack on what is ailing us as a nation. They will simply delay the inevitable adjustment that is needed, as happened when the infamous case of *Plessy v. Ferguson* installed the "separate-but-equal" doctrine for sixty years, until the Supreme Court jettisoned it in *Brown v. Board of Education.*

The school voucher movement is an example of an indirect approach that delays or deters us from dealing with the inevitable, underlying issues of inequality. Expensive vouchers for a relative few families out of the many thousands in a school system may make lawmakers feel as if they have done something positive. But voucher experiments delay our day of reckoning. They hold out the promise for a relatively few disadvantaged students to escape low-performing schools, but they do not hold out any hope of ever doing the same for *all* children. It would be too expensive, and neither the infrastructure nor the will is there to absorb every disadvantaged child into a better-performing private or public school. In fact, focusing on such indirect strategies ensures that this will never happen because it avoids the hard work of building consensus for that necessary course. We need to frontally address how we can bring about a transformative integration—a quality, middle-class educational experience—for all students rather than focus on the red herring of giving just a few children this option.

The Vision

I am imagining a society with public and private markets that encourage rather than discourage race and class inclusion. I am imagining a society where people of all races and classes have many more meaningful opportunities. Right now the choices available to the masses are rather limited. An inclusive society, rather than a separatist one, would offer much more in the way of choice and opportunity for all Americans. Encouraging markets to move in an integrated direction would also be a cheaper, more effective remedy for social inequality over the long haul than any government program could offer. It would also have the salient benefit of improving quality of life for everyone. But to get there, we need to have the kind of courage and vision that the civil rights movement itself necessitated. Since its founding, our country has evolved with each passing century, slowly completing a struggle to extend the privileges and opportunities of citizenship to everyone. For baby boomers, it was only in their lifetimes, as a result of the civil rights movement, that America came to accept the notion that all people, of whatever race, were inherently equal and entitled to the full privileges of citizenship. Our challenge for this new century is to move beyond mere acceptance of those values and make them true for everyone.

My optimistic vision for America in the twenty-first century is a new, socioeconomically integrated order, one where affordable housing is well dispersed throughout all communities, and there are no high-poverty schools. Racial enclaves might persist in this new order as a matter of preference; indeed, pockets of homogeneity may be necessary to make the larger project of integrating a community or an institution viable. It has been argued that a minority group will need to be large enough to form its own club in order to engender the kind of civic participation by minority and other groups that is necessary to make a heterogeneous community successful.[6] Homogeneity and group identity can and should be accommodated within a vision of inclusion, integration, and cross-cultural coalition building. Institutions and organizations that focus on supporting specific groups—from a Korean community center to Morehouse College—will have an important, continued role to play in nurturing individuals and making the voices of their constituents heard. The point, in a new integrationist order, is to give everyone more choices and greater opportunity. Above all, in my mind's eye, the black poor would not be singled out for derision and separation from the rest of society. They would be integrated into a society that has learned to be open and not fear the "other." At minimum, all children would able to attend schools that offer them a meaningful shot at a world-class education and the opportunity to move beyond circumstances of birth and chance.

Middle-income and affluent people would also have greater options in this new integrationist order. Those who wished to could find numerous stable racially and economically integrated communities that offer public schools they might actually want to send their children to. Encouraging the creation of more of these types of communities would eliminate much of the cost of our separatist system. The socioeconomically integrated communities would not have the ultra-high price tag of the white enclave, and if the middle and professional classes actively participated in the public schools in these neighborhoods, quality education might be available for free. Because socioeconomically integrated communities would have a mix of housing types, they would likely be developed at higher densities and therefore would have few of the problems associated with sprawl, like an unforgiving daily commute. Residents could walk to many of the amenities they need. Entry-level workers would be able to own a home near where they work.

In sum, every community in the United States would have a share of modest housing. Every public school would have students from a range of racial, ethnic, and economic backgrounds. No schools would be overwhelmingly poor.

The multicultural islands that I discussed in Chapter 2 are a window onto the transformative integration of the races and classes that I have in mind. By "socioeconomic integration" I mean communities and school environments where former strangers have come together and different races and classes feel comfortable with one another. Such true integration is transformative for those who experience it and for society as a whole. It connects people who are most disadvantaged by segregation to mainstream opportunities that are essential to upward mobility. It enables the privileged to live a saner, less expensive existence, one where they can confidently participate in public institutions and exist in a diverse society without fear.

Yes, this vision is utopian compared to our current reality. But sometimes utopian visions do come to pass. The greatest social changes in the United States were premised on optimistic visions rather than pessimistic ones. In 1954, the integrationist vision that animated the *Brown* decision, and ultimately the civil rights movement, seemed impossibly idealistic. In the 1990s, the impressive improvements in reducing concentrated poverty and the modest declines in economic segregation show that separatism is not inevitable. The ultimate goal is to cultivate a cultural shift of the magnitude of that achieved by the civil rights movement, which harnessed the better nature of Americans. The ultimate goal in a new integrated order is to create or rekindle a spirit of "we."

As with prior movements, the inclusive, full-opportunity society I envision must evolve over time. It took several decades for real estate markets to develop into a system for race and class exclusion. It might take at least that long for a dramatically different ethos to take hold. What we hold dear today—our separated milieus and the advantages they afford—could be viewed as anachronistic, if not absurd, decades hence. The idea that society would be ordered so as to benefit the lucky few rather than the diverse masses, and the missed opportunity of a rich mixing of people from various cultures and classes, could seem just as backward to future generations as slavery does to us today.

Reimagining Democracy, Building Coalitions for Change

How might we realize such a utopian vision? It will require a reimagining of democratic processes. Currently, separatism fosters a narrow conception of self-interest that blinds our many-hued citizenry to the possible benefits of building alliances with seemingly strange bedfellows. There are two possible paths we could take as our nation grows increasingly diverse. The fear impulse could move us toward further balkanization, greater rancor, and ever wider division in our politics. Or enlightened individuals could do the hard work of educating others to see our common needs and recognize our collective self-interest. If, as I contend throughout this book, the majority of Americans are harmed by our current tendency to institutionalize separation, a coalition of seemingly disparate groups might be formed to educate citizens on the perils of this reality and to encourage the establishment of a different, more empowering order. New, emerging political majorities could be formed by building coalitions across political and geographic boundaries of race, class, and culture—whether urban or suburban, inner city or edge city. Wise local and national leaders have begun to call for an explicit recognition that there are many potential allies within the sprawling American metropolis, if they could only break out of their parochial, or single-issue, endeavors to see it.[7]

Grassroots coalition building based upon actual—as opposed to perceived—self-interest is the only possible path to a truly inclusive society. More than thirty years ago, the National Advisory Commission on Civil Disorders (the Kerner Commission) called for a program of "enrichment" along with "integration" designed to disperse African Americans from the inner city. Among its several recommendations, the commission called for scattered-site public housing and more affordable housing outside of ghettos—recommendations that were largely ignored, even in the wake of urban riots.[8] Why would it be any different decades hence, when the terms of recent policy debates have centered not on *whether* to give the affluent a tax cut but on *how large* of a tax cut to give the affluent? There is no shortage of sound ideas for bringing about more socioeconomic integration. Since 1973, for example, Montgomery County, Maryland, has required that as much as 15 percent of all new housing developed throughout the county be for low- and moderate-income families. What is missing is an insistent movement to alter our present separatist course in all communities.

Any movement for race and class integration, then, must come from the grass roots. It has been argued that national and state political leaders "do not create social movements around race"; rather they "mediate energy for change that is created below the surface."[9]

To build such a movement we must recognize and address sensitively the problem of faction. Race and class barriers exist even among the so-called disadvantaged groups. Blacks and Latinos are beginning to experience serious friction rather than recognizing the enormous potential we have as common allies. We need to forgo zero-sum fights and instead build alliances between blacks and Latinos around issues that expand "the pie" for everyone. Listening to and including the wise leadership that exists in poor communities will also be a necessary course that is not often taken.[10] And it will sometimes take agreeing to disagree. As Bayard Rustin, the early architect of nonviolent social protest that animated the civil rights movement argued, political participation on the part of a range of interest and identity groups is necessary to any project of social reform. "The issue is which coalition to join and how to make it responsive to your program," he wrote. "Necessarily there will be compromise. But the difference between expediency and morality in politics is the difference between selling out a principle and making smaller concessions to win larger ones."[11] The inner-city advocate, for example, must recognize that he will not get very far in advancing the interests of highly marginalized minority populations without being part of a broader coalition that wields serious influence, which, in the case of doing anything progressive, usually requires a political majority.

A reinvigorated democracy—one that creates new political majorities out of currently disconnected interest and identity groups—can only come about with a sustained, intentional effort at building networks and relationships. In a rapidly diversifying America, were we to succeed in forming enduring relationships and coalitions across such boundaries, we would be building a truly inclusive American democracy for the first time.[12]

The problem of factional interests and friction between

seemingly unnatural allies will be overcome most easily by the collection and dissemination of objective data. Geographically mapped information has a way of breaking down barriers. It explains in tangible terms who is benefiting and who is not in a given metropolitan region, and why. One of the most powerful tools in the hands of a community organizer is geographic information systems software, which enables access to the kind of hard data that once was the exclusive province of governments and universities.[13] In contrast to the civil rights era, we no longer have obvious targets for mobilization of a movement. In many ways, the costs and inequalities described in this book are hidden from public view, or they are seen as the "natural" result of merit-based markets rather than the result of decades of conscious policy choices. A deeper understanding of how our separated universes came to be, and of just how disadvantaged most people are as a result, could spur people to organize and act. There are seeds of such a movement.

Moving Forward: How We Get There

There are at least three ongoing strands of coalition and community building that are relevant to advancing an agenda of true inclusion: (1) coalitions in metropolitan regions that are trying to bring about more equity in the allocation of resources, benefits, and social burdens; (2) organizations that are committed to physical development and building social capital in low-income, mostly minority communities; and (3) coalitions that work to foster sustainable development and counter the forces of suburban sprawl. All of these coalitions and interest groups—the regionalists, the community developers and builders, and the smart growth and sustainable development advocates—are working directly or indirectly on parts of the separatist problem, although sometimes, in the case of unthoughtful growth controls, in ways that are quite counter-productive. Together, they could seed a movement for a trans-formative integration of the races and classes. That could happen by infusing these ongoing efforts with an explicit dis-cussion of how a *frontal* assault on race and class segregation can advance their specific causes.

The Regionalists: Coalitions for Regional Equity

There is a groundswell of advocacy for an explicit discussion about equity in metropolitan regions. The Twin Cities metro-politan area in Minnesota, for example, has garnered attention for building a multiracial, multicity coalition that achieved a great deal of regional cooperation. In an area with seven coun-ties and 188 municipalities, one would think it would be futile to attempt any cross-border cooperation, much less tackle the inequity that such geographic separation of citizens into their own local fiefdoms produces. Recognizing the debilitating effects of extremely uneven distribution of economic growth and of social services needs, however, some visionary leaders began a labor-intensive effort to build a broad, majority coali-tion for reform in the state legislature.

Among the issues they would ultimately tackle were fair-share affordable housing and regional tax-base sharing, as well as coordinating land use and transportation planning and cre-ating a strong regional entity for cohesive governance. Over a period of several years, a coalition of twenty-six organizations was built that included mayors from declining suburban com-munities, inner-city community groups, environmental groups, transit advocates, and churches. Organizers understood that older, inner-ring suburbs held the balance of power in state leg-islatures and that building an alliance between representatives from the central cities and the several inner-ring suburbs would create a narrow majority. Objective, geographically mapped data—and several years of sharing this information in hundreds of presentations and meetings—provided a critical organizing tool that built bridges between communities not inclined to see themselves as allies. When mayors from older suburbs, like then-mayor Jesse Ventura, who represented a declining, predominately white, blue-collar community, real-ized that a fair-share affordable housing bill would not increase their obligations because their communities already had more than a fair share of modest housing, they became very strong supporters of the bill because it would open up the affluent developing suburbs to ordinary working people. Ulti-mately, this coalition of central- and inner-city and older sub-urban interests was able to get five seminal legislative reforms passed, including fair-share affordable housing, a regional council that sets the direction for land use and transportation in the entire region, and a system of tax-base sharing whereby each municipality must contribute 40 percent of its annual growth in tax revenue into a regional pool to be shared with other localities. The overall result is a fiscally healthier, more sustainable region that benefits everyone because there is much less risk of any concentrated social distress overwhelming weaker cities and hence destabilizing the region.[14]

Business groups, which recognize that economies don't stop at local borders, have often been the chief sponsors of efforts to examine and mitigate the impacts of grave regional dispari-ties. It was the Commercial Club of Chicago, for example, that initiated Chicago Metropolis 2020, an organization designed to draw people from across the region into developing a blueprint for addressing hypersegregation of the poor, inequality in education and training, and sprawl and balkanization. Other groups, such as the Metropolitan Alliance of Congregations, West Town Leadership United, the Chicago Affordable Housing Coalition, Chicago ACORN, and Latinos United have joined in the chorus, advocating for affordability and fairness in housing in the Chicago region.

Such direct appeals to equity issues are rare among regional civic organizations, most likely because the politics surrounding these efforts is so difficult. Still, coalitions of the type formed in the Twin Cities and Chicago will be necessary to address the "hard" issues, ones that will feel like a loss of privilege to some suburban voters, particularly those that benefit most from exclusion. Opening up new communities to affordable housing, opening up all school districts to all comers, or achieving a sharing of tax-base wealth to mitigate the effects of concentrated poverty are all relevant to any movement for integration. The regionalists have begun a process of education necessary to form a political majority for change, one that redirects democratic politics in state legislatures and makes revolutionary new policy choices possible.

The Community Builders and Developers

Community developers and community builders have been the vanguard of efforts to empower and stabilize marginal low-income communities, particularly those of color. Since 1960, more than 3,600 community development corporations (CDCs) have been established in low-income, usually minority, communities. About one-fifth of CDCs are faith based. A mainstay black church will use the seeds of church member offerings to create housing, schools, and small businesses. When the riots of the late 1960s and early 1970s left the West Garfield Park neighborhood on the West Side of Chicago in a shambles, a small neighborhood church, Bethel Lutheran, said, "No to despair, and yes to life," giving birth to Bethel New Life in 1979—a place-based, faith-based CDC. Now a venerable institution with 348 employees, Bethel New Life has, with its many partners, injected over $110 million into this credit-starved community. Their mission, in the words of the prophet Isaiah, is to "put an end to oppression, to every gesture of contempt, and to every evil word ... give food to the hungry and satisfy those who are in need" so that "the darkness ... will turn to the brightness of noon." And they are doing just that. As Isaiah predicted, they are "known as the people who rebuilt the walls, who restored the ruined houses."[15] They focus and build on the assets and strengths of West Garfield Park and are holistic in approach, "understanding the connections between a decent place to live and a living wage job for healthy families, and child care, quality education, transportation and access to health care."[16]

This CDC movement, while vital, has focused inwardly on renewal of marginalized places. Even the most successful CDCs, like New Community Corporation in Newark, or the Banana Kelley and MBD development corporations, which spurred a stunning transformation of formerly blighted "Fort Apache" in the South Bronx, have not stemmed the tide of out-migration of middle-class people to suburban locales. Typically, concentrated poverty endures in their target communities. Nor have they managed to create large numbers of jobs for community residents.[17] In short, they have not appreciably improved the opportunities available to the people in the communities they fervently serve. Still, community developers can provide a critical link for people in their target neighborhoods, helping them access the jobs and institutions—like banks and service providers—often located elsewhere that can improve lives and life chances.

Some community developers are moving in a new direction. Longtime participants in community development and community building in low-income neighborhoods have begun to frontally address issues of regional equity—to examine how economies and labor markets have come to be ordered and consider how their constituents' interests should be advanced in this wider context.[18] There is an emerging movement for "equitable development" that forces an explicit discussion about inequality and seeks to "promote and manage regional economic growth in a way that maximizes benefits for residents of low-income communities of color."[19]

Community developers and all other organizations that represent the interests of low-income people should be interested in the project of bringing about more socioeconomic integration because it will directly address the gaps of opportunity their target constituents face. Community developers and builders would be especially relevant to the hard work of building stable integrated communities and institutions that meaningfully benefit and include, rather than displace, low-income people.

The Anti-Sprawl Advocates: Coalitions for "Smart Growth" and Sustainable Development

The growing concern with sprawl creates an interesting possibility for alignment of urban and suburban, white and minority, affluent and poor interests. Quality-of-life issues became politically potent in the late 1990s. In the November 1998 elections, there were 240 ballot initiatives designed to limit urban sprawl or manage growth; 72 percent of them passed.

More than thirty states have also undertaken some form of growth management. Since the mid-1990s, much of this work has been pursued under the rubric of "smart growth," a phrase coined by former Maryland governor Parris Glendening. Its principal tenet is to develop metropolitan regions "in ways that allow us to thrive environmentally, economically, and socially while still providing all the assets of the American Dream and conserving our landscape."[20] This enlightened notion of economic development that is both socially equitable and environmentally sound may seem too much to hope for, and at the outset of the smart growth movement, it apparently was. Cynics of growth controls point out that the smart growth mantra is too easily used to mask what is essentially an exclusionary impulse. Too often citizen backlash over traffic congestion, school crowding, and loss of open space has created a groundswell of popular support for legislation that, at bottom, prevents others from coming to "ruin" what established suburban home owners already have. The tenor of the smart growth movement began to change in November 2000 after growth-management initiatives in Arizona and Colorado were defeated in the face of well-organized resistance from affordable housing advocates. Smart Growth America, a coalition of more than eighty national and local organizations was formed in late 2000 and directly took on as part of its mission the preservation and expansion of affordable housing. The coalition includes advocacy groups that place a premium on issues of equity, including the National Low-Income Housing Coalition, the Enterprise Foundation, and the National Neighborhood Coalition.[21]

At the same time, in the past two decades, a citizen-driven, sustainable development movement has taken root across the country. Broad coalitions for sustainable development tend to be forged based upon the collection, dissemination, and monitoring of objective information, usually indicators of community well-being. There are over 1,400 local, environmentally focused sustainable development organizations in existence in the United States. They tend to emphasize citizen participation in determining what community indicators to monitor and in developing a vision for the community's future. In Jacksonville, Florida, for example, the community issues an annual report that tracks seventy-four quality-of-life indicators in nine categories of citizen interest, including education (e.g., high school graduation rates); natural environment (e.g., days air quality is in the good range); and social environment (e.g., people believing racism is a problem). The annual report is itself a community organizing and consensus building exercise.[22] Often such efforts influence land-use decisions as well as the public and private policies that shape a community.

Advocates for low-income people and for cities and older suburbs need to be much more involved in the smart growth and sustainable development movements. It is highly relevant to enhancing the viability of central cities and older suburbs and even more important to expanding opportunities and choices for low-income minorities. Steering growth to the urban core has a number of benefits. It saves millions in public resources by building on existing infrastructure rather than sinking funds into new roads, sewers, and utility lines. It renders cities and older suburbs more vibrant and attractive, especially as an alternative to intense traffic congestion and a withering daily commute. It makes the centers of job growth more accessible to the urban poor, especially when mass transit and bus routes for marginalized communities are improved. It cuts down on loss of open space and uncontrolled growth on the outer fringe. Above all, steering growth inward will contribute mightily to the vitality of existing developed neighborhoods where many people of color live. Coalitions for smarter and more sustainable growth, then, are highly relevant to the project of cultivating successful socioeconomic integration.

Those who come to the growth issues solely from an environmental perspective should also be interested in enhancing race and class integration because more people will feel inclined to choose neighborhoods in the densely developed urban core as they become comfortable living with difference.

Race and class issues hover below the surface of the smart growth and sustainable development debates. It is time to bring them out into the open in order to advance a mutually beneficial agenda. It is time for those in the smart growth and sustainable development movements who have not done so to account for their failure to address the issue of inequity, especially of the racial kind. This is what it means to take the "hard" path. There will be no such accounting, however, without the insistent advocacy of civil-rights and community organizations that are committed to racial and economic justice. They must join in and shape this debate. Currently that is not happening to the degree necessary, although there are inspiring examples, like Bethel New Life discussed above. It has evolved into a holistic institution that embodies sustainable development principles. Its new motto is "Smart Growth in an Urban Community Context," which includes an agenda of encouraging citizen involvement in planning, developing housing and commercial projects around transit stops, training former welfare recipients for living-wage jobs in the environmental remediation field, and redeveloping polluted urban brownfields. Most importantly, Bethel New Life is actively working to ensure that regional planning and smart growth discussions are infused with a "justice agenda." It participates in regional planning and advocates for critical reinvestment in sustainable development in the inner city.[23]

Faith-based organizations have an especially critical role to play. They can bring their moral persuasion and values to bear in raising issues of equity and socioeconomic inclusion in the smart growth debate. At the very least, an inclusive agenda demands that individuals, including those living in advantaged communities, make a personal commitment to accepting some social responsibility. Faith-based organizations have enormous credibility and unique standing to argue this case.[24] In the Detroit metropolitan area, for example, one of the driving forces behind the creation of a new multicounty regional transit authority was a multiracial, city-suburban church-based organization called MOSES (Metropolitan Organizing Strategy Enabling Strength). A new regional entity that will provide greater access and connection between the inner city of Detroit and its surrounding suburbs is an important feat for one of the most racially segregated regions in the country.[25]

In addition to the regionalists, the community builders, and the smart growth and sustainable development advocates, there are many other types of interests that could be brought into this fold. Education advocates, for example, should join with smart growth and community advocates to combat the vicious cycle of sprawled growth that starves school districts in older communities of needed revenues and encourages the flight of the middle class to ever newer school districts on the suburban fringe.[26] And leaders of cities and older suburbs should also participate in this movement because it will enable more middle-class families to see their localities and public schools as viable, attractive options. In sum, all of the organizations currently working to bring about a little more justice and sanity to our mutual existence will be vital in this work.

Nothing transformative will come to pass, however, without an unprecedented activism on the part of those who currently suffer under our separatist system. Far too many people and interests, wittingly or unwittingly, benefit from our fragmented condition. As Frederick Douglass, one of my personal heroes, once said: "Power concedes nothing without a demand. It never did and it never will."[27]

I have said nothing about the role of state or federal government in this endeavor. This omission is intentional. Any government intervention on behalf of socioeconomic integration or equity—such as a state mandate that all municipalities must have their fair share of affordable housing, or a federal mandate that all recipients of federal transportation funds take affirmative steps to eliminate race and class segregation—presupposes an altered politics and a public mandate for inclusion. The hard but achievable work of bringing about public support for such a change of policy has yet to be done.

Revolutionary Possibilities in Public Policy

Revolutionary change can be wrought by powerful new multirace, multiclass coalitions that pursue smart new policies. Again, such change presupposes an advocacy base that may not yet exist but certainly is within the realm of possibility. It also presupposes a political rhetoric that has broad saliency. In opinion polls, for example, whites support race-oriented civil rights measures when they are cast in terms of giving minorities the same rights as whites, rather than creating special privileges.[28] I suggest the pursuit of what I call "choice logic," offering a series of policy directions that would give all of us more choices, and more of the benefits, of integration or integrated institutions. At the same time, we must vigilantly guard against the incorrect assumption that the playing field is level.[29] Persistent *current* racial discrimination and exclusion, and its decades-long historic practice, mean that some groups, especially the minority poor, deserve focused attention to ensure that they have the kind of meaningful choices that others enjoy.

Meaningful integration will not come about by any command-and-control forcing of race and class mixing. The answer lies, I believe, in the changes that have already begun to happen in communities across the country. Three trends that emerged in the prosperous 1990s offer insightful lessons and hope. First, record economic growth, combined with a housing shortage in many metropolitan areas, a sharp decline in crime, and a backlash against the quality-of-life challenges associated with suburban sprawl, has made "colorful" urban neighborhoods a newly viable option for many. Second, also due in part to record prosperity and some changes in public housing, we witnessed a dramatic decline in concentrated poverty in much of the country. As many former welfare recipients joined the ranks of the employed and were bolstered by increases in the earned income tax credit that rewarded work, more poor folks were able to move from extremely poor neighborhoods to just working poor ones.[30] Third, although public schools unfortunately became more segregated in the 1990s, as I described in Chapter 6, the school choice movement blossomed in that decade.

All three of these trends constituted an expansion of choices for low- and moderate-income families, as well as for the middle-income and affluent people who might prefer socioeconomically integrated communities and public schools.

By expanding choices, the possibilities for integration are enhanced. Among the policy directions that new coalitions for a renewed democracy might consider are programs that would (1) empower more low-income people to escape the most distressed neighborhoods and create more integration elsewhere; (2) encourage more middle-class people to inhabit low-income areas in ways that create stable integration; and (3) encourage middle-class people to return to public schools by giving them more attractive choices, while at the same time giving lower-income parents more quality choices.

Anti-Discrimination Enforcement: A National Commitment to Housing Choice

Before addressing the specifics of how to promote integration by building on existing trends, there is one general strategy to consider. Any society that claims to be an equal opportunity democracy, as we do, must eliminate to the utmost extent possible all racial barriers to free choice in regard to housing. There are a phalanx of federal and state anti-discrimination and civil rights laws that prohibit discrimination in housing, lending, banking, and other services that affect one's ability to choose where to rent or buy a home. Vigorous enforcement of these laws is essential for meaningful expansion of housing options for minority individuals. It is quite easy to become complacent and assume that discrimination is a thing of the past. As recent studies demonstrate, it is not.[31] Race still matters to an unfortunate degree, especially for many blacks and Latinos who attempt to buy a home, procure a loan or insurance, or merely find out whether that nice two-bedroom apartment in a better neighborhood is still available.

We should recommit ourselves to the fundamentally American value of opportunity for all and prosecute anti-discrimination and civil rights laws with renewed vigor. Eradicating discrimination, as much as possible, from real estate markets will help accelerate the trend of modest declines in racial segregation. It may not be a sexy or bold idea, but it is necessary, year in and year out, to be consistent and vigilant in enforcing laws and sending the message that discrimination of any kind is intolerable. Commitment and leadership make a huge difference in shaping the attitudes of market actors. When private actors receive the signal that they may discriminate with impunity, either because of government indifference or thin enforcement budgets, they respond accordingly. When fair housing enforcement essentially shut down at the Department of Justice during the Reagan years, for example, complaints of housing discrimination rose precipitously.[32] The Reagan administration's hostility to civil rights was curious, given conservatives' professed beliefs in free markets. There is no reason why anyone of any political persuasion should be against aggressive enforcement of existing anti-discrimination law; it is fully consistent with our shared fundamental ideals. Stopping discrimination at its source expands opportunities and markets. It will be especially important in the future, when the majority of individuals aspiring to participate in our national economy will be racial and ethnic minorities.

Unfortunately, the traditional civil rights organizations have not focused much on housing, choosing instead to place their emphasis on race-based litigation strategies concerning education and employment. While I do not wish to denigrate those efforts, I would argue that housing strategies are most directly relevant to improving the lives and opportunities for low-income and minority people and to bringing about a fairer, more socially cohesive society. We should seriously advance a national commitment to housing choice, that is, eliminating all discriminatory barriers to free choice of where to live.

Anti-discrimination enforcement, though necessary, is not a sufficient condition for achieving true integration. Additional affirmative strategies will be needed to overcome decades of entrenched biases toward separation. Past policies that have led to entrenched separation must be met with affirmative counterweights. Assuming a baseline of commitment to enforcing civil rights and fair housing laws, I will now explore three policy directions that will build upon encouraging market trends, moving us toward a more integrated, full-opportunity society.

Break up the ghetto.

Lyndon Johnson's War on Poverty, declared in 1964, suggested that we could somehow eradicate poverty altogether. That may not be possible. Poverty has existed, and likely will continue to exist, throughout human history. An infinitely more achievable goal would be to eradicate *concentrated* poverty. There is no reason why being poor should equate with living in a neighborhood where more than 40 percent of your neighbors are also poor—the accepted definition among social scientists for concentrated poverty. Such neighborhoods tend to serve as incubators for social distress that is very hard to eradicate. Large numbers of adults are not working, violence and violent death are a constant presence, crime and teenage pregnancy rates soar, and opportunities to rise to something better are extremely limited. That is an existence no child deserves.

If we believe in the ideal of social mobility in this country, and if we want to save ourselves a multitude of social and fiscal costs, we will pursue sound policies that could lead to the eventual eradication of anything approaching ghetto conditions. Such a goal is eminently achievable in our lifetime. In the 1990s, 2.5 million poor people left concentrated poverty communities.[33] We should empower millions more to do so. A concerted effort will be necessary to create a healthy dynamic of mobility in high-poverty neighborhoods, one where people who wish to leave have meaningful options for moving out, and where others begin to see these neighborhoods as viable options and move in. Returning such a market dynamic to the most distressed of places would be the least expensive route to revolutionary social change, in my view. Abolishing the black ghetto altogether would have the seminal benefit of eradicating a deeply stigmatic stereotype, which, as I describe in Chapter 7, is at the core of race and class tensions in the United States. It would also afford the most poor and isolated among us the enormous social benefits of experiencing more in the way of socioeconomic integration. As the *Gautreaux* case (described in Chapter 7) demonstrated, integration matters most for those who currently have little choice or mobility. Above all, those trapped in high-poverty communities who are willing to work and strive beyond their circumstances of birth deserve a choice about whether to stay where they are or move elsewhere.

So how do we do it? One strategy is to give new and existing Section 8 federal housing vouchers to eligible residents of high-poverty communities. Coalitions for integration might advocate for a reauthorization and dramatic expansion of HUD's Moving to Opportunities (MTO) program. *And* they could help create a more enlightened national and local political context for such efforts. Given that there is significantly more demand for Section 8 housing vouchers than our political willingness to fund them, it makes sense to focus on putting interested residents of the most impoverished communities first in line for such mobility options, with concerted efforts to help them find a socioeconomically integrated neighborhood where they can actually use the voucher. The logical place to start with any expansion and improvement of MTO would be with the public housing residents who are currently being displaced by HUD's Hope VI program, which is generally demolishing the worst public housing to create new mixed-income developments with fewer public housing units.[34]

Another strategy is to offer attractive tax incentives for owner-occupied home ownership in the most distressed neighborhoods. Just as ghetto residents need more options to live elsewhere, those who have the wherewithal to buy or rehabilitate a home, including ghetto residents, need an incentive to move into or stay in a high-poverty neighborhood. Just as socioeconomic integration can be created when poor people move into middle-class settings, it can also be created when new stakeholders move into high-poverty neighborhoods or when current residents who have risen from poverty decide to stay.

An infusion of such mobility—people moving in and out of the most distressed neighborhoods—could have the effect of accelerating the eradication of concentrated poverty. This would produce other important benefits: a lessening of crime and the social distress that high poverty incubates, a less threatening environment for the people who live in or near formerly high-poverty neighborhoods, and improved perceptions of urban neighborhoods that in turn improve race and class relations.

To those who are concerned about the potential of such efforts to displace the very poor, one way of fighting such dis-

placement and the attendant net reduction in affordable housing stock would be to build consensus for meaningful inclusion
of low-income people, particularly low-income minority people, *everywhere*. Again, that will not happen without sustained, insistent advocacy on the part of groups who care
about such populations. They must demand a seat at the table
of institutions and coalitions that can shape development patterns, and other interest groups must understand their own
long-term interests in such inclusion.

These are just two of the policy ideas that could expand
choices for low-income people and help eradicate the ghetto.
There are many others, such as a more sensitive deployment of
the Hope VI program, continued expansion of the earned
income tax credit, raising the minimum wage, and other policies that raise income for low-income people who work. Most
importantly, an intelligent mobility strategy for low-income
minorities presupposes that those who are given a housing
voucher can use it somewhere that will not simply recreate
race and class segregation. Ideally, they should have the option
of moving into a middle-class neighborhood. Coalitions for
integration will need to continue the difficult fight to develop
affordable housing, especially in job-rich suburbs. My point,
however, is not to advance specific proposals but to underscore
the fact that revolutionary new possibilities are within our
reach, if we will only acknowledge the seeds of change at our
disposal. Ghetto conditions are not inevitable.

*Encourage the middle class to return to minority neighbor-
hoods in ways that create stable integration.*

Attracting new home owners to an urban neighborhood
increases the tax base of the city. In cities like Washington,

D.C., which has been hemorrhaging middle-class families for decades, especially black ones, an infusion of new home owners who pay taxes and have a powerful stake in improving otherwise politically marginal neighborhoods is a good thing. But, as with all good things, too much of it can be a problem. Our goal should not be gentrification or displacement but the cultivation of neighborhoods that are economically and racially stable. When middle-income or affluent people move into an impoverished area, this contributes not just to its physical regeneration but the creation of economic and racial diversity that offers enormous potential benefits for the community as a whole and its formerly marginalized residents. The trick is to have a strategy for intelligently responding to gentrification, so that low- and moderate-income folks are included *and* they have a voice and role in charting the destiny of their communities. A sense of community does not happen naturally. In those islands of stable diversity, people of goodwill, longtime activists and newcomers alike, must work at building bonds of trust and addressing those issues that affect the quality of life and vitality of the community.

We are limited only by our imagination. Attracting the middle-class to cities and urban neighborhoods does not exclude the possibility of providing housing options for low- and moderate-income people. On the contrary, the infusion of tax revenue that comes with this new populace *enhances* the options available to cities for creating, retaining, and expanding their affordable housing stock throughout the city.[35] The point is for city leaders, policymakers, and low-income housing advocates to commit to and work together on advancing a goal of creating vibrant, mixed-income communities. There is a risk that city leaders, feeling that they already have more than their fair share of poor people, may focus exclusively on accelerating

gentrification and displacement, a process that ultimately leads
to the exporting of some poorer residents across the city border into distressed older suburbs. This has been happening in
the District of Columbia. But any city leader who adheres to a
logic of merely accelerating such displacement is being short-
sighted and missing a larger opportunity.

American cities have their share of the poor to deal with,
especially the minority poor. It would take many decades of
unbridled gentrification reaching its tentacles into all manner
of distressed neighborhoods to change that reality and render
the American metropolis more like its European cousin. (European separatism has pushed lower-income people to the suburban fringe, reserving the great cities for the more elite classes.)
American cities that embrace the principle of inclusion and
cultivate vibrant socioeconomically integrated neighborhoods
will be rewarded in the exciting, diverse future that lies ahead.
It will help cities overcome a perception that has fueled a mass
exodus of middle-class families—the idea that cities are crime-
ridden, unsafe places with bad schools, or worse—while also
greatly reducing the social distress, and attendant fiscal costs,
that concentrated poverty produces.

A socioeconomically integrated neighborhood has a salutary natural order that is lacking in neighborhoods where a
majority or plurality of the residents are beaten down. There
are social markets as well as economic ones. Middle-class parents and citizens tend to make demands on governments and
institutions, take action to address issues that affect community quality of life, and attract resources and investment that,
all too often, elude impoverished communities. The middle
class also forms the backbone of an insistent consumer base
for public institutions that the elite professional class can
afford to simply bypass. This is part of the reason why the five-

decade hemorrhaging of the middle class from central cities and their school systems has been so devastating. Tragically, similar demands by low-income folks often go unheeded. Middle-class people also infuse a social order into the neighborhoods they inhabit. They get up and go to work everyday and model this behavior for those around them. As the work of William Julius Wilson has shown, a neighborhood devoid of large numbers of working men and women will be hard-pressed to overcome the forces set against it.[36] Rendering formerly distressed neighborhoods more socioeconomically integrated will have enormous, exponential benefits. Focusing on socioeconomic integration strategies may be even more critical for those distressed older suburbs that saw a rise in poverty concentration in the 1990s. All municipalities have an obligation to actively cultivate the development of housing for those on the lowest rungs of the economic ladder. Communities that do this in a manner that integrates low-income minority people into middle-class settings will benefit most.

There are several strategies for cultivating socioeconomic integration, one of which is inclusionary zoning—requiring all new development to include a percentage of low-income housing. There are also strategies for mitigating gentrification in a way that produces stable integration.[37] My purpose is not to offer a laundry list of policy recommendations but to underscore that wise, sound, and cost-effective strategies exist for cultivating mixed-income, and mixed-race, residential living.

Predominately minority neighborhoods, in particular, offer rich, interesting opportunities for class mixing, even of the one-race kind. They also offer a context for learning that will be sorely needed in the majority-minority America of the future. Whites who choose such environments will have the opportunity to test and stretch their capacity for being among, and outnumbered by, people of other races and, hence, for adjusting to and participating in our nation's emerging demographic reality. When millions of whites learn that the sky does not fall when they or their children are outnumbered racially, we will have finally begun to render the metaphor of America's melting pot a reality.

Black professionals could be just as much a part of the influx who reconsider poor minority neighborhoods as the affluent, often gay whites who are typically associated with urban gentrification. Black enclaves offer the black middle class the possibility of reconnecting of with their lower-income brethren. Ultimately, it is incumbent on the black middle class to love, respect, and reach out to poor black people. I am not suggesting that this is solely a job for the black middle class, but we, of all people, should reject the classism that works against the black poor. For the millions of middle-class blacks who have moved to "buppie" enclaves precisely to escape the hood, the separatist tendencies of real estate markets have meant that low-income black people eventually migrate to neighborhoods in close proximity. Rather than erect walls and flock to private schools, those in the black middle class should roll up their sleeves and do the hard work of building communities and institutions—particularly public schools—that bring all black people along.

Expand school choice and cross-jurisdictional choice.

Now I come to the most vexing hurdle of all: How do we approximate the integrationist, equal opportunity vision of public schools conjured by the architects of *Brown v. Board of Education,* given our separated state of living? As I argued in Chapter 6, class integration has profound impacts on low-income and minority kids. The best avenue to bringing about equality of educational opportunity, and equality of outcomes, in my view, is to bring about more socioeconomic integration in American public schools. My hope is that as we create more stable, socioeconomically integrated neighborhoods, we can create or harness the civic infrastructure to encourage all inhabitants of these neighborhoods to participate in public schools. In the meantime, I believe the best hope we have for achieving more integration and more quality in education, given existing neighborhood demographics and legal constraints, is to accelerate the school choice movement.

This movement toward choice has been accompanied by a dramatic increase in the number of families who now educate their kids in an environment other than a neighborhood public school.[38] At the same time, opinion polls suggest that there is now majority support for the general proposition that all families, regardless of race or ability to pay, should be able to choose a good school for their children.[39] Perhaps this explains the growth of two choice-oriented strategies: charter schools and controlled choice. Charter schools cultivate more parental involvement and put pressure on failing schools to turn around or risk closure, creating a vibrant social market for children that may also attract more middle-class families who welcome quality public school options that are available at no cost. Controlled choice typically involves an intentional plan of economic integration, using income rather than race as a factor in assigning students to school. School districts in Cambridge, Massachusetts; Wake County and Charlotte-Mecklenburg, North Carolina; South Orange–Maplewood, New Jersey; Manchester, Connecticut; St. Lucie County, Florida; and San Francisco, California, have adopted economic integration plans in recent years. They are known as controlled-choice plans because they enable parents to have some choice in school assignments.[40] A version of this model has worked for the most part in Wake County, North Carolina, where children from Raleigh and its surrounding suburbs participate in a unified school district. After more than twenty-five years of using race-based busing, the school board opted for an income desegregation plan, whereby no more than 40 percent of any school's students are eligible for free or reduced-price lunch and no more than 25 percent of the school's students perform below grade level. Only about 9 out of 122 schools exceed the income guidelines, and Wake County overall remains one of the highest-performing school districts in the state, with more than 80 percent of students scoring at grade level or higher. The school superintendent spoke passionately to the *Boston Globe* about the policy of economic integration and its logic: "This policy . . . is a reminder that we don't have any throwaway children. I know how high-poverty schools can overwhelm. I know the defeatedness of that. I'm going to make every effort for that not to happen."[41]

A third revolutionary idea whose time may have come is the concept of universal choice. Why not do away with all jurisdictional barriers to choice? A growing groundswell of sentiment favors the notion that every family deserves the opportunity to choose a quality school for their child. Suppose that groundswell were translated into a grassroots movement for empowering ordinary families to choose a good school, regardless of where they live or their ability to pay. Such a movement might pressure state legislators to recognize that because all local school districts are creatures of the state, the state should allow the educational resources it funds to be open to any families living in the state. Were this to happen, a visionary state could implement a requirement that all publicly funded schools be open to residents both inside and outside their local school jurisdiction, without nonresidents having to pay reciprocal tuition or the often insurmountable cost of moving to a home in a different neighborhood. It would be left to democratic processes to determine how such a vision might come to pass.⁴²

I have offered three general policy directions that have increased race and class integration as their animating goal. If they were implemented, the end result would be an expansion of choices for individuals of every hue and economic station. These suggestions are not a panacea for all of society's ills nor an exhaustive list of what can or should be done to improve the quality of life and vitality of the American metropolis. However, they are ideas and strategies that can begin to move us toward greater socioeconomic cohesion and less inequality of opportunity. They are starting points for actions we might take to promote a fairer society, one with more choices for everyone and more daily interaction and understanding between the races and classes. Such possibilities are achievable if the majority of people who now suffer under American separatism would organize and act to reclaim democratic processes. It is time for people who care to imagine a different, more inclusive order—one that will benefit everyone.

Conclusion

Black people have always been a gauge for how well America is doing in meeting our national ideals.⁴³ By no means have I intended to denigrate black neighborhoods or black institutions in this book. Nor am I suggesting that black institutions should cease to exist in any new socioeconomically integrated order. On the contrary, they could be powerful engines of race and class inclusion. What I am suggesting, however, is that the rest of society should stop fearing us and ordering themselves in a way that is designed to avoid us where we exist in numbers. America created slavery, Jim Crow, and the black ghetto. America has shaped stereotypes grounded in fear of black people, especially black males. Our residential patterns reflect that fear. America has to get beyond fear of black people and fear of difference to begin to order itself in a way that is consistent with its ideals.

The spirit of oneness that prevailed in the days and weeks following the tragedy of September 11 is a rare approximation of the ethos I believe we should be trying to cultivate. The reaction of America to the victims in the towers of the World Trade Center was the closest we came as a nation in recent memory to a moment where race and class differences seemed to be suspended. It was not a perfect moment. There were ugly attacks on people who were or appeared to be Muslim. Yet a spirit of oneness, a sense of what could be, also prevailed. From the immigrant waiters of the Windows on the World to the masters of the universe dominating Wall Street, we were all Americans at that moment. The most refreshing dynamic in our collective 9/11 moment was that black people were no longer the villain. The ugly side was that now some other group was. Still, for a brief time, a careful observer might have sensed what an altered American consciousness might look like—what we might achieve in more than a fleeting way in the new century. Maybe we can break out of the racial narrative that has defined social discourse in this country since its inception, one where the darkest group is most feared and excluded. Above all, each of us needs to develop the quality of empathy. If we take the time to see that the racial or economic "other" sitting next to us—if we even allow ourselves such proximity— is not that different from ourselves, we will have begun an important personal and national developmental process. Empathy. In our bewilderingly diverse future, it is the human quality that will be most fundamental to our nation's progress.

ACKNOWLEDGMENTS

I could not have written this book without the support and assistance of many people. I wish to thank you all; your help has meant more than I can say.

Peter Edelman believed in this project from the very beginning, carefully read and gave me feedback on an early book prospectus, and introduced me to Esther Newberg, who became my book agent. Esther immediately understood why this book should be published by PublicAffairs, helped make it happen, and supported me throughout. Vernon Jordan vouched for me and vouched for PublicAffairs, helping both writer and publisher appreciate that this was an excellent fit. Peter Osnos valued my argument and helped me develop as a writer. Kate Darnton was a fabulous editor who wielded her pencil gently but effectively. She patiently helped me clear away the chaff and hone in on the essential. The production team at PublicAffairs, including Nina D'Amario and Melanie Peirson Johnstone, was terrific at every stage of a very compressed schedule.

Peter Byrne read the entire manuscript and gave me extremely helpful comments. He also consented to be interviewed for the book, offering the critical insights of a real-world integrator. Palma Strand read several chapters and offered invaluable comments over the course of several conversations that greatly advanced my understanding of the challenges of integration and coalition building. She was extremely generous in arranging a meeting of women in her home that gave me the opportunity to speak directly with accidental and ardent integrationists in South Arlington, Virginia. Nina Pillard, James Forman and Paul Dimond all read and gave me very helpful feedback on certain chapters. Jonathan Weiss helped me better understand the smart growth movement. Carrie Menkel-Meadow and Emma Coleman Jordan offered helpful advice and support throughout. I also received excellent feedback from my colleagues when I presented an early and later a final chapter of the book to the Georgetown Law Center faculty workshop.

Many people shared their unique perspectives on American separatism with me, some in formal interviews, others in informal conversations. I greatly appreciate their time and willingness to share. All of their voices were critical to helping me comprehend the complexities of the subject matter and to bringing alive our nation's challenges and possibilities.

Judy Areen, my dean at the Law Center generously supported me with summer writing grants. Vicki Jackson, in her capacity as Associate Dean for Research, generously supported my request for extra research assistants.

My many research assistants over the last few years left no stone unturned in helping me complete this project. Thad Hackworth, Marie Grant, Hank Willson, Kim Murakawa, Nicole Devero, Jeff Epstein, and Aaren Jackson all made heroic and invaluable contributions. The faculty support staff of the Law Center library, including Tracey Bridgman and Christopher Knott, and several research assistants employed by the library, especially Lorelei Klein, provided invaluable, timely assistance. The Law Center staff, especially John Showalter, Derreck Brown, and Rada Hayes, provided very helpful technical support and assistance.

Many friends and family provided much needed moral support, love and patience as I wrote this book. I am especially grateful to all of them for being forgiving of my being so selfish with my time. My stepmother, Louise White Cashin, was an especially constant, supportive cheerleader. Finally, I wish to thank my devoted husband, Marque Chambliss, for being there for me in every imaginable way as I wrote this book, and for sacrificing much more than he should have had to in our first year of marriage.

I have tried to be as accurate as possible in citing and interpreting sources and supporting arguments throughout this book. Inevitably there will be errors, for which I apologize.

NOTES

Introduction

1. Joseph Lelyveld, *How Race Is Lived in America: Pulling Together, Pulling Apart* (New York: Times Books, 2001), 367 (the poll, conducted in June 2000, surveyed 1,107 people who said they were white and 943 who said they were black).

2. See "Views on Race in America," *Boston Globe*, December 21, 1997, http://www.boston.com (in an opinion poll, 76 percent of blacks and 73 percent of whites responded that "integration" would be better for race relations than "people of different races living apart in separate communities"); Camille Zubrinsky Charles, "Processes of Racial Residential Segregation," in *Urban Inequality: Evidence from Four Cities*, ed. Alice O'Connor, Chris Tilly, and Lawrence Bobo (New York: Russell Sage Foundation, 2001), 263–264 (concluding from a comprehensive study that all racial groups—whites, blacks, Hispanics, and Asians—desire "substantial integration" as well as a strong representation of people from their own ethnic group).

3. Ana M. Aizcorbe, Arthur B. Kennickell, and Kevin B. Moore, "Recent Changes in U.S. Family Finances: Evidence from the 1998 and 2001 Survey of Consumer Finances," *Federal Reserve*

Bulletin 89 (January 2003): 1, 7–8, and Table 3 (showing black median net worth at $19,000 in 2001 compared to $120,990 for whites). For a general comparison of black-white wealth disparities, see Melvin L. Oliver and Thomas M Shapiro, *Black Wealth/White Wealth: A New Perspective on Racial Inequality* (New York: Routledge, 1995).

4. Richard Morin, "Misperceptions Cloud Whites' View of Blacks," *Washington Post,* July 11, 2001 (reporting on a national opinion survey sponsored by the *Washington Post,* the Henry J. Kaiser Family Foundation, and Harvard University); Steven A. Tuch, Lee Sigelman, and Jason A. Macdonald, "Trends: Race Relations and American Youth, 1976–1995," *Public Opinion Quarterly* 63, no. 1 (1999): 109–148.

5. The social science research supporting these claims is discussed in detail in Chapter 1.

6. Bruce Lambert, "Study Calls L.I. Most Segregated Suburb," *New York Times,* June 5, 2002.

7. Allan Richter, "Black and White on Long Island: Like Oil and Water," *New York Times,* June 16, 2002.

8. See Elizabeth Warren and Amelia Warren Tyagi, *The Two-Income Trap: Why Middle-Class Mothers and Fathers Are Going Broke* (New York: Basic Books, 2003).

Chapter 1: Won't You Not Be My Neighbor?

1. Ron French, "Mistrust Keeps Races Living Apart," *Detroit News,* January 14, 2002.

2. Ron French, "Metro Area Leaders: Segregation Not an Issue," *Detroit News,* January 28, 2002.

3. Jodi Upton, "Livonia Mirrors Area's Barriers to Integration," *Detroit News,* January 27, 2002.

4. Ibid.

5. U.S. Census Bureau, detailed tables for Census Tracts 5133 and 5501, Wayne County, Michigan, Census Summary File 1, 2000, http://factfinder.census.gov/servlet/DTTable?_ts=52676755170 (percentages calculated by author based upon populations of blacks and whites relative to total populations for each census tract respectively).

6. John O. Calmore, "Race/ism Lost and Found: The Fair Housing Act at Thirty," *University of Miami Law Review* 52 (1998): 1067, 1101 (citing research by David Cutler, Edward Glaeser, and Jacob Vigdor).

7. John T. Metzger, "Clustered Spaces: Racial Profiling in Real Estate Investment," report prepared for the International Seminar on Segregation and the City, Lincoln Institute of Land Policy, Cambridge, Mass., July 26–28, 2001.

8. Given my own limitations of time and skill, I can only conjecture about how Native Americans feel about integration, as the social science research frequently renders them invisible in this discourse.

9. John Yemma, "Rethinking Integration," *Boston Globe*, September 17, 1997.

10. "The Personal Gap Narrows," in "A Roper Center Data Review: Mending the Fabric," *Public Perspective* 12, no. 3 (May–June 2001) (citing Surveys by the Gallop Organization).

11. Pew Research Center for the People and the Press, "No Consensus on the Census," Survey Reports, May 13, 2001, http://people-press.org/reports/print.php3?PageID=104 (last accessed July 19, 2002).

12. Boston Globe Poll, "Views on Race in America," http://www.boston.com/globe/nation/packages/rethinking_integration/views_on_race_poll.htm, last accessed February 6, 2002.

13. "Mending the Fabric: A Roper Center Data Review," *Public Perspective* 12, no. 3 (May–June 2001) (citing an NBC News/*Wall Street Journal* survey conducted March 2–5, 2000).

14. The most comprehensive attempts to explain residential segregation point either directly or indirectly to attitudes about race. A multicity study conducted in the early nineties attempted to test the extent of tolerance for integration among the races and found some clear limitations. When asked to identify the racial composition of their ideal neighborhood, all racial groups preferred living with substantial numbers of their own race even as they expressed a desire for a moderate level of integration. Whites expressed the strongest degree of racial solidarity; they were the only racial group that needed to be in a clear majority. White participants in the study stated a mean percentage of 52 percent white for their

ideal neighborhood. Whites were also more likely than other races to prefer a neighborhood that was completely of their own race, although only 11 percent of whites identified an all-white neighborhood as ideal. Blacks, Latinos, and Asians were content to have their group be a preponderance of the neighborhood, i.e., 40 to 45 percent. Camille Zubrinsky Charles, "Processes of Residential Segregation," in *Urban Inequality: Evidence from Four Cities*, ed. Alice O'Connor, Chris Tilly, and Lawrence Bob (New York: Russell Sage Foundation, 2001), 233, Figure 4.6 (interpreting the Multi-City Study of Urban Inequality).

15. In fact, blacks at every income level are more segregated from whites at the same income level than are higher-income whites from lower-income whites. See Douglas S. Massey and Nancy A. Denton, *American Apartheid: Segregation and the Making of the Underclass* (Cambridge: Harvard University Press, 1993), 10–11, 84–88.

16. Tom Brokaw Special Report, "Why Can't We Live Together?" *Dateline NBC*, June 27, 1997; see Myron Orfield, *American Metropolitics: The New Suburban Reality* (Washington, D.C.: Brookings Institution Press, 2002), 11–12.

17. Edward L. Glaeser and Jacob L. Vigdor, "Racial Segregation in the 2000 Census: Promising News," Brookings Institution Center on Urban and Metropolitan Policy, April 2001, 7 (noting that half of all black people live in metropolitan regions with a dissimilarity index of 75 or higher, such that 75 percent of all blacks would have to move in order to be evenly dispersed throughout the region in numbers consistent with their percentage of the overall population).

18. Pew Research Center for the People and the Press, "No Consensus on the Census" (54 percent of whites cite the rise of U.S. population as a "bad thing"); see note 14 above.

19. Jodi Upton and Gordon Trowbridge, "Efforts to Integrate Are 'Just an Illusion'; Race Guides Where and How Most Blacks, Whites Live in Metro Detroit," *Detroit News*, January 14, 2002.

20. Charles, "Processes of Residential Segregation," 240–244.

21. In the 1970s when blacks in the Detroit area were asked about their ideal neighborhood, the most popular choice was half black

and half white. See Reynolds Farley et al., "Continued Racial Residential Segregation in Detroit: Chocolate City, Vanilla Suburbs Revisited," *Journal of Housing Research* 4 (1993): 29. Other investigations of African American preferences from the 1970s through the 1990s also showed that the majority of blacks preferred a 50–50 integrated neighborhood. See Maria Krysan and Reynolds Farley, "The Residential Preferences of Blacks: Do They Explain Persistent Segregation?" *Social Forces* 80, no. 3 (2002): 937, 940. In a national survey conducted in the 1990s, when this question was repeated to blacks, the most preferred neighborhood was 73 percent black and the second most popular choice was half black. Charles, "Processes of Residential Segregation," 237, Figure 4.9. In this same national survey, Latinos and Asians, however, most preferred the option of 50–50 integration with whites. Ibid., 242, 244, Figures 4.11 and 4.13.

22. Krysan and Farley, "The Residential Preferences of Blacks," 940, 969.

23. Sam Fulwood, *Waking from the Dream: My Life in the Black Middle Class* (New York: Anchor Books, 1996), 204–205 (quoting Pam Harris, an accountant with an Atlanta real estate management firm).

24. Erin Texeira, "Prince George's: A Dream Revised, *Baltimore Sun*, January 18, 1999 (quoting Alvin Thornton, former chair of the Prince George's County school board and associate provost of Howard University).

25. Charles, "Processes of Residential Segregation," 231; John Yinger, "Evidence on Discrimination in Consumer Markets," *Journal of Economic Perspectives,* Spring 1998, 23.

26. Roy L. Brooks, *Integration or Separation?* (Cambridge: Harvard University Press, 1996), 189 (quoting John Edgar Wideman).

27. Natalie Hopkinson (resident of Bloomingdale, a predominately black but rapidly gentrifying neighborhood in northwest Washington, D.C.), "I Won't Let D.C. Lose Its Flavor," *Washington Post*, June 17, 2001.

28. Michael Getler, "Labeling Racism," *Washington Post*, July 1, 2001; Michael Getler, "Buying Into the Hood," *Washington Post*, June 24, 2001.

29. See note 14 above.

30. Jonah Goldberg, "Keeping Whitey Out," *National Review Online*, October 8, 2002. http://www.nationalreview.com/goldberg/goldberg061801.shtml.

31. Wil Haygood, "Race in American Life: Ideals Giving Way to Reality," *Boston Globe*, September 14, 1997.

32. Tamar Jacoby, *Someone Else's House: America's Unfinished Struggle for Integration* (New York: Free Press, 1998), 523.

33. Brooks, *Integration or Separation?* 105.

34. Haygood, "Race in American Life"; "'Resegregation' Attracts Converts Among Blacks," *Boston Globe*, September 14, 1997.

35. See, generally, Ellis Cose, *The Rage of a Privileged Class* (New York: HarperCollins, 1993); Fulwood, *Waking from the Dream*; Lawrence Otis Graham, *Member of the Club: Reflections on Life in a Racially Polarized World* (New York: HarperCollins, 1995); Brent Staples, *Parallel Time: Growing Up in Black and White* (New York: Pantheon Books, 1994).

36. David B. Wilkins, Elizabeth Chambliss, Lisa A. Jones, and Haile Adamson, *Harvard Law School Report on the State of Black Alumni: 1869–2000* (Cambridge: Harvard Law School, 2002), 51.

37. Jane Gross, "A Black Enclave in the Hamptons Offering Comfort and Sanctity," *New York Times*, July 16, 2002.

38. Allan Richter, "Black and White on Long Island: Like Oil and Water," *New York Times*, June 16, 2002.

39. John Yemma, "The New Segregation: Black Community Reexamining School Busing," *Boston Globe*, September 15, 1997.

40. Wil Haygood, "Back to Business, Savannah's Black Leaders Say Past Holds Lessons for Future," *Boston Globe*, September 16, 1997.

41. "Testimony: Segregation Revisited," *New York Times Magazine*, September 15, 2002 (quoting George H. Ray Jr., Charles Redfern, and Bettye Golden Holloway).

42. Beverly Tatum, "Identity Development in Adolescence," in *Why Are All the Black Kids Sitting Together in the Cafeteria? and Other Conversations About Race* (New York: Basic Books, 1997), 52–74.

43. Tamar Lewin, "Growing Up, Growing Apart: Fast Friends Try to Resist the Pressure to Divide by Race," *New York Times*, June 24, 2000, http://www.nytimes.com/library/national/race/062500lewin -kids.html (accessed July 8, 2002).

44. Ibid. "There is a consensus that the split [between black and white kids in the very integrated South Orange-Maplewood, New Jersey, School District] is mostly, though hardly exclusively, a matter of blacks' pulling away"; "I think the black kids feel like they're black and the white kids feel like they're white because the black kids feel like they're black"; "Everybody gets along, but I think the white kids are more friendly toward black or interracial kids, and the black kids aren't as interested back, just because of stupid stereotypical stuff like music and style."

45. Lynne Jensen, "Landlord Was Not Colorblind, Jury Rules: Discrimination Could Net $100,000," *New Orleans Times-Picayune*, March 7, 2002; "In Their Own Words," July 2002, http://www.nationalfairhousing.org/html/Updatearchive/julyup-date/pg3.htm; Greater New Orleans Community Data Center, "Lakeview Neighborhood," http://www.gnocdc.org/orleans/5/37/snapshot.html.

46. Recent cases, http://www.fairhousing.com/news_archive/may2002.htm, (last accessed September 15, 2002.

47. Associated Press State and Local Wire, "Landlord Admits to Racial Discrimination," May 13, 2002.

48. David C. Savage, "Reach of Fair Housing Act Crux of High Court Case," *Los Angeles Times*, December 2, 2002, A1.

49. Recent cases, http://www.fairhousing.com/news_archive/releases/cafhc4-9-2002.htm, (last accessed September 15, 2002.)

50. Margery Austin Turner et al., *Discrimination in Metropolitan Housing Markets: National Results from Phase I HDS 2000*, Final Report, November 2002, http://www.huduser.org /publications/pdf/Phase1_Report.pdf (accessed November 25, 2002), 3:1–3:19.

51. Ibid., 8:1.

52. Ibid., 8:11.

53. Ibid., 6:16.

54. Ibid.

55. Urban Institute, *What We Know About Mortgage Lending Discrimination*, Report for U.S. Department of Housing and Urban Development, September 1999.

56. Association of Community Organizations for Reform Now (ACORN), "Giving No Credit Where Credit Is Due," 1998, http://www.acorn.org/ACORNarchives.

57. U.S. Department of Housing and Urban Development, *Unequal Burden: Income and Racial Disparities in Subprime Lending in America*, April 2000, http://www.hud.gov/library/bookshelf18/pressrel/subprime.html; U.S. Department of Housing and Urban Development, *Curbing Predatory Home Mortgage Lending,* June 2000, http://www.huduser.org/publications/hsgfin/curbing.html.

58. John Yinger, *Closed Doors, Opportunities Lost: The Continuing Costs of Housing Discrimination* (New York: Russell Sage Foundation, 1995), 244; George C. Galster, "More Than Skin Deep: The Effect of Housing Discrimination on the Extent and Pattern of Racial Residential Segregation in the United States," in *Housing Desegregation and Federal Policy*, ed. John M. Goering (Chapel Hill: University of North Carolina Press, 1986), 133.

59. Calmore, "Race/ism Lost and Found," 1071.

Chapter 2: Bucking the Trend

1. Ingrid Gould Ellen, *Sharing America's Neighborhoods: The Prospects for Stable Racial Integration* (Cambridge: Harvard University Press: 2000), 21.

2. Ibid.

3. Phillip Nyden et al., "Chapter 13: Conclusion," *Cityscape: A Journal of Policy Development and Research* 4, no. 2 (1998): 269, n. 1, http://www.huduser.org/periodicals/cityscape/vol4num2/current.html.

4. Lois M. Quinn and John Pawasarat, "Racial Integration in Urban America: A Block Level Analysis of African American and White Housing Patterns" (University of Wisconsin–Milwaukee, Employment and Training Institute, December 2002, revised January 2003), 10, http://www.uwm.edu/Dept/ETI/integration/integration.htm. Admittedly, the authors of this study may have been

self-serving in creating a new, subjective definition of "integration" that placed the city of Milwaukee high in the rankings of
"integrated" cities while leaving cities with fewer blacks that typically did better than Milwaukee under traditional indices of "segregation" low in their ranking. The study was heavily criticized
on this account; see, e.g., Joel McNally, "Poof! Segregation Van-
ishes?" *Capital Times*, February 1, 2003. However, the empirical
findings using this new definition of "integration" do not appear
to have been disputed. The controversy this study attracted centered on what the most appropriate or useful measure of integration or segregation should be, given that cities with many blacks
tend to be more segregated than cities with few blacks.

5. Nyden et al., "Chapter 1: Neighborhood Racial and Ethnic Diversity in U.S. Cities," *Cityscape: A Journal of Policy Development and
Research* 4, no. 2 (1998): 7, 9–13, http://www.huduser.org/
periodicals/cityscape/vol4num2/current.html.

6. Barbara Ferman, Theresa Singleton, and Don DeMarco, "Chapter
3: West Mount Airy, Philadelphia," *Cityscape: A Journal of Policy
Development and Research* 4, no. 2 (1998): 41 (citing Juliet Salt-
man, *A Fragile Movement: The Struggle for Neighborhood Stabi-
lization* [New York: Greenwood Press, 1990]).

7. Ibid., 29–54. Unless otherwise noted, all of the factual or anecdotal information about West Mount Airy that appears in this
chapter is supported at ibid., 29–54. Any statements of opinion
are my own.

8. Ibid., 40. West Mount Airy also had a disproportionate number
of Jews who were active within the Havura movement within
Judaism, which placed key emphasis on community and family,
was disproportionately made up of highly educated, liberal Jews,
and being religiously orthodox, required that no driving take
place on the Sabbath. Hence the fact that West Mount Airy
enabled such residents to walk to their synagogues contributed to
neighborhood stability.

9. Ibid., 44 (citing Gary Orfield, "The Movement for Housing Inte-
gration: Rationale and Nature of the Challenge," in *Housing
Desegregation and Federal Policy*, ed. John Goering [Chapel Hill:
University of North Carolina Press, 1986]).

10. Darryl Carter, "Not Just Black and White," *In These Times*, March 18, 2002, 18.

11. Oralander Brand-Williams, "The Cost of Segregation Part III: Where We're Headed; Shaker Heights: City Works at Integration," *Detroit News*, January 28, 2002.

12. Richard A. Smith, "Creating Stable Racially Integrated Communities: A Review," *Journal of Urban Affairs* 15 (1993): 115, 128–131.

13. Andrew Gordon, Hubert Locke, and Cy Uberg, "Chapter 10: Ethnic Diversity in Southeast Seattle," *Cityscape: A Journal of Policy Development and Research* 4, no. 2 (1998): 213, http://www.huduser.org/periodicals/cityscape/vol4num2/current.html (quoting an anonymous interviewee). Unless otherwise noted, all of the factual or anecdotal information about Southeast Seattle that appears in this chapter is supported at ibid., 197–216. Any statements of opinion are my own.

14. Ibid., 213 (quoting an anonymous interviewee).

15. Ibid., 215–216.

16. Nyden et al., "Chapter 13," 265.

17. Ibid., 266.

18. Ibid., 264–265.

19. Ron French, "Success Stories Offer Lesson," *Detroit News*, January 28, 2002.

20. Rona Marech, "Of Race and Place: San Antonio/Oakland Flavors Meld in Community East of Lake," *San Francisco Chronicle*, May 31, 2002, http://www.sfgate.com/cgi-bin/article.cgi?file=/c/a/2002/05/31/EB175201.DTL (quoting Rob Jamal Jackson, 30, an African American man who co-teaches a hip-hop class at the East-Side Arts Alliance and lives with his wife on East 17th street).

21. Nyden et al., "Chapter 1," 11–13.

22. Marech, "San Antonio/Oakland Flavors."

23. Nyden et al., "Chapter 13," 262.

24. Nyden et al., "Chapter 1," 12; see also pages 11–13 for other factual assertions.

25. French, "Success Stories."

26. Ferman et al., "Chapter 3," 46 (citing Leonard Heumann, "The Definition and Analysis of Stable Racial Integration: The Case of

West Mount Airy, Philadelphia" [Ph.D. diss., University of Pennsylvania, 1973], and Samuel Brown, "Community Attachment in a Racially Integrated Neighborhood" [Ph.D. diss., University of Pennsylvania, 1990]).

27. Gordon et al., "Chapter 10," 212.
28. Ibid., 214.
29. Ibid., 215.
30. Ferman et al., "Chapter 3," 50–51.
31. All of the factual assertions about Montclair are supported in Lisa Funderburg, "Integration Anxiety," in *The American Civil Rights Movement: Readings and Interpretations*, ed. Raymond D'Angelo (Guilford, Conn.: McGraw-Hill/Dushkin, 2001), 526–533. Any statements of opinion are my own.
32. Ibid., 530.
33. Ferman et al., "Chapter 3," 54.
34. Funderburg, "Integration Anxiety," 532–533.
35. For example, the most recent, fully comprehensive report on the status of African Americans, *A Common Destiny: Blacks and American Society*, which was composed by more than thirty eminent social scientists and scholars, unanimously concluded that gaps in socioeconomic status between whites and blacks have narrowed mainly under two conditions: (1) general economic growth and expansion; and (2) broad, government-backed efforts at antidiscrimination, integration, and greater inclusion. Gerald D. Jaynes and Robin M. Williams Jr., eds., *A Common Destiny: Blacks and American Society* (Washington, D.C.: National Academy Press, 1989). "[A]t the time [the 1989 report] represented the best consensus of social scientific thinking and ... there are strong reasons to believe that the same not only holds true for African Americans but also characterizes the experiences of many Latino and Native Americans as well." Lawrence D. Bobo, "Inclusion's Last Hour?: Affirmative Action Before the Bush Court," January 17, 2003, http://ccsre.stanford.edu/EV_events_BoboInclusion.htm.
36. *Grutter v. Bollinger*, 123 S. Ct. 2325 (2003) (citing *Loving v. Virginia*, 388 U.S. 1 [1967] and *Plyer v. Doe*, 457 U.S. 202 [1982]).
37. Ibid. (citing *Brown v. Board of Education*, 347 U.S. 483 [1954]).

Chapter 3: Institutionalized Separatism

1. See, generally, Myron Orfield, *American Metropolitics* (Washington, D.C.: Brookings Institution Press, 2002), 9–21.

2. In this book I focus on the four broad racial categories that have been used by most demographers who research and interpret census trends: whites, blacks, Latinos, and Asians. I recognize that there are many hues, many subgroups, and much more complexity than these categories imply. American Indians or Native Americans are particularly invisible when it comes to demographic analyses. The story of race relations is always more complicated than anyone who is trying to provide a brief synthesis can convey.

3. William H. Frey, Population Studies Center, University of Michigan, *Census 2000 Shows Large Black Return to the South, Reinforcing the Region's "White-Black" Demographic Profile* (Ann Arbor: PSC Publications, May 2001), 2, 4, and 6 (Figure 1), http://www.frey-demographer.org/reports/rro1–473.pdf (accessed February 16, 2004).

4. See, for example, Edward L. Glaeser and Jacob L. Vigdor, "Racial Segregation in the 2000 Census: Promising News," Survey Series (Washington, D.C.: Brookings Institution, April 2001).

5. In the stubbornly segregated largest cities of the Midwest and Northeast it could take another 70 years just to reach the upper bound of the range of moderate segregation. See Douglas S. Massey and Nancy A. Denton, *American Apartheid: Segregation and the Making of the Underclass* (Cambridge: Harvard University Press, 1993), 221.

6. "Ethnic Diversity Grows, Neighborhood Integration Lags Behind" (report, Lewis Mumford Center, University of Albany, April 3, 2001, revised December 18, 2001), http://mumford1.dyndns.org/cen2000/WholePop/WPreport/page1.html (last visited Jan. 22, 2004), 4.

7. Glaeser and Vigdor, "Racial Segregation," 4–5.

8. Ibid., 7.

9. "Ethnic Diversity Grows," 30.

10. Ibid., 14.

11. Ibid., 21.

12. Ibid., 18–19.

It could be argued that I am overstating the case about Latino separation because about half of the Latino population is white. See Orlando Patterson, "Race by the Numbers," *New York Times*, May 8, 2001.

The Census Bureau uses the term "Hispanic" to cover a congeries of Latin peoples. Technically, this term does not connote race. Hispanics can be white, Indian, black, Asian, some other race, or some combination of races. About half of Hispanics—48 percent—identified themselves as white in the 2000 census. This is not surprising, however, as the question about race on the census form offers Hispanics the options of identifying themselves only as white, black, American Indian, or one of several Asian or Pacific Islander subgroups, or "some other race." A separate question regarding ethnicity offers the option of identifying oneself as Hispanic—a bureaucratic invention of the Census Bureau that started appearing on all census forms in 1980. Campbell Gibson and Kay Jung, "Historical Census Statistics on Population Totals by Race, 1790 to 1990, and by Hispanic Origin, 1970 to 1990, for the United States, Regions, Divisions, and States" (Working Paper Series no. 56, Population Division, Bureau of the Census, Washington, D.C., September 2002), http://www.census.gov/population/www/documentation/twps0056.html (last accessed January 22, 2004).

Most Latinos in America are of Mexican (58.5 percent), Puerto Rican (9.6 percent), or Cuban (3.5 percent) origin—the three largest subgroups in 2000. But the fastest-growing Hispanic subgroups—"the New Latinos"—hail from the Dominican Republic and a diverse set of countries in Central America—like El Salvador—and South America. John R. Logan, "The New Latinos: Who They Are, Where They Are" (report, Lewis Mumford Center for Comparative Urban and Regional Research, University of Albany, September 10, 2001), http://mumford1.dyndns.org/cen2000/HispanicPop/HspReport/HspReportPage1.html (last accessed January 22, 2004).

Apart from Census bureaucratese, there is a 500-year history of

Latino culture in the United States. Admittedly, this culture defies simplistic characterization; under the Latino umbrella is a rich mix of subcultures emanating from different countries of origin. But Latinos generally retain language and native culture over succeeding generations to a much higher degree than the major white ethnic groups of European descent. And Latino culture is certainly distinct from that of the vast majority of whites of European descent. In this sense, when I speak of whites in this book I am speaking of non-Hispanic whites.

13. Data taken from U.S. Census Bureau American Factfinder, http://factfinder.census.gov/home/saff/main.html?_lang=en.

14. Glaeser and Vigdor, "Racial Segregation," 10–11, 14; Roberto Suro and Audrey Singer, *Latino Growth in Metropolitan America: Changing Patterns, New Locations*, Survey Series (Washington, D.C.: Brookings Institution, July 2000); U.S. Census Bureau American Factfinder, http://factfinder.census.gov/home/saff/main.html?_lang=en.

15. Alan Berube, *Census Matters 2000: Racial Change in the Nation's Largest Cities: Evidence from the 2000 Census* (Washington, D.C.: Brookings Institution Center on Urban and Metropolitan Policy, April 2001).

16. Ibid. Percentages generated using data taken from the Brookings report and the U.S. Census Bureau American Factfinder at http://factfinder.census.gov/home/saff/main.html?_lang=en.

17. Some explain white out-migration solely in economic terms. For demographer William Frey, Milwaukee's situation is typical of the cities that whites are leaving: "I don't think there is anything unique to Milwaukee. . . . It's a place where the status quo lives on: a blue-collar, industrial city in which people are leaving for something better and the people who stay are left holding the bag." Mark Lisheron and Bill Bishop, "Growth of Creative Hubs Redefines 'White Flight,'" *Austin American-Statesman*, September 1, 2002.

18. John R. Logan, "The New Ethnic Enclaves in America's Suburbs" (report, Lewis Mumford Center for Comparative Urban and Regional Research, University of Albany, July 9, 2001),

http://mumford1.dyndns.org/cen2000/suburban/SuburbanReport/
page1.html (last visited January 22, 2004).

19. John R. Logan et al., "Separating the Children" (report, Lewis
Mumford Center, University of Albany, May 4, 2001, revised
December 28, 2001), http://mumford1.dyndns.org/cen2000/
Under18Pop/U18Preport/page1.html (last accessed January 22,
2004).

20. The white suburban population rose by a mere 5 percent in the
1990s. Meanwhile, the number of blacks in suburbs increased by
38 percent, and the number of Latinos and Asians in suburbs
exploded, rising 72 percent and 84 percent, respectively. Asians
are the most suburbanized minority group—58 percent live in
suburbs, while nearly half of Latinos call suburbia home. African
Americans lag behind, with only 39 percent living in suburbs.
Logan, "New Ethnic Enclaves," 1, 2.

21. "Ethnic Diversity Grows," 3 (80.2% white, 6.7% black, 7.9%
Hispanic, 3.9% Asian).

22. Ibid. (51.4% black, 33.0% white, 11.4% Hispanic, 3.3% Asian).

23. Bill Saporito, "The Rap on Bush and Cheney," *Time*, July 22,
2002, 22.

24. Barbara Ehrenreich, "Nickel-And-Dimed, On (Not) Getting By in
America," *Harper's Magazine* 298 (January 1999): 37. In 2003,
the median national wage needed to afford a modest two-bedroom rental unit was $15.21 per hour, significantly more than the
federal minimum wage of $5.15. "Out of Reach 2003: America's
Housing Wage Climbs," National Low Income Housing Coalition, available at http://www.nlihc.org/oor2003/index.php
(accessed February 14, 2004).

25. Ehrenreich, "Nickel-And-Dimed."

26. Douglas S. Massey and Mitchell L. Eggers, "The Spatial Concentration of Affluence and Poverty During the 1970s," *Urban
Affairs Quarterly* 29 (1993): 299, 306, 308. According to the federal government, in 2000, a family of four with an annual income
of $17,029 was "poor." Affluence, on the other hand, is defined
as income exceeding four times the poverty level—$68,116 or
higher for a family of four, although the average person probably

thinks of affluence in much more gilded terms than $70,000 a year for a household. Douglas S. Massey and Mary J. Fischer, "The Geography of Inequality in the United States, 1950–2000," paper prepared for the Brookings-Wharton Conference on Urban Affairs, Brookings Institution, Washington, D.C., October 24–25, 2002, 4.

27. If we were to step back from the neighborhood level, we could tell a happier story. Across entire metropolitan areas, class segregation has declined substantially since 1970. In other words, over the latter half of the twentieth century, rich and poor families have come to inhabit the same metropolitan areas, but rising class segregation at the neighborhood level has ensured that they are buffered from one another. Ibid., 27.

28. Ibid., 30.

29. Massey and Denton, *American Apartheid*.

30. Mary J. Fischer, "The Relative Importance of Income and Race in Determining Residential Outcomes in U.S. Urban Areas, 1970–2000, *Urban Affairs Review* 38, no. 5 (May 2003): 691–692.

31. Paul A. Jargowsky, *Stunning Progress, Hidden Problems: The Dramatic Decline of Concentrated Poverty in the 1990s*, Living Census Series (Washington, D.C.: Brookings Institution, May 2003).

32. Paul A. Jargowsky, "Take the Money and Run: Economic Segregation in U.S. Metropolitan Areas," *American Sociological Review* 61 (1996): 984, 990–991.

33. Fischer, "Relative Importance of Income and Race," 25; Alan J. Abramson et al., "The Changing Geography of Metropolitan Opportunity: The Segregation of the Poor in U.S. Metropolitan Areas, 1970 to 1990," *Housing Policy Debate* 6 (1995): 45, 59.

34. Sheldon Danziger and Peter Gottschalk, *America Unequal* (Cambridge: Harvard University Press and the Russell Sage Foundation, 1995); Frank Levy, *The New Dollars and Dreams: American Incomes and Economic Change* (New York: Russell Sage Foundation, 1998).

35. David Cay Johnston, *Perfectly Legal: The Covert Campaign to*

Rig Our Tax System to Benefit the Super Rich—And Cheat Everybody Else (New York: Portfolio, 2003), 30–31, 35.

36. Ibid., 33–35.

37. Paul Krugman, "For Richer: How the Permissive Capitalism of the Boom Destroyed American Equality," *New York Times Magazine*, October 20, 2002, 62.

38. Shannon Mullen, "The House of Big," *New Jersey Monthly*, March 1, 2002, 64.

39. Robert H. Frank, *Luxury Fever* (New York: Free Press, 1999), 146.

40. Massey and Fischer, "Geography of Inequality," 29.

41. John R. Logan, "Separate and Unequal: The Neighborhood Gap for Blacks and Hispanics in Metropolitan America" (report, Lewis Mumford Center for Comparative Urban and Regional Research, University of Albany, October 13, 2002), http://mumford1.dyndns.org/cen2000/SepUneq/SUReport/SURep-Page1.htm (last accessed January 23, 2004).

42. To illustrate my point, consider four fictional affluent families with incomes above $60,000. Depending on their respective race and class, they will live in different circumstances. The black family will live in a neighborhood with a median income of $45,000; the Latino family, $49,000; the white family, $60,000; and the Asian family, $64,000. For blacks and Latinos, the neighborhood gap is widest and growing fastest at the top of the income spectrum—their white counterparts at the top of the income scale are much farther ahead in terms of neighborhood returns. But this gap appears across the income scale. Ibid., Table 3.

The slight average advantage Asians enjoy over whites is deceptive. This advantage, which also applies across the income spectrum, is declining over time. But more importantly, this national average advantage for Asians disappears in the metropolitan areas where Asians are most concentrated—places like New York, Los Angeles, Honolulu, San Jose, and San Francisco. In those places, Asians tend to live in neighborhoods with much less economic standing than their white counterparts. Ibid., Tables 11 and 12 and accompanying text.

43. Douglas S. Massey and Mary J. Fischer, "Does Rising Income Bring Integration? New Results for Blacks, Hispanics, and Asians in 1990," *Social Science Research* 28 (1999): 316–326; Massey and Denton, *American Apartheid*.

44. Massey and Denton, *American Apartheid*, 17–18.

45. Ebenezer Howard, *Garden Cities of Tomorrow* (London: Swan Sonnenschein, 1902).

46. *Village of Euclid v. Amber Realty Co.*, 272 U.S. 365 (1926).

47. *Ambler Realty Co. v. Village of Euclid*, 297 F. 307, 316 (N.D. Ohio 1924).

48. *Village of Belle Terre v. Boraas*, 416 U.S. 1 (1974).

49. *Berman v. Parker*, 348 U.S. 26 (1954).

50. Jerry Frug, "Symposium: Surveying Law and Borders; The Geography of Community," *Stanford Law Review* 48 (1996): 1047, 1070–1071.

51. U.S. Bureau of the Census, *1997 Census of Governments* (Washington, D.C.: Bureau of the Census, 1999).

52. Nancy Burns, *The Formation of American Local Governments: Private Values in Public Institutions* (New York: Oxford University Press, 1994), 75–95; Gregory R. Weiher, *The Fractured Metropolis: Political Fragmentation and Metropolitan Segregation*, (Albany: State University of New York Press, 1991), 184–185.

53. David Rusk, *Cities Without Suburbs* (Baltimore: Johns Hopkins University Press, 1993), 34–35.

54. Paul Kantor, *The Dependent City Revisited* (Boulder: Westview Press, 1995), 164–167.

55. In Los Angeles County, for example, a study of thirty municipalities created between 1950 and 1970 found that most of the new municipalities showed increasing income and racial homogeneity compared to older, existing towns. Gary Miller, *Cities by Contract: The Politics of Municipal Incorporation* (Cambridge: MIT Press, 1981), 134.

56. Weiher, *The Fractured Metropolis*, 13–15, 113.

57. Peter Hall, *Cities of Tomorrow: An Intellectual History of Urban Planning and Design in the Twentieth Century* (Oxford: Blackwell, 1988), 291–294; Kenneth Jackson, *Crabgrass Frontier: The Suburbanization of the United States* (New York: Oxford University Press, 1985), 203–218.

58. Jackson, *Crabgrass Frontier*, 203–209, 213–218.

59. Michael Jones-Correa, "The Origins and Diffusion of Racial Restrictive Covenants," *Political Science Quarterly* 115 (Winter 2000–2001): 541; Ken Fireman, "Racist Clause Comes Back to Haunt Bush; Deed on Home Had Whites-Only Covenant," *N.Y. Newsday*, July 14, 1999.

60. Massey and Denton, *American Apartheid*, 51.

61. Jackson, *Crabgrass Frontier*, 203–209, 213–218.

62. Frug, "Geography of Community," 1068.

63. Melvin L. Oliver and Thomas M. Shapiro, *Black Wealth / White Wealth: A New Perspective on Racial Inequality* (New York: Routledge, 1995).

64. Frug, "Geography of Community."

65. Raymond A. Mohl, "Race and Space in the Modern City: Interstate–95 and the Black Community in Miami," in *Urban Policy in Twentieth-Century America,* ed. Arnold R. Hirsch and Raymond A. Mohl (New Brunswick, N.J.: Rutgers University Press, 1993), 102, 134–136.

66. Between 1956 and 1998, the federal government spent over $411 billion on highways. Senate Budget Committee, *Budget Bulletin: Informed Budgeteer*, 105th Cong., 2nd sess., no.8, March 30, 1998. The most recent transportation legislation, enacted in 1998, authorized an additional $217 billion in spending for surface transportation, including highways and mass transit. *The Transportation Equity Act for the 21st Century*, Public Law 105–178, 112 Stat. 107 (June 9, 1998); see Benjamin K. Olson, "The Transportation Equity Act for the 21st Century: The Failure of Metropolitan Planning Organizations to Reform Federal Transportation Policy in Metropolitan Areas," *Transportation Law Journal* 28 (2000): 147, 156. Historically, the majority of surface transportation funds have been allocated to highway spending. Conservatively, if one assumes that just half of the "TEA–21" funds are allocated to highway construction, total federal highway spending since 1956 will have exceeded $500 billion.

67. Sheryll D. Cashin, "Localism, Self-Interest, and the Tyranny of the Favored Quarter: Addressing the Barriers to New Regionalism," *Georgia Law Journal* 88 (2000): 1985, 2007, n. 115 (citing sources).

68. Frug, "Geography of Community," 1069.

69. Ibid., 1071.

70. Michael H. Schill and Susan M. Wachter, "The Spatial Bias of Federal Housing Law and Policy: Concentrated Poverty in Urban America," *University of Pennsylvania Law Review* 143 (1995): 1285, 1290–1308.

71. Frug, "Geography of Community," 1069; Schill and Wachter, "The Spatial Bias," 1285, 1290–1308.

72. Arnold R. Hirsch, *Making the Second Ghetto: Race and Housing in Chicago, 1940–1960* (Cambridge: Cambridge University Press, 1983), 223, 242–243.

73. Massey and Denton, *American Apartheid*, 37–38.

74. All information concerning cluster profiling is drawn from John T. Metzger, "Clustered Spaces: Racial Profiling in Real Estate Investment," paper prepared for the International Seminar on Segregation and the City, Lincoln Institute of Land Policy, Cambridge, Mass., July 26–28, 2001.

75. Ibid.

76. Ibid.

77. Sam Fulwood III, *Waking from the Dream: My Life in the Black Middle Class* (New York: Anchor Books, 1996), 190.

78. Burns, *Formation of American Local Governments*, 6, 75–95, 102.

79. David Dillon, "Fortress America: More and More of Us Are Living Behind Locked Gates," *Planning* 60, no. 6 (1994): 9.

80. Edward J. Blakely and Mary Gail Snyder, *Fortress America: Gated Communities in the United States* (Cambridge: Brookings Institution Press, 1997), 152, 155–156 (quoting a participant from a study on community and place).

Chapter 4: The Dilemma of the Black Middle Class

1. David J. Dent, "The New Black Suburbs," *New York Times Magazine*, June 14, 1992, 18, 24 (quoting Radamase Cabrera, an urban planner and resident of Prince George's County).

2. Marita Golden, "Prince George's Convert," *Washingtonian*, July 2003, 35, 36.

3. Most of the empirical claims made in this chapter are supported in an extensive research article I recently published: Sheryll D. Cashin, "Middle-Class Black Suburbs and the State of Integration," *Cornell Law Review* 86 (2001): 729.

4. Myron Orfield, *American Metropolitics: The New Suburban Reality* (Washington, D.C.: Brookings Institution Press, 2002), 11; Gary Orfield and Carol Ashkinaze, *The Closing Door: Conservative Policy and Black Opportunity* (Chicago: University of Chicago Press, 1991), 81 (noting that "[h]ousing and neighborhood choice was seriously … limited for higher-income blacks" in the Atlanta area in the 1980s and that "rental and homeownership markets, particularly in the more desirable suburbs, remained largely closed even to blacks with sufficient incomes"); Mary Patillo-McCoy, *Black Picket Fences: Privilege and Peril Among the Black Middle Class* (Chicago: University of Chicago Press, 1999), 27 (noting that the black middle class has always been in a constant process of out-migration as it attempts to leave poor neighborhoods "but has never been able to get very far"); while black middle-class enclaves have developed in close proximity to poor neighborhoods, as the number of black middle-class persons has increased, the size of black middle-class enclaves has expanded and created greater physical separation in an otherwise contiguous "Black Belt" (ibid.).

5. Orfield, *American Metropolitics*, 2. For the listing of "at-risk" suburbs in the D.C. metro area, see Metropolitan Area Research Corporation, "Washington, D.C.–Baltimore Region: Community Classification," Metropolitan Area Research Corporation, http://www.metroresearch.org/maps/national_report/DC_clus.pdf (accessed August 24, 2003).

6. "The 2002 Challenge Index," *Washington Post*, December 5, 2002; Jay Mathews, "High Schools Aim for More College-Level Classes," District Extra, *Washington Post*, December 5, 2002; "School Guide: Washington Area Education," *Washington Post*, http//www.washingtonpost.com/wp-dyn/education/schoolguide (accessed January 26, 2004).

7. Erin Texeira, "Prince George's: A Dream Revised," *Baltimore Sun*, January 18, 1999. For most recent rankings based upon

school test performance among Maryland school districts, see "How do we compare to all other school districts?" http://mdk12.org/data/worksheets/wspindex.asp (accessed February 16, 2004).

8. Avis Thomas-Lester, "Fleeing Residents Cite County's Shortcomings, Schools, Lack of Amenities Criticized," *Washington Post*, June 21, 2001.

9. Ibid.

10. For information about individual schools, see "School Guide: Washington Area Education," *Washington Post,* http//www.washingtonpost.com/wp-dyn/education/schoolguide/ (accessed January 26, 2004).

11. Dalton Conley, *Being Black, Living in the Red: Race, Wealth, and Social Policy in America* (Berkeley: University of California Press, 1999), 68–79.

12. Fedstats, "Crimes Reported in Prince George's County Maryland, Crime 2000," http://www.fedstats.gov/mapstats/crime/county/24033.html (accessed February 15, 2003) (showing 72 murders and 4,174 aggravated assaults); Fedstats, "Crimes Reported in Montgomery County Maryland, Crime 2000," http://www.fedstats.gov/mapstats/crime/county/24031.html (accessed February 15, 2004) (showing 12 murders and 873 aggravated assaults).

13. Todd Shields, "For Some Black Pr. Georgians, Charles Is a Better Place to Be," *Washington Post*, June 22, 1997 (noting the increased migration of upwardly mobile African Americans from Prince George's County to Charles County).

14. Craig Whitlock and David S. Fallis, "County Officers Kill More Often Than Any in U.S.; Official Ruled Shootings Justified in Every Case—Even of Unarmed Citizens," *Washington Post*, July 1, 2001.

15. See James Forman Jr., "Diversity Alone Won't Stop Police Violence," *Washington Post*, July 15, 2001. To his credit, when he was the chief county prosecutor, current County Executive Jack Johnson prosecuted eleven officers in seven cases but won no convictions, and he made an issue of police wrongdoing in his campaign for county executive. Most accountability for police

brutality in Prince George's County has come from federal Justice Department investigations rather than citizen outcry. See, e.g., Jamie Stockwell and Ruben Castaneda, "Pr. George's Agrees to Curb Excessive Force by Police," *Washington Post*, January 23, 2004.

16. Nancy Burns, *The Formation of American Local Governments: Private Values in Public Institutions* (Oxford: Oxford University Press, 1997).

17. Cashin, "Middle-Class Black Suburbs," 758. In addition to the empirical studies cited in Cashin, see Andrew A. Beveridge and Jeannie D'Amico, *Black and White Property Tax Rates and Other Homeownership Costs in 30 Metropolitan Areas: A Preliminary Report* (New York: Queens College of the City University of New York, Department of Sociology, Program for Applied Social Research, 1994). Also see Diana Jean Schemo, "Suburban Taxes Higher for Blacks, Analysis Shows," *New York Times*, August 17, 1994.

18. Thomas-Lester, "Fleeing Residents."

19. Golden, "Prince George's Convert," 36.

20. Thomas-Lester, "Fleeing Residents."

21. Sara Kehaulani Goo, "County Residents Hunger for More Dining Options," *Washington Post*, June 21, 2001. The Borders bookstore chain is a notable exception. It goes beyond market profiles and attempts to make its stores fit markets it finds. Using that method, Borders "dug deep" into Prince George's County to find a location that would enable it to reach affluent black customers, opening a store at the Boulevard at Capital Centre. Krissah Williams, "For Sales, Focus on Local Interests, Borders Tries New Marketing Approach in Prince George's," *Washington Post*, November 24, 2003.

22. Golden, "Prince George's Convert," 37.

23. For an extensive analysis of the phenomenon of commercial disinvestment in contemporary black suburbs and the likely reasons for such disinvestment, including the risk that racial information leads investors to undervalue the assets of blacks, see Mary Jo Wiggins, "Race, Class, and Suburbia: The Modern Black Suburb as a 'Race-Making Situation,'" *University of Michigan Journal of*

Law Reform 35 (2002): 749. One recent study of the ten-county Atlanta region found that residents of affluent black neighborhoods were more likely to have to leave their neighborhood and drive some distance in order to dine at a non–fast-food restaurant, to grocery shop, or to see movies as compared to residents of white neighborhoods that had *less* aggregate buying power. Ruling out income or buying power differences as an explanation, the researchers concluded that the disparity was likely due to "inaccurate or stereotyped marketing profiles of black neighborhoods or racial bias in business decision making." Amy Helling and David S. Sawicki, "Race and Residential Accessibility to Shopping and Services," *Housing Policy Debate* 14, no. 1–2 (2003): 69, 96–97.

24. Civil Rights Forum on Communications Policy, "When Being Number One Is Not Enough: The Impact of Advertising Practices on Minority-Owned and Minority-Formatted Broadcasting Stations" (online report, January 1999), http://www.fcc.gov/Bureau/Mass_Media/Informal/ad-study/adsynposis.html (accessed January 26, 2004). In one case, a firm was quoted as encouraging advertisers to avoid urban stations and "instead buy time on those that would offer 'prospects, not suspects.'" Paul Farhi, "Advertisers Avoiding Minority Radio; FCC Study Cites Washington Market for Black and Hispanic 'Dictates,'" *Washington Post*, January 13, 1999.

25. Orfield and Ashkinaze, *The Closing Door*, 115–116, 127.

26. Thomas-Lester, "Fleeing Residents."

Chapter 5: White Separatism

1. Median income figures used in this chapter are based upon the 2000 census.

2. Myron Orfield, *American Metropolitics: The New Suburban Reality* (Washington, D.C.: Brookings Institution Press, 2002), 3. For the categorization of Fairfax City as an affluent suburban job center, see Myron Orfield, "Washington Metropolitics: A Regional Agenda for Community and Stability," (Metropolitan Area Research Corporation, 1999), http://www.metroresearch.org/maps/region_maps/DC_report.pdf.

3. Lewis Mumford Center, "Ethnic Diversity Grows, Neighborhood Integration Lags Behind," (Lewis Mumford Center, April 3, 2001), 6, http://mumford1.dyndns.org/cen2000/WholePop/WPreport/page1.html

4. United States Kerner Commission, *Report of the National Advisory Commission on Civil Disorders* (Washington, D.C.: U.S. Government Printing Office, 1968), 1. The only difference from the Kerner Commission prediction is that there are now many gradations. To assess race and class inequality in America solely in terms of the black and white races would offer an inaccurate portrayal. Other races, nationalities, and ethnic groups populate and lay claim to America's promise. Added to this complexity is the fact that neither blacks nor whites are monolithic in their experience of race and class separation.

5. Orfield, *American Metropolitics*, 2–3, 33, Table 2.3.

6. Myron Orfield, *Metropolitics: A Regional Agenda for Community and Stability* (Washington D.C.: Brookings Institution Press, 1997), 2, 5.

7. Orfield, *American Metropolitics*, 2. For the categorization of Alexandria as an "at-risk" suburb, see Orfield, "Washington Metropolitics."

8. This was a 2002 ranking produced by the *Washington Post*, which now no longer provides such comparisons across schools districts. For intradistrict information on top schools, see *Washington Post*, "Washington Post Top Schools Index," 2003, http://www.washingtonpost.com/wp-dyn/education/schoolguide/topschools (accessed January 30, 2004).

9. *Washington Post*, "School Guide: Washington Area Education," http://www.washingtonpost.com/wp-dyn/education/schoolguide/ (accessed January 30, 2004).

10. Liz Seymour, "School Bonds Pass Easily; Fairfax, Loudon Pass Big Proposals," *Washington Post*, November 7, 2001.

11. Fairfax County complete chart '98–'02: Fairfax County, Virginia, 2002 Crime and Police Activity Statistics, http://www.co.fairfax.va.us/ps/police/pdf/Page3–02.pdf (accessed January 30, 2004). Montgomery County Department of Police, "Montgomery County Police Release: Crime Statistics for 2002," http://www.

montgomerycountymd.gov/mc/services/police/media/crimestats1.
html (accessed January 30, 2004).

12. Fedstats, "Crimes Reported in Fairfax County Virginia, Crime
2000," http://www.fedstats.gov/mapstats/crime/county/51059.
html (accessed February 15, 2004); Fedstats, "Crimes Reported in
Prince George's County Maryland, Crime 2000," http://www.fed-
stats.gov/mapstats/crime/county/24033.html (accessed February
15, 2003).

13. Michael D. Shear, "Kilgore Promises Crackdown on Gangs,
Attorney General Warns of Growing Va. Problem," *Washington
Post*, May 29, 2003.

14. Kenneth Bredemeier, "Fairfax County," *Washington Post*, March
19, 2003.

15. Sheryll D. Cashin, "Localism, Self-Interest, and the Tyranny of
the Favored Quarter: Addressing the Barriers to New Regionalism," *Georgia Law Journal* 88 (2000): 1985, 2004. All of the factual claims made about favored-quarter communities in this
chapter are generally supported at ibid., 2004–2015.

16. See, for example, Richard Voith, "Transportation Investments in
the Philadelphia Metropolitan Area: Who Benefits? Who Pays?
And What Are the Consequences?" working paper, Federal
Reserve Bank of Philadelphia, No. 98–7, 1998, http://
www.phil.frb.org/files/wps/1998/wp98-7.pdf (accessed January
30, 2004) (finding "considerable evidence that investments in
transportation infrastructure have significant effects on the relative attractiveness of local communities" and, hence, local land
values, and that the weight of the evidence suggests that "highway
investments do guide development patterns").

17. Orfield, *Metropolitics*, 6–8.

18. Cashin, "Localism," 2004–2005 (citing research by Myron
Orfield).

19. Voith, "Transportation Investments," 4 ("Communities fortunate
enough to be net recipients of public infrastructure funds will
have an advantage in competing for people and firms, and communities that fail to receive transportation investments and pay
taxes or user fees that are spent in other communities will be at a

disadvantage"); and Cashin, "Localism," 2007–2009 (citing research and arguments).

20. See, generally, Orfield, *Metropolitics;* and Cashin, "Localism," 2012 (citing additional research and arguments by Myron Orfield).

21. Anthony Downs, *New Visions for Metropolitan America* (Washington, D.C.: Brookings Institution Press, 1994), 13–14.

22. See Cashin, "Localism," 2013 (citing the literature and conclusions regarding the costs of sprawl).

23. Ron French and Oralandar Brand-Williams, "Blacks Pay Harsh Price While Whites Suffer Less," *Detroit News*, January 21, 2002.

24. See, generally, Elizabeth Warren and Amelia Warren Tyagi, *The Two-Income Trap: Why Middle-Class Mothers and Fathers Are Going Broke* (New York: Basic Books, 2003).

25. Patricia Sullivan, "In a Seller's Market, the Familiar Frenzy," *Washington Post*, April 12, 2003; Daniela Deane, "Low Rates Keep Sales Blooming, But Price Counts," *Washington Post*, April 12, 2003.

26. Jaime Green, "Clarendon Envy; Trendy Shops, Great Places to Stroll, Cute Little Houses—That Go for Half a Mil. What Do These People Do for a Living?" *Washington Post*, April 28, 2002.

27. Manny Fernandez, "Thriving in Public; Some Students Shun Private Option, Choose D.C. Schools," *Washington Post*, June 13, 2001. Students excelled at Wilson High School; one turned down admission to Yale University to attend the University of Wisconsin after graduating near the top of her class with a 4.2 GPA. She said that her public school experience caused her to shun the "sheltered" lifestyle of premier undergraduate universities. Ibid.

28. Ron French and Oralandar Brand-Williams, "Black Cost: Fewer Jobs, Black Cost: Infant Mortality, Black Cost: Lack Of Shopping, White Cost: Overdevelopment, White Cost: Commuting, White Cost: Suburban Sprawl, White Cost: High Mortgages, Black Cost: Crime, *Detroit News*, January 21, 2002.

29. U.S. Department of Transportation, "Safety Belts and Teens: 2003 Report," National Highway Traffic Safety Administration, March 2003, http://www.nhtsa.dot.gov/people/injury/airbags/

buckleplan/buasbteenso3/BUA%2oSBTeens.pdf (accessed January 30, 2004).

30. William Lucy, "Mortality Risk Associated with Leaving Home: Recognizing the Relevance of the Built Environment," *American Journal of Public Health* 93 (2003): 1564.

31. "We're Exactly Where You Want to Be!" Advertisement for Ryan Homes new Liberty Run Community in Fauquier County, *Washington Post*, April 12, 2003, F2.

32. Grubman wanted to get his twin four-year-old daughters into the 92nd Street Y Nursery School and agreed to endorse AT&T stock if Sanford Weill, chairman of Citigroup and an AT&T director, put in a good word for him. Michael Powell, "Manhattan's Elite Don't Kid Around; Preschool Admission Rivals Any Boardroom Battle," *Washington Post*, November 15, 2002.

Chapter 6: Schools

1. Henry E. Cauvin, "Two Tried to Bring Gun to School, Police Say," *Washington Post*, February 13, 2004; Neely Tucker, "Teen Dated Man Accused in Her Death; Wilson Student's Affair Revealed in D.C. Court," *Washington Post*, March 14, 2000.

2. *Washington Post*, "School Guide: Washington Area Education," http//www.washingtonpost.com/wp-dyn/education/schoolguide (accessed February 2, 2004).

3. Justin Blum and David A. Fahrenthold, "Student Slain in Shooting at Ballou," *Washington Post*, February 3, 2004; Sylvia Moreno and Justin Blum, "Ballou Slaying Rooted in Territorial Rivalry, Pride, Not Drugs, Fuels Antagonism," *Washington Post*, February 9, 2004.

4. *Pearson v. Murray*, 182 A. 590 (Md. 1936).

5. *Sweatt v. Painter*, 339 U.S. 629 (1950). See "The Handbook of Texas Online," at http://www.tsha.utexas.edu/handbook/online/articles/view/SS/fsw23.html (providing interesting details on the life of Herman Marion Sweatt).

6. *McLaurin v. Oklahoma State Regents for Higher Education*, 339 U.S. 637 (1950).

7. *Smith v. Allwright*, 321 U.S. 649 (1944).

8. See *Shelley v. Kraemer*, 334 U.S. 1 (1948) (prohibiting enforcement of racially restrictive housing covenants); *Morgan v. Virginia*, 328 U.S. 373 (1946) (prohibiting discrimination in transportation in interstate commerce). Among other realms, Marshall made inroads into the treatment of blacks in the military, in commerce, and in the criminal justice system (in regard to minority participation on juries). See, generally, Juan Williams, *Thurgood Marshall: American Revolutionary* (New York: Times Books, 1998).

9. *Board of Education of Oklahoma City v. Dowell*, 498 U.S. 237, 251 (1991) (Marshall, J., dissenting).

10. David Rusk, *Cities Without Suburbs* (Washington, D.C.: Woodrow Wilson Center Press, 1993), 34–35 (citing number of school districts surrounding Detroit); Erica Frankenberg, Chungmei Lee, and Gary Orfield, *A Multiracial Society with Segregated Schools: Are We Losing the Dream?* (Cambridge: Civil Rights Project, 2003).

11. *San Antonio v. Rodriguez*, 411 U.S. 1 (1973).

12. See Advocacy Center for Children's Educational Success with Standards, "Finance Litigation," http://www.accessednetwork.org/litigation/index.htm (accessed September 18, 2003) (providing an overview of the litigation to date in forty-five states).

13. James Ryan, "Schools, Race, and Money," *Yale Law Journal* 109 (1999): 249, 259–260.

14. Ryan, "Schools, Race, and Money," 285–286, n. 89. "Greater needs require greater resources: Disadvantaged students simply cost more to educate, requiring additional educational programs and non-academic services such as health care and counseling.... A number of state school finance systems recognize this fact and provide additional funding to high poverty schools." Ibid., 285–286.

15. Patricia F. First and Barbara M. DeLuca, "The Meaning of Educational Adequacy: The Confusion of DeRolph," *Journal of Law and Education* 32 (2003): 185, 203. ("The bottom line is that despite litigation in nearly every state over the past two decades, interdistrict disparities in the United States still exist.")

16. *Dowell,* 498 at 262–263 (citing *Swan v. Charlotte-Mecklenburg,* 402 U.S. 1, 18 [1971]).

17. Ibid., 265.

18. *Freeman v. Pitts,* 503 U.S. 467 (1992).

19. *Missouri v. Jenkins,* 515 U.S. 70 (1995).

20. Peter Applebome, "A Wave of Suits Seeks a Reversal of School Busing," *New York Times,* September 26, 1995, A1.

21. Peter Applebome, "Schools See Re-emergence of 'Separate but Equal,'" *New York Times,* April 8, 1997, A10 (citing Gary Orfield, *Deepening Segregation in American Public Schools* (Cambridge: Harvard Project on School Desegregation, 1997)(regarding changes between 1991 and 1994).

22. See Roslyn Arlin Mickelson, "Symposium: Do Southern Schools Face Rapid Resegregation? The Academic Consequences Of Desegregation and Segregation: Evidence from the Charlotte-Mecklenburg Schools," *University of North Carolina Law Review* 81 (May 2003): 1513, 1543–1544, 1556–1558.

23. Frankenberg et al., *A Multiracial Society,* 37 (including Table 10).

24. Ibid., 31, Figure 6; 34, Figure 8.

25. The average Asian student attends a school that is 46% white, 12% black, 19% Latino, 22% Asian, and 1% Native American. Asian students' diverse experiences are due in part to their low numbers; as of 2000, Asians were only 4% of the student population, although their numbers are rapidly increasing. Ibid., 4, 27, 30–33.

26. These figures are based on the numbers of students who received free or reduced-price lunch during the 1999–2000 school year, which is a rough proxy for poverty. John R. Logan, *Choosing Segregation: Racial Imbalance in American Public Schools, 1990–2000* (Albany, N.Y.: Lewis Mumford Center, 2002), http://www.albany.edu/cpr/LoganChoosingSegregation2002.pdf (accessed May 15, 2003).

27. Frankenberg et al., *A Multiracial Society,* 35.

28. Ibid., 5, 57, Table 21. These figures were computed based upon the numbers of white, non-Latino students in these schools systems as of 2000.

29. U.S. Department of Education, Office of Education Research, National Center of Education Statistics, "Characteristics of the 100 Largest Public Elementary and Secondary School Districts in the U.S., 2000–2001," http://nces.ed.gov/pubs2002/100_largest/table_09_1.asp (accessed October 2, 2003). In New York, Los Angeles, Miami-Dade, and Houston, more than 70 percent of students were eligible for free or reduced-price lunch. This figure was not available for Chicago.

30. Tom Vander Ark, Executive Director of Education, Gates Foundation, personal communication with the author, February 9, 2003.

31. Ibid. All quotes are from Vander Ark.

32. Paul Dimond, "School Choice and the Democratic Ideal of Free Common Schools Open to All," in *The Institutions of Democracy: Public Schools*, ed. Marvin Lazerson and Susan Furhman (Oxford: Oxford University Press, forthcoming) (draft on file with author).

33. Jay P. Greene, Greg Forster, and Marcus A. Winters, "Apples to Apples: An Evaluation of Charter Schools Serving General Student Populations," Education Working Paper No. 1, Manhattan Institute, July 2003, http://www.manhattan-institute.org/html/ewp_01.htm (accessed on September 24, 2003).

34. Ryan, "Schools, Race, and Money," 256–257, 287.

35. Ibid., 287, n. 165, citing James S. Coleman et al., *Equality of Educational Opportunity* (Washington, D.C.: U.S. Department of Health, Education, and Welfare, 1996).

36. Ibid., 280–288 (summarizing the conflicting debate and noting that a confluence of empirical research suggests that such an oppositional culture develops in high-poverty schools).

37. Richard Kahlenberg, Online Dialogue Series: Economic School Integration, http://www.ideas2000.org (accessed August 12, 2003).

38. See, generally, James Rosenbaum et al., "The Urban Crisis; The Kerner Commission Report Revisited: Can the Kerner Commission's Housing Strategy Improve Employment, Education, and Social Integration for Low-Income Blacks?" *University of North Carolina Law Review* 71 (1993): 1530–1531.

39. Ibid., 1542–1545, for discussion of Laura's experience.
40. Richard Kahlenberg, *Economic School Integration, Idea Brief No. 2,* (New York: Century Foundation, February 2000), 4.
41. Lynn Olson and Craig D. Jerald, "The Achievement Gap," *Education Week,* January 8, 1998, 10. The Title I federal compensatory education funding for low-income schools has not produced the kind of achievement gains one would hope for. For a more detailed overview, see ibid., and Ryan, "Schools, Race, and Money," 284–296.
42. Michael A. Fletcher, "Education Support Defended; Bush Says Improvement of Schools 'Not Just About Money,'" *Washington Post,* January 9, 2003.

     The No Child Left Behind Act requires states to administer standardized reading and math tests to students each year in grades 3 through 8. Schools must make steady progress toward raising achievement levels on the exams, with all students required to reach state-defined proficiency levels by 2014. Schools deemed failing for two consecutive years must begin transferring students to better schools—even to those filled to capacity—and use public money to hire private firms to tutor students. If a school continues to be designated as failing, it must replace its principal and teachers or reopen as a charter school.
43. See editorial, "Many Children Left Behind," *San Francisco Chronicle,* September 18, 2002.

     A key to getting the legislation out of Congress was Rep. George Miller's (D-Calif.) insistence that schools serving poor students get the resources they need to succeed. After months of negotiation, Congress authorized $5.8 billion in additional Title I spending, the federal education program for poor children. But in his budget, Bush has proposed only $1 billion in additional Title I funding, and those funds came from eliminating 65 federal programs—38 of them education programs. Overall, Bush's education budget represents the smallest increase in the past seven years.
44. Frank Akpadock, "The Social and Economic Impacts on the African-American Community of Incarcerated Black Males Between the Ages of 18 and 35, 1996–2000," report,

Youngstown State University, January 2003, http://cc.ysu.edu/psi/
incarcerated_black_males.pdf.

45. Fox Butterfield, "Study Finds Big Increase in Black Men as
Inmates Since 1980," *New York Times,* August 28, 2002; Justice
Policy Institute, "Cellblocks or Classrooms? The Funding of
Higher Education and Corrections and Its Impact on African-
American Men," August 2002, http://www.justicepolicy.org/arti-
cle.php?list=type&type=20, (accessed February 2, 2004) (noting
that in 2000 there were 791,600 black men in jail or prison and
603,032 enrolled in colleges and universities, whereas in 1980
there were 143,000 black men behind bars compared to 463,700
enrolled in college).

46. The average annual cost of undergraduate tuition and fees and
room and board for a full-time student across all types of institutions (public and private, four-year and two-year) is $11,454. The
average cost of a college education at a four-year public college is
$9,199. U.S. Department of Education, National Center for Edu-
cation Statistics, *Tuition Costs of Colleges and Universities*
(Washington, D.C.: U.S. Department of Education, 2003),
http://nces.ed.gov/fastfacts/display.asp?id=76 (last accessed on
February 15, 2004).

The average annual cost of housing a prisoner is upward of
$20,000. James J. Stephan, U.S. Department of Justice, Bureau of
Justice Statistics, *State Prison Expenditures, 1996* (Washington,
D.C.: U.S. Department of Justice, August 1999), iv,
http://www.ojp.usdoj.gov/bjs/pub/pdf/spe96.pdf (noting average
annual operating expenditure per state prison inmate in 1996 was
$20,100 and per federal prison inmate was $23,500); David Fire-
stone, "U.S. Figures Show Prison Population Is Now Stabilizing,"
New York Times, June 9, 2001 ("State prisoners now cost an
average of $23,000 a year to house"); Brent Staples, "Prison
Class: What Ma Barker Knew and Congress Didn't," *New York
Times,* November 25, 2002 ("The cost of housing this country's
inmates exceeds $20,000 per person per year—more than the
price of in-state student enrollment at many of America's best
public universities").

47. Justice Policy Institute, "Cellblocks or Classrooms?"

48. See the introduction of this book and accompanying Note 3.
49. Frankenberg et al., *A Multiracial Society,* 4.
50. Sara Rimer, "Schools Try Integration by Income, Not Race," *New York Times,* May 8, 2003.
51. Frankenberg et al., *A Multiracial Society,* 5, 28-29.

Chapter 7: The Cost of the Ghetto

1. Sue Anne Pressley, "On a Road in SE, No Deliverance from the Killing," *Washington Post,* January 2, 2004.
2. Frank Main, "Residents of Dearborn Homes Protest Surge of Gang Violence," *Chicago Sun-Times,* August 14, 2001.
3. Felicia R. Lee, "Tested," *New York Times,* November 11, 2001.
4. Maribel Morey, "Former Cabrini Green Gang Members Speak at Notre Dame," *The Observer* (via University Wire), February 19, 2001.
5. Bob Herbert, "L.A.'s Streets of Death," *New York Times,* June 12, 2003.
6. Helen Epstein, "The New Ghetto Miasma, Enough to Make You Sick?" *New York Times Magazine,* October 12, 2003, 98.
7. Ibid.
8. The five dimensions of segregation are measured as follows:

   Unevenness: the degree to which blacks are distributed so that they are overrepresented in some areas and underrepresented in others.
   Isolation: the degree to which blacks are distributed so that they rarely share a neighborhood with whites.
   Clustered: the degree to which black neighborhoods form one large contiguous enclave.
   Concentrated: the degree to which blacks live within a very small area.
   Centralized: the degree to which black neighborhoods are spatially centralized around an urban core.

   "A high score on a single dimension is serious because it removes blacks from full participation in urban society and limits their access to its benefits. As segregation accumulates across multiple dimensions, however, the effects intensify. . . . Not only are blacks more segregated than other groups on any single dimension of segregation, but they are also more segregated on all dimensions simultaneously; and in an important subset of U.S. metropolitan areas, they are very highly segregated on at least four of the five dimensions at once, a pattern we call hypersegregation." Douglass Massey and Nancy Denton, *American Apartheid* (Cambridge: Harvard University Press, 1993), 74. Massey and Denton's analysis of the 1990 census showed that about one-third of African Americans living in the sixty largest metropolitan areas, where the majority of black people reside, lived in hypersegregation. Ibid., 74–77.

The 2000 census showed that in the 300 largest metropolitan areas in the country, 30 percent of all black people live in neighborhoods that are at least 80 percent black. Edward L. Glaeser and Jacob L. Vigdor, "Racial Segregation in the 2000 Census: Promising News," Survey Series (Washington, D.C.: Brookings Institution, 2001), http://www.brook.edu/dybdocroot/es/urban/census/glaeserexsum.htm (accessed January 27, 2004).

9. Glaeser and Vigdor, "Racial Segregation in the 2000 Census."

10. Paul A. Jargowsky, "Stunning Progress, Hidden Problems: The Dramatic Decline of Concentrated Poverty in the 1990s" (Washington, D.C.: Brookings Institution, 2003), http://www.brook.edu/es/urban/publications/jargowskypoverty.htm (accessed January 27, 2004).

11. Ibid.

12. Massey and Denton, *American Apartheid,* 77.

13. William J. Wilson, *The Truly Disadvantaged: The Inner City, the Underclass, and Public Policy,* 3rd ed. (Chicago: University of Chicago Press, 1990); Jonathon Kozol, *Savage Inequalities: Children in America's Schools* (New York: HarperPerennial Press, 1992); Alex Kotlowitz, *There Are no Children Here: The Story of Two Boys Growing Up in the Other America* (New York: Anchor Books, 1992).

14. William J. Wilson, *When Work Disappears: The World of the New Urban Poor* (New York: Knopf, 1996), 12–19.

15. James F. Rosenbaum et al., "Can the Kerner Commission's Housing Strategy Improve Employment, Education, and Social Integration for Low-Income Blacks?" *University of North Carolina Law Review* 71 (1993): 1519, 1527–1540. There is a direct correlation, for example, between educational attainment and concentrated poverty: "In real-world terms, the difference between living in a relatively disadvantaged neighborhood (one standard deviation below the mean) and living in an advantaged neighborhood (one standard deviation above the mean) is 3.65 points on the standardized achievement test. In comparison to other effects, this difference is more than one-third the effect of being black, more than half the difference between white and Hispanic students, and twice the effect of attending a private school. Moreover, the parallel difference in terms of time spent on homework (.890 hours per week) is comparable to the effect of private school attendance (.916 hours per week) and is almost twice as much as the black/white disparity (.466 hours per week). James W. Ainsworth, "Why Does It Take a Village? The Mediation of Neighborhood Effects on Education Achievement," *Social Forces* 81, no. 1 (2002): 117, http://gateway.proquest.com/openurl?ctx_ver= z39.88–2003&res_id=xri:pqd&rft_val_fmt=ori:fmt:kev:mtx: journal&genre=article&rft_id=xri:pqd:did=000000208348111& svc_dat=xri:pqil:fmt=html&req_dat=xri:pqil:pq_clntid=5604.

16. Margery A. Turner and Christopher Hayes, "Poor People and Poor Neighborhoods in the Washington Metropolitan Area," (Urban Institute, 1997), http://www.urban.org/urlprint.cfm? ID=6565, (accessed January 27, 2004).

17. Ron French and Oralandar Brand-Williams, "Blacks Pay Harsh Price While Whites Suffer Less," *Detroit News*, January 21, 2002, http://www.detnews.com/specialreports/2002/segregation2/ b01–395704.htm (accessed January 28, 2004), citing research by George Galster of Wayne State University.

18. Thomas P. Bonczar, U.S. Department of Justice, Bureau of Justice Statistics, *Prevalence of Imprisonment in the U.S. Population, 1974–2001* (Washington, D.C.: U.S. Department of Justice, August 2003), 1, http://www.ojp.usdoj.gov/bjs/pub/pdf/piuspo1. pdf (accessed February 15, 2004).

19. Katherine Beckett and Theodore Sasson, *The Politics of Injustice: Crime and Punishment in America* (Thousand Oaks, Calif.: Pine Forge Press, 2000), 91, 97 (noting, inter alia, that half of black males ages 18–35 in Washington, D.C., and 56 percent of this group in Baltimore are under criminal supervision and that the numbers are even higher in certain areas within these cities).

20. National Criminal Justice Commission, *The Real War on Crime: The Report of the National Criminal Justice Commission,* ed. Steven R. Donziger (New York: HarperPerennial, 1996), 102; Loic Wacquaint, "Deadly Symbiosis: When Ghetto and Prison Meet and Mesh," in *Mass Imprisonment: Social Causes and Consequences,* ed. David Garland (London: Sage Publications, 2001), 82–93; Paige M. Harrison and Allen J. Beck, *Bureau of Justice Statistics Bulletin: Prisoners in 2002,* U.S. Department of Justice, July 2003, http://www.ojp.usdoj.gov/bjs/pub/pdf/p02.pdf (accessed January 30, 2004), 9.

21. Nancy LaVigne et al., *A Portrait of Prisoner Reentry in Maryland* (Urban Institute, 2003), http://www.urban.org/Uploaded-PDF/410655_MDPortraitReentry.pdf (accessed January 28, 2004).

22. David Wessel, "Studies Suggest Potent Race Bias in Hiring," *Wall Street Journal,* September 4, 2003.

23. Justice Commission, *The Real War,* 126 (noting that the stereotypical association of minority urban youths with crime has hampered efforts to create corporate summer job programs).

24. Beckett and Sasson, *The Politics of Injustice.*

25. Marc Mauer, "The Causes and Consequences of Prison Growth in the United States," in *Mass Imprisonment: Social Causes and Consequences,* ed. David Garland (London: Sage Publications, 2001), 9–10.

26. Harrison and Beck, *Prisoners in 2002.*

27. Katherine Beckett and Bruce Western, "Governing Social Marginality: Welfare, Incarceration, and the Transformation of State Policy," in *Mass Imprisonment: Social Causes and Consequences,* ed. David Garland (London: Sage Publications, 2001), 35–47.

28. Ibid.

29. Nancy Burns, *The Formation of Local Governments: Private Val-*

ues in Public Institutions (New York: Oxford University Press, 1994); Kenneth Jackson, *Crabgrass Frontier: The Suburbanization of the United States* (New York: Oxford University Press, 1985).

30. Petula Dvorak and Clarence Williams, "Everyday Violence Still Claims Its Victims," *Washington Post*, October 19, 2002.

31. John R. Logan, "The New Ethnic Enclaves in America's Suburbs" (University of Albany, Lewis Mumford Center for Comparative Urban and Regional Research, 2001), http://mumford1.dyndns.org/cen2000/suburban/SuburbanReport/page1.html (accessed January 28, 2004).

32. Mark Rom, "Health and Welfare in the American States," in *Politics in the American States: A Comparative Analysis,* 3rd ed., ed. Virginia Gray and Herbert Jacob (Washington, D.C.: CQ Press,1996), 399, 407–408 (discussing the differing public perceptions between AFDC welfare mothers and social security recipients).

33. Lise Funderburg, "Integration Anxiety," in *The American Civil Rights Movement: Readings and Interpretations*, ed. Raymond D'Angelo (Guilford, Conn.: McGraw-Hill/Dushkin, 2001), 531 (quoting Elliott Lee).

34. Richard Cohen, "Common Ground on Crime," *Washington Post*, December 21, 1993 (quoting Jesse Jackson).

35. Rosenbaum, "Kerner Commission's Housing Strategy," 1519.

36. Epstein, "New Ghetto Miasma."

Chapter 8: The 50–50 Nation

1. Michael N. Danielson, *The Politics of Exclusion* (New York: Columbia University Press, 1976), 29 (citing a study conducted by Oliver Williams).

2. John J. Harrigan, *Political Change in the Metropolis* (New York: Harper Collins, 1993), 166.

3. Ronald Smothers, "Ending Battle, Suburb Allows Homes for Poor," *New York Times*, April 12, 1997. Ethel Lawrence was deceased by the time the groundbreaking occurred.

4. Sheryll D. Cashin, "Localism, Self-Interest, and the Tyranny of the Favored Quarter: Addressing the Barriers to New Regional-

ism," *Georgia Law Journal* 88 (2000): 1985, 2019–2020 (citing empirical studies).

5. Richard Child Hill, "Separate and Unequal: Governmental Inequality in the Metropolis," *American Political Science Review* 68 (1974): 1557, 1558–1559.

6. Margaret Weir, "In the Shadows: Central Cities' Loss of Power in State Politics," *Brookings Review* (Spring 1995): 18–19.

7. Margaret Weir, "Central Cities' Loss of Power in State Politics," *Cityscape: A Journal of Policy and Research* (May 1996): 23.

8. This happened in the state of Washington, for example, when the state legislature enacted the Basic Education Act of 1977 ostensibly to equalize per-pupil spending throughout the state after years of relying upon inequitable local levies to fund education. The immediate impact was a reduced reliance on local levy funds and a substantial increase in state funding to school districts across the state. However, the increase in state funding over time led to an overall shift in resources away from districts with substantial poor and minority student populations and toward districts educating predominantly white, relatively affluent students.

   Between 1976 and 1990, the share of state and local revenues received by districts educating the highest percentage of students eligible for free and reduced-price lunches fell 4.9 percent, while the share of districts with the lowest percentage of such students rose 2.5 percent. Diane W. Cipollone, "Defining a 'Basic Education': Equity and Adequacy Litigation in the State of Washington," *Campaign for Fiscal Equity, Inc.,* vol. 1, no 5 (December 1998): 20, www.accessednetwork.org/resources/WASHINGtwo.PRI.PDF (accessed on February 4, 2004).

9. Sheryll D. Cashin, "Federalism, Welfare Reform, and the Minority Poor: Accounting for the Tyranny of State Majorities," *Columbia Law Review* 99 (1999): 552, 587–588, citing empirical studies, including William N. Evans et al., "Schoolhouses, Courthouses, and Statehouses after Serrano," *Journal of Policy Analysis and Management* 16 (1997): 10; and Neil D. Theobald and Faith Hanna, "Ample Provision for Whom? The Evolution of State Control over School Finance in Washington," *Journal of Education Finance* 17 (1991): 7, 22–25.

376 NOTES TO PAGES 268–274

10. Caroline Hoxby, "All School Finance Equalizations Are Not Created Equal," *Quarterly Journal of Economics* 116 (2001): 1189–1190.

11. This history on school finance in New Jersey is culled from Jeffrey Metzler, "Inequitable Equilibrium: School Finance in the United States," *Indiana Law Review* 36 (2003): 561, and recent developments reported at: http://www.accessednetwork.org/litigation/lit_nj.html#ReNJ (accessed February 4, 2004).

12. Metzler, "Inequitable Equilibrium," 589 (giving a recent history of school finance struggles in Vermont).

13. *DeRolph v. State*, 677 N.E.2d 733, 737–738 (Ohio 1997) ("DeRolph I"); *DeRolph v. State*, 754 N.E.2d 1184, 1190 (Ohio 2001) ("DeRolph III").

14. Patricia F. First and Barbara M. DeLuca, "The Meaning of Educational Adequacy: The Confusion of *DeRolph*," *Journal of Law and Education* 32 (April 2003): 185; Mary J. Amos, "*DeRolph v. State*: Who Really Won Ohio's School Funding Battle?" *Capital University Law Review* 30 (2002): 153; editorial, "*DeRolph*'s Fourth Down: Court Finally Ends Its Reign as Superlegislature of School Funding," *Columbus Dispatch*, December 15, 2002.

15. Metzler, "Inequitable Equilibrium," 564 (stating inequitable equilibrium hypothesis).

16. See, generally, William Julius Wilson, *The Truly Disadvantaged: The Inner City, the Underclass, and Public Policy* (Chicago: University of Chicago Press, 1987); William Julius Wilson, *When Work Disappears: The World of the New Urban Poor* (New York: Knopf, 1996).

17. Steven J. McDonald, "How Whites Explain Black and Hispanic Inequality," *Public Opinion Quarterly* 65 (2001): 562–573. In a survey of white Floridians, when asked to explain why blacks on average have "worse jobs, income, and housing than white people," the most frequent response (46.4 percent) was "lack of motivation." When asked the same question concerning Latinos, the most frequent response (41.0 percent) was "no chance for education." Only 31.2 percent of respondents ascribed Latino inequality to "lack of motivation."

18. Joshua Green, "In Search of the Elusive Swing Voter," *Atlantic Monthly* 293 (January/February 2004), http://www.theatlantic. com/issues/2004/01/green-voter.htm (accessed February 4, 2004).

19. Jeffrey Toobin, "The Great Election Grab: When Does Gerrymandering Become a Threat to Democracy?" *New Yorker,* December 8, 2003.

20. Myron Orfield, *American Metropolitics: The New Suburban Reality* (Washington, D.C.: Brookings Institution, 2002), 28–46, 155–162.

21. Green, "Elusive Swing Voter."

22. Toni Morrison, "The Talk of the Town," *New Yorker,* October 5, 1998, 32.

23. Interview with the Reverend Richard Tolliver of St. Edmund's Episcopal Church, November 8, 2001, discussing a meeting he attended in the Old Executive Office Building during Clinton's second term in office.

24. David Kusnet, *Speaking American: How the Democrats Can Win in the Nineties* (New York: Thunder's Mouth Press, 1992). David Kusnet was Clinton's chief speech writer from 1992 through 1994. His book, *Speaking American,* was required reading for all White House policy wonks in the early days of Clinton's presidency.

25. Editorial, "An Appraisal: Bill Clinton's Mixed Legacy," *New York Times,* January 14, 2001.

26. Mike Allen and Helen Dewar, "Bush Bypasses Senate on Judge Pickering Named to Appeals Court During Recess," *Washington Post,* January 17, 2004.

27. Laura D'Andrea Tyson, "The Bush Tax Cuts Are Sapping America's Strength," *Business Week,* August 11, 2003, 22.

28. Dana Milbank and Jonathan Weisman, "Middle-Class Tax Share Set to Rise; Studies Say Burden of Rich to Decline," *Washington Post,* June 4, 2003.

29. Albert R. Hunt, "Unshared Sacrifices," *Wall Street Journal,* April 10, 2003.

30. Tyson, "Bush Tax Cuts."

31. Andres Martinez, "Paul O'Neill, Unplugged, or What Would

Alexander Hamilton Have Done?" *New York Times*, January 14, 2004. Ron Suskind, *The Price of Loyalty: George W. Bush, the White House, and the Education of Paul O'Neill* (New York: Simon and Schuster, 2004).

32. David Cay Johnston, *Perfectly Legal: The Covert Campaign to Rig Our Tax System to Benefit the Super Rich—and Cheat Everybody Else* (New York: Portfolio, 2003), 71–91.

33. Robert J. Shiller, "Mind the Gap," *New York Times*, May 15, 2003.

Chapter 9: What to Do About It

1. David Brooks, "The Americano Dream," *New York Times*, February 24, 2004.

2. Paul Dimond, "School Choice and the Democratic Ideal of Free Common Schools Open to All," in *The Institutions of Democracy: Public Schools*, ed. Marvin Lazerson and Susan Fuhrman (Oxford: Oxford University Press, forthcoming) (draft on file with author).

3. Myron Orfield, "Comment on Scott A. Bollen's 'In Through the Back Door: Social Equity and Regional Governance,'" *Housing Policy Debate* 13 (2003): 659, 664.

4. Ibid., 664–665, citing Henry Mayer, *All on Fire: William Lloyd Garrison and the Abolition of Slavery* (New York: St. Martin's Press, 1998); and Daniel Levering Lewis, *W.E.B. DuBois: Biography of Race, 1868–1919* (New York: Henry Holt, 1993).

5. Ibid., 665.

6. Dora L. Costa and Matthew E. Kahn, "Civic Engagement and Community Heterogeneity: An Economist's Perspective," *Perspectives on Politics* 1 (March 2003).

7. Myron Orfield, *Metropolitics: A Regional Agenda for Community and Stability* (Cambridge: Brookings Institution Press, 1997); Myron Orfield, *American Metropolitics: The New Suburban Reality* (Washington, D.C.: Brookings Institution Press, 2002); David Rusk, *Inside Game / Outside Game* (Washington, D.C.: Brookings Institution Press, 1999); David Rusk, *Cities Without*

Suburbs (Washington, D.C.: Woodrow Wilson Center Press, 1993); John A. Powell, "Opportunity-Based Housing," *Journal of Affordable Housing and Community Development* 12 (Winter 2003): 188; Angela Glover Blackwell, "Promoting Equitable Development," *Indiana Law Review* 34 (2001): 1273; Jeremy Nowak, "Neighborhood Initiative and the Regional Economy," *Economic Development Quarterly* 11 (February 1997). I discuss the possibilities for metropolitan coalition building in detail in Sheryll D. Cashin, "Localism, Self-Interest, and the Tyranny of the Favored Quarter: Addressing the Barriers to New Regionalism," *Georgia Law Journal* 88 (2000): 1985.

8. Report of the National Advisory Commission on Civil Disorders (Kerner Commission), March 1968.

9. Orfield, "Comment on Bollen," 666 (noting that Abraham Lincoln initially opposed the abolition of slavery and Lyndon Johnson initially opposed civil rights, but both leaders were ultimately forced by grassroots movements to pursue the progressive course).

10. Blackwell, "Promoting Equitable Development."

11. Michael Anderson, "The Organizer," *New York Times Book Review*, November 9, 2003 (quoting Bayard Rustin from *Time on Two Crosses: The Collected Writings of Bayard Rustin*, ed. Devon W. Carbado and Donald Weise [San Francisco: Cleis Press, 2003]).

12. I am indebted to my colleague Palma Strand, a scholar of democracy and democratic processes, for advancing my thinking on the role of organizing and building relationships in creating true democracy.

13. Blackwell, "Promoting Equitable Development," 1277, n. 26.

14. For a detailed summary of this five-year process of coalition building and legislative maneuvering, see Orfield, *Metropolitics*.

15. Isaiah 58:9–12.

16. All quotes regarding Bethel New Life appear on its Web site. For an overview of Bethel New Life's mission, history, and wondrous works, see http://www.bethelnewlife.org (last accessed January 4, 2004).

17. Rusk, *Inside Game / Outside Game,* 52–59. For a forceful defense

of the success of CDCs, see Paul Grogan and Tony Proscio, *Comeback Cities: A Blueprint for Urban Neighborhood Revival* (Boulder: Westview Press, 2000), 1–14, 90–96.

18. Jeremy Nowak, "Neighborhood Initiative and the Regional Economy," *Economic Development Quarterly* 11 (February 1997): 3–10; Blackwell, "Promoting Equitable Development."

19. Blackwell, "Promoting Equitable Development," 1278.

20. Parris Glendening, foreword to *Solving Sprawl: Models of Smart Growth in Communities Across America*, by F. Kaid Benfield, Jutka Terris, and Nancy Vorsanger (New York: Natural Resources Defense Council, 2001).

21. Jonathan Weiss, "Preface: Smart Growth and Affordable Housing," *Journal of Affordable Housing and Community Development* 12 (Winter 2003): 165, 167.

22. Sustainable Communities Network, "Quality Indicators for Progress: Jacksonville, Florida," available at http://www.sustainable.org/casestudies/SIA_PDFs/SIA_florida.pdf (accessed September 23, 2003).

23. See note 15, above.

24. Brian Siebenlist, "The Role of Faith-Based Organizations in Smart Growth and Regionalism," in Leah Kalinosky and Kathy Desmond, *National Neighborhood Coalition, Smart Growth, Better Neighborhoods: Communities Leading the Way* (Washington, D.C.: National Neighborhood Coalition, 2000).

25. Orfield, "Comment on Bollen," 662.

26. Jonathan Weiss, "Smart Growth and Schools," *Planetizen*, November 14, 2003, http://www.planetizen.com/oped/item.php?id=111 (accessed February 6, 2004).

27. Frederick Douglass, Speech Before the West Indian Emancipation Society (August 4, 1857), in Philip S. Foner, *The Life and Writings of Frederick Douglass* (New York: International Publishers, 1950), 437.

28. Orfield, "Comment on Bollen," 667.

29. "Prioritizing this notion of 'choice' can obscure the legacy and persistence of racial discrimination in housing and falsely suggest that there is now a 'level playing field' in the housing market

rather than one that actually coerces impoverished people of color." Powell, "Opportunity-Based Housing," 189–190.

30. Paul Jargowsky, *Stunning Progress, Hidden Problems: The Dramatic Decline of Concentrated Poverty in the 1990s* (Washington, D.C.: Brookings Institution, 2003).

31. See Chapter 1, pp. 32–38.

32. Douglass Massey and Nancy Denton, *American Apartheid: Segregation and the Making of the Underclass* (Cambridge: Harvard University Press, 1993), 207.

33. Jargowsky, *Stunning Progress.*

34. Alexander Polikoff, "Unlikely Times," in Owen Fiss, *A Way Out: America's Ghettos and the Legacy of Racism* (Princeton: Princeton University Press, 2003), 90.

35. Peter Byrne, "Two Cheers for Gentrification," *Howard University Law Journal* 46 (2002): 405.

36. William Julius Wilson, "When Work Disappears: New Implications for Race and Urban Poverty in the Global Economy," *Ethnic and Racial Studies* 22, no. 3 (1999); William Julius Wilson, *The Truly Disadvantaged: The Inner City, the Underclass, and Public Policy* (Chicago: University of Chicago Press, 1987).

37. For a summary of state and local policy strategies that local community leaders and municipal agencies can use to manage new investments in ways that produce equitable outcomes and promote "diverse mixed-income/mixed-wealth neighborhoods" that are "strong, stable and welcoming to all," see "Equitable Development Toolkit," PolicyLink, http://www.policylink.org (accessed September 24, 2003).

38. Dimond, "School Choice."

39. Ibid. (citing the 2002 Phi Delta Kappan annual poll).

40. Sara Rimer, "Schools Try Integration by Income, Not Race," *New York Times*, May 8, 2003. For a thorough defense of controlled choice, see Richard D. Kahlenberg, *All Together Now: Creating Middle-Class Schools Through Public School Choice* (New York: Century Foundation Press, 2001).

41. Anand Vaishnav, "Desegregation by Income Gets Wary Reception in N.C.; Raleigh, Like Cambridge, Embarks on Reassignments,"

Boston Globe, June 3, 2002.

42. For similar proposals that would allow parents to choose among public schools without regard to where they live, see Dimond, "School Choice"; Elizabeth Warren and Amelia Warren Tyagi, *The Two-Income Trap: Why Middle-Class Mothers and Fathers Are Going Broke* (New York: Basic Books, 2003), 35–36.

43. Lani Guinier and Gerald Torres, *The Miner's Canary: Enlisting Race, Resisting Power, Transforming Democracy* (Cambridge: Harvard University Press, 2002).

INDEX